P9-CSB-937

Multinational Accounting
A Research Framework
for the Eighties

Research for Business Decisions, No. 46

Gunter Dufey, Series Editor

Professor of International Business and Finance
The University of Michigan

Other Titles in This Series

HF
5686
.I56
.M84

Multinational Accounting
A Research Framework
for the Eighties

Edited by
Frederick D. S. Choi

UMI RESEARCH PRESS
Ann Arbor, Michigan

FEB 2 1 1985

458568

Copyright © 1981
Frederick D. S. Choi
All rights reserved

Produced and distributed by
UMI Research Press
an imprint of
University Microfilms International
Ann Arbor, Michigan 48106

Library of Congress Cataloging in Publication Data

Multinational accounting.

(Research for business decisions ; no. 46)
Bibliography: p.
Includes index.
1. International business enterprises—Accounting.
I. Choi, Frederick D. S., 1942-   . II. Series.
HF5686.I56M84   657'.95   81-16448
ISBN 0-8357-1267-2   AACR2

Dedicated to Gerry Mueller in the spirit of *Festschrift*

Contents

Part III: Overview

List of Tables

Gernon: Internal Performance Evaluation

Dukes: Foreign Currency Financial Statement Translation

Hiramatsu: International Accounting Research in Japan

Preface

Interest in multinational accounting as a specialized field of inquiry is today at an all time high. This heightened intellectual curiosity has been spurred by such post-World War II developments as the emergence of the multinational enterprise as a significant economic and social force, the abandonment of stable currency systems in global monetary affairs, rising resource and commodity prices as a worldwide malady, the international diversification of investment portfolios—both direct and indirect, efforts to harmonize widely divergent national accounting and economic systems, and the high priority being accorded accounting as a positive development force by third world countries.

Despite its recent evolution, the field of international accounting research has developed very rapidly. Starting with a pioneering dissertation written by Gerhard G. Mueller in the late 1950s, the academic literature now boasts at least three university texts, four major anthologies, several dozen research monographs, and literally hundreds of journal articles devoted exclusively to the international dimension of accounting. University research centers specializing in multinational accounting are also growing in number, not to mention the research sponsored by national, regional, and international accounting organizations. We enter the decade of the 1980s, therefore, with a level of academic attention to multinational accounting that is vastly larger than that which existed only ten short years ago.

Given a fairly respectable international accounting research base, I believe the time has come to take stock of what has been done to date and to engage in some thoughtful prognostication as to future research opportunities in the field. A major objective of this book is to provide accounting researchers with a framework for viewing contemporary international accounting research issues and to highlight promising avenues of future inquiry. Hopefully, many more researchers will be motivated to join the effort to extend further the boundaries of this challenging and exciting field of human thought and knowledge.

To this end I have asked those actively engaged in international accounting research to express their views on various subjects of current and future import. As the question of research methodology is dependent on the research question addressed, methodological issues covered are writer-specific. Given the limited scope of this anthology, it was not possible to cover all researchable topics in the field.

In formulating a framework for appraising multinational accounting research issues, three vantage points are employed. The first considers the various facets of multinational accounting: institutional, topical, methodological, technical, and educational. The second focuses on specific types of research: behavioral, comparative, empirical, descriptive, and historical. Each research mode draws on a specific topic as a frame of reference. Normative considerations are implicit in each of the foregoing research categories; hence, the absence of a separate "normative" designation. The third vantage point examines accounting research from a cross-national perspective. Research developments are accordingly monitored in Europe, Asia, North America and Latin America.

I wish to thank Richard Wood, editor-in-chief of UMI Research Press, and Professor Gunter Dufey, series editor, for their personal encouragement and support of this project. Thanks are also due Mrs. Donna Jacobs who very ably managed the design and production of this book. Finally, a sincere "mahalo" (thank you) to the authors of the essays included herein. While many of the writers have not personally met one another, all share one thing in common. This is their association with Professor Gerhard Mueller, an individual who has done more than anyone else to advance the cause of international accounting research. We have all benefitted from the many stimulating discussions we have had with this international accounting pioneer. The contributions in this book are a collective expression of our appreciation.

New York City
1981

Frederick D. S. Choi
Editor

Part I

Dimensions

Introduction

Multinational accounting is today an important specialization in the accounting field. As a body of knowledge, it provides a new base for the organization of accounting data and concepts. As an area of inquiry, it is providing new directions for accounting research as a means of adding to our knowledge.

Being a relatively young field, the boundaries of academic research in multinational accounting are neither clearcut nor fixed. Some, for example, view multinational accounting research as the quest for a universal accounting system that could be adopted by all nation-states. Others view it as the study and codification of the varieties of accounting principles and practices which exist worldwide. Still others view multinational accounting as the study of the accounting and reporting problems associated with companies whose operations transcend national borders.

To provide some perspective, five basic distinctions are drawn in the subject matter of multinational accounting. As with any classification scheme, borderlines between classifications are not precise. Nevertheless, it is useful to relate multinational accounting issues to different developmental fronts within the field. These developmental fronts encompass issues that are 1) topical, 2) methodological, 3) technical, 4) institutional, and 5) educational in tenor.

Ultimately, the criterion for selecting a given research question for study is its importance. In the absence of a formal priority scheme, international accounting research problems are often selected for study according to personal whim or convenience. This void is significantly narrowed by Scott, author of the first essay in this section. Based on an earlier study, Scott engages in a systematic attempt to rank order various international accounting problems according to their relative importance.

In the second essay, Smith and Shalchi offer a critical review of prior international accounting research from a methodological point of view. Noting the absence of a systematic approach to the study of international accounting issues, the authors proffer research methodologies that promise increased rigor in future research contributions to the field.

What distinguishes international accounting as a unique field of inquiry are the number of technical accounting issues that defy purely domestic solutions. Employing the combined perspectives of an accounting academic as well as that of a professional consultant with a major New York consulting firm, Seidler identifies a number of research issues that promise to challenge the ingenuity of accounting researchers for many years to come.

The growing institutionalization of the international accounting field is the focus of the fourth essay in this section. Brennan's penetrating glimpse into the internal workings of various international standards-setting bodies reflects his experiences as former Secretary of the International Accounting Standards Committee. Accounting researchers are directed to areas of investigation that are felt to be more productive than those previously pursued.

And what about international accounting education? Are there issues here worthy of academic attention? Radebaugh's reply is a hearty "yes, indeed!" The growing importance of international accounting is exerting increased pressures upon collegiate schools of business to incorporate the international dimension into traditional accounting curricula. Compliance with such pressures at a time when university budgets are strained and enrollments are on the decline pose program, curricula, and faculty challenges of no small proportion.

Topical Priorities in Multinational Accounting

GEORGE M. SCOTT
University of Connecticut

Introduction

This essay is based in part on the author's study, *Eighty-eight International Problems in Rank Order of Importance—A DELPHI Evaluation* (with Pontus Troberg), which was published as a monograph in 1980 under the auspices of the International Accounting Section of the American Accounting Association (AAA). It examines five of the highest ranked problems that were identified in the DELPHI evaluation with the objective of encouraging additional research in international accounting.

The DELPHI Study

Systematically soliciting expert opinion, the DELPHI Technique uses sequential questionnaires that encourage participants to refine their opinions on a subsequent questionnaire in light of the findings developed from the preceding questionnaire. Multiple questionnaires promote intensive study and agreement among expert participants who have been exposed to other viewpoints via the questionnaire results feedback process.

This DELPHI study had four phases. First, international accounting experts from numerous countries were identified, and information about the general approach to the study was forwarded to them. Second, each participating expert submitted a minimum of three international accounting problems that he considered most important.

During the third phase of the study, this author categorized the problems according to their general topics (e.g., international auditing, international taxation, etc.) and returned the entire list of problems in the form of a questionnaire to the participants. To evaluate the relative importance of each of the ninety-one problems, the participants used a scale of one to four, with one being most important. The experts were also requested to state why they thought each problem was important or was not important. The average value of importance for each problem was calculated. Additionally, the opinions of the participants were summarized and classified into two groups for each problem: those opinions indicating that the problem was important and those opinions indicating that the problem was not important.

During the final phase, a new questionnaire was distributed. This questionnaire was thirty-seven single-spaced pages in length and asked the experts to do three things. First, a participant was requested to read each problem, consider its average importance (the measure of importance was included for each question), and analyze the statements about the importance and the lack of importance of the problem. Second, after evaluating the "importance" statements, the experts again numerically indicated the perceived importance of the problem. Third, the participants were asked to suggest research or other approaches that might be useful to help study and resolve the problem. This new questionnaire contained a total of eighty-eight problems. (A few of the problems from the preceding questionnaire were combined as recommended by the participants.) The results of this questionnaire were then analyzed and served as the basis for the published monograph.

Thirty-eight experts completed the first DELPHI questionnaire, and forty-one experts completed the second (last) DELPHI questionnaire. Participants who completed the last questionnaire represented citizenship in nine different countries and/or residence in fourteen different countries. These participants included twenty-three academics and eighteen non-academics. Among the non-academics, twelve were associated with public accounting firms and six were associated with corporations.

The objectives of the DELPHI study were to: a) identify the major international accounting problems; b) rank these problems in their importance relative to each other; and c) tentatively establish the research methodology that might be applied to each. The major achievements of the study were as follows:

1. Eighty-eight more or less separate accounting problems were identified, all contributed by the participants.
2. All eighty-eight problems were placed in rank order of importance as evaluated by the forty-one participants in the last questionnaire.
3. Experts tended to agree about the relative importance of the problems; in fact, greater agreement existed at the conclusion of the study than at its inception. This ranking enables researchers to assess the merits of investigating a particular problem.

4. A rich variety of research projects and other investigations of the problems were suggested. Some suggestions are merely general statements; others relate to organizational changes thought to be needed; still others suggest the need for a specific, defined research project or the application of a specific research method.

Table 1 displays the twelve problems assessed as the most important out of the total of eighty-eight problems evaluated; due to space limitations all eighty-eight problems are not listed in this article. Two problems tied for the most important rank, two others tied for the third most important rank, and two tied for the eleventh rank.

The Problem of Lack of Accounting Educators

To this author, the most surprising result of the DELPHI study was the selection of this first-place problem: "There is a lack in many countries of adequately trained accounting educators." This outcome is particularly noteworthy because it is strikingly similar to the result of another DELPHI study that dealt more narrowly with accounting in developing countries.[1] In that study the most important "accounting education" problem, among twelve major problems placed in the education category, was "Lack of Qualified Accounting Instructors at the College Level" (p. 202); this problem was dubbed the "professor problem." The study concluded, in part, as follows:

> The Committee has examined the study results to determine if any accounting education problem can be identified as the critical linch-pin problem such that its amelioration will serve as a catalyst by beneficially affecting other problems; international cooperation focused narrowly to such a key problem would multiply the effects of this cooperation. The Committee believes that the study results suggest this critical problem to be the professor—specifically, the quality of professors in the developing countries and the employment conditions which influence their dedication to teaching. If international cooperation can improve the quality of the professors and these conditions, many of the other problems—such as curriculum problems—are likely to be commensurately relieved in due course as a consequence of professors' attention to these problems; but attention to some other problem may well provide only a short term cosmetic effect for that problem and have little or no effect on other problems. . . . (pp. 211-212).

Thus, the importance of the "professor problem" in the preceding study was reaffirmed by the more recent "eighty-eight problems" study. But it is not just the most important accounting education problem in developing countries; the professor problem is one of the two most important international accounting problems of all types in all countries.

Table 1.   Six Most Important Problems, (most important first)

(Based on a 4 point scale, 1 = extremely important;
2 = moderately important; 3 = less important; 4 = not important)

Rank	Problem	Rating
1.	*Problem.* There is a lack in many countries of adequately trained accounting educators.	1.64
1.	*Problem.* In a world of shifting exchange rates, it is difficult to measure the economic effect of exchange rate changes on a particular company having dealings with foreign affiliates or other foreign operations, or the net effect of these rate changes on a system of interrelated companies in different countries; in some circumstances the swings in the parities of currencies are largely unrelated to the operations of affiliated companies in that country.	1.64
3.	*Problem.* An auditor's report may not be easily or properly interpreted by readers in another country because it is prepared on the basis of the auditing standards and using accounting terminology of another country, or because different types of attestations are used in various countries which have different meanings.	1.68
3.	*Problem.* Different rates and structural characteristics of inflation in different countries make it difficult to achieve comparability of financial status and results among companies in different countries for external financial reporting.	1.68
5.	*Problem.* The lack of uniformity in approaches of inflation accounting as indicated by the emergence of different inflation accounting systems in different countries, (such as different versions of current-value accounting) further hampers comparability among unrelated companies as well as among affiliated companies in different countries.	1.74
6.	*Problem.* The lack of international accounting standards greatly diminishes the usefulness of financial statements to users in countries other than the country on whose accounting standards the statements are based.	1.81
7.	*Problem.* (Added from ROUND TWO) Basic priciples of independence and ethics differ among countries' auditors.	1.84
8.	*Problem.* Translation gains and losses other than on currency conversion transactions-in-process often do not reflect economic reality.	1.85
9.	*Problem.* The necessity in many countries to conform to financial accounting and reporting to the tax law impedes the development of sound accounting standards and affects the international comparability of the published financial statement.	1.86
10.	*Problem.* Too many translation approaches are now in existence around the world.	1.89
11.	*Problem.* There is no extensive program to promote the development of accounting education in those countries where this education is lagging.	1.92
11.	*Problem.* There is a lack in many countries of adequately trained indigenous accountants.	1.92

Readers may note, too, that other "accounting educator" problems rated in the top third of the eighty-eight problems study. These were the two tied for eleventh place in importance (see table 1); number nineteen, which suggested the need for international guidelines for accounting education; and number twenty-two, which states that "there is inadequate exchange of accounting educators among the countries of the world."

Three approaches to the number one "accounting educators" problem were suggested by the eighty-eight problems study participants, but none was a specifically research approach. Most participants believed that "exchanges of accounting educators" would be must useful. The second best approach, according to participants, would be "special regional centers for educating accounting educators."[2] Third, participants advocated "more admission of foreign students to U.S. accounting Ph.D. programs."

Unfortunately, the eighty-eight problems study did not suggest what academic research could be usefully employed for this problem. This author suggests three research approaches.

Perhaps a research program intended to deal with the "accounting educator" problem should first measure the magnitude of the problem on a country-by-country basis. If the magnitude of the problem is known for each country, forceful arguments can be made for resources or policies to deal with the problem, and these arguments will be more readily accepted. The magnitude of the "accounting educators" problem might be examined in these terms:

1. The quantities of accounting educators (both in total and in terms of full-time equivalents) relative to demand for accounting educators within the society. An indicator of demand might be an index of the level of industrialization. Because no one indicator is likely to be statistically above suspicion, probably several should be employed in order to build an overwhelming case for a country's need. The absolute position of these indicators in comparison with those of other countries could clearly indicate the extent of shortage in terms of numbers of accounting educators in a particular society.
2. The training of the accounting educators. If one assumed that quality of education is correlated to quantity of education as indicated by degree level, a researcher could rank all countries on the average level of education of accounting educators. Of course, this measurement approach may be fraught with difficult judgments.

In combination, or as a composite measure, these measures may persuasively show that specific countries have a severe shortage of accounting professors. However, the research methodology would have to be carefully developed. In addition, the study would have to be undertaken in several, and preferably a great many, countries and would require identical measurement procedures. Only in this way would useful comparisons be established.

A second research approach is analysis of the social, political, economic, or institutional phenomena that inhibit the marketplace in some countries from responding to the need for more accounting educators. Again, this research would need to be carried out in several countries and would require identical research methodologies in each in order to provide comparative information. For example, perhaps professors' salaries in several countries are inflexibly applied without regard to the opportunity-cost differences in the marketplace among the academic disciplines. Consequently, accounting educators, who are in scarce supply and have extensive opportunities outside of universities, are offered salaries that are little or no more that those offered educators in other disciplines who are in plentiful supply.

A third worthwhile research study would analyze various countries' attempts to increase the number or quality of accounting educators. This study would include, at least, the identification and description of the programs undertaken, as well as an assessment of their effectiveness. Such a study might indicate that certain types of programs have no lasting effects, but that one or more types of programs have proved to be unusually effective at increasing the quality or number of accounting educators. The 1980-81 Committee on Accounting Development of the International Accounting Section of the American Accounting Association is now developing such a study that is intended to determine how accounting in developing countries can be improved. The charge to this Committee (which is chaired by the author) is as follows:

1. Review and summarize research and other activities to date on the development of accounting in developing countries.
2. Outline several action programs to promote this accounting development.

Measurement of Exchange Rate Change Impact

Strongly reinforced by related problems in the top ten (see exhibit 1), the other "most important" problem is this: "In a world of shifting exchange rates, it is difficult to measure the economic effect of exchange rate changes on a particular company." Problem eight, "Translation gains and losses . . . often do not reflect economic reality," and problem ten, "Too many translation approaches" are directly related. Problems three and five pertaining to inflation can also be related to the problem of the economic effect of exchange rate changes. Differences in inflation rates and structure undoubtedly are related to the economic effect of exchange rate changes in complex ways. For example, inflation can precipitate exchange rate changes, and exchange rate changes often add fuel to the inflation fires.

   To correct the problem of the economic effect of exchange rate changes, participants recommended that "a body of knowledge relating to the economic effects of exchange rate needs to be developed." Next, they recommended "studies of the impact of FASB 8." (FASB 8 is now in process of being altered, and an exposure draft of proposed changes is in existence.) Third, participants suggested "Harmonizing currency translation internationally." Also significant are approaches to problem eight, "Translation gains and losses . . . often do not reflect economic reality." The most recommended approach to problem eight is this: "The real meaning of translation gains and losses should be researched and set forward clearly." And the next-most recommended approach to problem eight is this suggestion: "The behavioral impact of exchange gains and losses on management needs to be explored, as does the perception of management about the significance of these gains and losses."

   The high ranking of several problems either directly or indirectly related to the economic effect of exchange rates—five problems among the top ten problems—suggests concern by the experts about several dimensions of exchange rate problems, rather than concern for a narrowly defined "accounting translation" problem. This author believes that two major problem areas must be exhaustively studied separately and sequentially in order to deal with the exchange rate and accounting translation problems. Specifically, the following studies are needed:

1. Understanding and measuring the economic effect of exchange rate changes on each country and on the companies within each country, and
2. Establishing translation rules that enable the effects of exchange rate changes to be portrayed in their financial statements.

The first of these areas entails separating exchange rate effects and inflation effects, which are interrelated. In turn, separation requires that both of the phenomena of exchange rates and inflation can be examined and that the relationships between these be researched. Then, before proper translation rules can be established in response to number two above, a theory of translation gains and losses must be developed that will enable these gains and losses to be measured in a manner that is a) consistent in its principles of application for a company, but also b) tailored to properly portray the economic context of each company's situation. To date, accounting standard setting bodies have devoted almost no attention to the first problem area noted above and have concentrated almost exclusively on the second. Unfortunately, the second problem area cannot be tackled until the first is solved; a body of knowledge pertaining to the "theory of translation gains and losses" must be established to serve as a framework within which translation rules can be developed. Accordingly, translation problems have not been resolved to date despite the allocation of considerable resources to these problems by standard setting bodies around the world.

Table 2 sets forth one logical approach suggested by this author for

Table 2. One Logical Approach for Dealing with "Economic Impact" Problem

Basic research to develop knowledge	research to develop a body of knowledge about the economic effects of exchange rate changes on companies	research to develop a body of knowledge about the economic effects of inflation on companies	research to develop a body of knowledge about the interaction of inflation and exchange rate changes
Framework within which translation rules can be developed	OBJECTIVES OF ACCOUNTING	development of a theory of translation gains and losses	generally accepted accounting principles related to other aspects of accounting
		development of currency translation principles	

dealing with the "economic impact" problem (problem one of table 1) and the translation gains and losses problem (problem eight of table 1).

Table 2 shows that accounting translation of foreign resources is fraught with complexity and that basic research in this area must be broad in scope. Prior to finding satisfactory solutions, the profession must: a) develop the three bodies of knowledge indicated in table 2, none of which presently exists to a satisfactory degree; b) develop a translation gains and losses theory that is largely derived from the three bodies of knowledge; and c) develop translation principles and practices that are consistent with the theory of translation gains and losses, are within the context of the existing objectives of accounting (and the general framework of accounting), and are within the generally accepted accounting principles pertaining to other accounting matters.

Given the magnitude and difficulty of the tasks described in table 2, it is little wonder that progress in the accounting translation area has been slow. Accountants are only now reaching a level of sophistication about the problems of translation and can now focus on the matters that must be dealt with before these problems can be solved.

At no point could the research suggested above be expected to be straightforward in its reliance on existing accounting dogma. For example, existing objectives of accounting or, certainly, generally accepted accounting principles could be inadequate and require revision in the context of accounting translation. Perhaps, translation principles consistent with the theory of translation gains and losses may require the use of another index to supplement or replace the exchange rate index. In a series of manuscripts the author has propounded four possible indices that merit research for possible currency translation usage.[3] These are the purchasing power parity index, the constructed rate index, the foreign currency translation index, and the major commodities index. Space does not permit a full elaboration of these approaches. However, a partial analysis of the constructed rate index (CRI) method is presented here as an example.

The CRI method is based on the ratios of price indices among countries and might be applied to translate foreign held resources; transactions in process in the world monetary system would continue to be translated with exchange rates. For example, the consumer price index (CPI) or another price index of Country X and of the U.S. can arbitrarily be assumed to be a base year index for the CRI method at the end of any year. The constructed rate "base relationship" would then be the relationship between the two CPIs at that year end and the current exchange rate (or the current purchasing power parity index) at that time. Subsequent changes in the consumer price indices used are converted to relative price changes and applied to the base relationship to calculate a new constructed rate for translation.

To illustrate the application of the CRI method, readers may assume that the U.S. CPI is 200% of its base year; Country X's CPI is 400% of its base year; the exchange rate is U.S. $1 to 3 Foreign Currency Units (FCU); and at this time a CPI/CRI base relationship is established as a basis for construction of future CRIs. This CPI/CRI base relationship is: 200%/400% = $1/3FCU. If at a subsequent year end the U.S. CPI is 300% and Country X's is 800%, the U.S. CPI has increased by 150% while the foreign CPI has increased by 200%. Accordingly, the following calculations can be made for the constructed index, which would serve as the "current index" for accounting translation for that year:

$1.5 \times \$1 = \$1.50$ where 1.5 represents 150% of the base CPI for the U.S.
$2.0 \times 3FCU = 6FCU$ where 2.0 represents 200% of the base CPI for Country X.

This yields a new ratio of $1.50/6FCU, or $1/4FCU. The new constructed rate is $1 to 4FCU for translation purposes. Obviously, relative price changes cause the CPI to change; an equal percentage CPI change for both countries would have no effect on the CRI. Thus, the CRI would reflect differences in internal price changes, and changes in exchange rates would not affect translation of foreign held resources.

The preceding example is only intended to illustrate the *possibility* that alternatives to the exclusive use of exchange rates may be both feasible and practical, and it does not indicate a position in favor of the CRI method. Both advantages and disadvantages of CRI can be cited. Major advantages are simplicity and ease of understanding; also price indices exist in all major countries (the CPI exists in most). Another advantage is the stability of a constructed rate; for most countries the CRI will exhibit a gradual trend over time so that consequent value changes would be minor and fairly predictable. Additionally, the CRI appears to be readily used with present FASB 8 or probable follow-on rules. (The historical CRI can be applied in all circumstances where a historical exchange rate is called for, and the current CRI can be applied wherever a current rate would be used). Finally, there would be no incentive to hedge translation losses in the exchange markets for the exchange markets are irrelevant to the CRI calculation.

Disadvantages of the CRI method should also be noted. The CRI method adjusts *only* for inflation, but other factors influence the economic value of foreign resources. In addition, selection of the most relevant inflation index for each country and selection of a base year may present difficulties. A final disadvantage is that a set of machinery would have to be put into place to develop the CRI method and make the periodic calculations required.

Foreign Auditors' Reports Not Easily Interpreted

Tied for third place in importance is the problem of difficulty with the interpretation of auditors' reports in other countries. A total of eleven approaches to its resolution were suggested by DELPHI participants. The four receiving the greatest number of votes are the following, in descending order of number of votes:

1. Collaborative effort with IFAC's Auditing Standards Committee.
2. Establishment of international auditing standards.
3. A survey to establish the impact of this problem on users.
4. A survey of auditing practices in different countries.

All but the first of these suggest the need for specific research.

However, this author suggests a more basic study than that suggested by the participants. This basic study might consist of two parts. The first part might attempt to *explain* differences in auditing procedures and reports among countries. Explanation will require examination of social, economic, and institutional differences among countries, such as could account for differences among countries in the preparation and meaning of auditors' reports. For example, perhaps due to differences in regulatory structures and processes and differences in the structure of industries and companies, auditors' reports in different countries are prepared in accordance with different auditing standards and accounting terminology; therefore, attestations in different countries have different meanings. The second part of the study would then attempt to evaluate which of these differences among countries *justify* differences in auditing procedures and reports. This research could then be usefully employed in attempting to eliminate unnecessary differences in audit procedures and reports among the countries.

Inflation and Inflation Accounting

The problems of different rates and structural characteristics of inflation and the lack of uniformity in approaches of inflation accounting are closely related. Therefore, these problems (the second problem three and problem five) are examined together here. In addition to emphasizing the importance of the exchange rate and currency translation problems, as already noted, these inflation problems are important in their own right and appear to make two conflicting statements. First, because of differing rates and structural characteristics of inflation, countries are less inclined to adopt a uniform inflation accounting approach, and there may be valid reasons why this should not be done. Yet, the need for comparability among the financial statements of companies in different countries requires uniformity of inflation accounting approaches. This dilemma is emphasized by the existence of several inflation accounting approaches, each annointed by the standard-setting bodies of one country. The entrenchment of these approaches makes eventual uniformity even more difficult to achieve. To accommodate structural diversity among the inflations of different countries, any internationally uniform inflation accounting approach must be especially flexible and, nevertheless, must achieve a degree of uniformity.

Three of the more interesting approaches suggested by the DELPHI participants to help resolve these two problems are the following:

1. Develop full disclosure standards for different approaches, together with a system that permits adjustment of the various approaches to a uniform basis.
2. Conduct experiments with accountants and investors to analyze their behavior in the face of financial reports from different nations prepared on a different inflation adjustment basis.
3. Conduct empirical research on how different characteristics of inflation affect decision-making behavior.

All three of these research approaches appear to have merit.

This author's research activities in inflation accounting suggest a research program that might effectively address this problem of lack of international uniformity of inflation accounting.[4] The initial program step might be an analysis of inflation structures in different countries. This analysis would determine if any inflation structure necessitated a particular inflation accounting approach, and it would determine which inflation accounting approaches seem preferable in certain sets of circumstances. The researcher might study these inflation structures: widely different inflation rates among industries within a country; different rates of inflation of labor and capital; inflation coupled with an overheating economy; stagflation (inflation during a recession); inflation in high growth, as opposed to inflation in low growth, industries, inflation in one major sector of an economy coupled with deflation in another; and deflationary conditions throughout the economy. These structures could be empirically examined by means of case studies of actual countries that illustrate different inflation structures. Cause and effect are more likely to be segregated, however, if computer simulation studies are used so that one variable can be altered while all others are held constant.

Next, the researcher would attempt to determine if any inflation structure appeared to require a unique inflation accounting approach. Very likely, this determination would be made in concert with an examination of any preferences for present inflation accounting approaches in each set of inflation structure circumstances. The critical choice criterion is the relative costs/benefits of each inflation accounting system. According to some evidence, perhaps the implementation and continuing costs of preparing inflation-adjusted financial statements a) do not differ markedly between systems and b) are not a major consideration. What remains critical, however, is the relative benefit of each inflation accounting system. Assessment of benefits is difficult, indeed, and useful research in this area has been scant. Inflation impacts companies in many different, complex, and interrelated ways. There is no general understanding of these impacts, and there is no uniform method of interpreting inflation-adjusted financial statements. Interpretation of inflation-adjusted financial information is a sorely neglected aspect of inflation accounting research.

If agreement were reached on the interpretation of financial statements prepared on the basis of different inflation-adjustment methods, the relative benefits of each method could be tentatively identified, and the world community of accounting standard setters could move toward a preferred method. Not only would each country's inflation accounting approach be improved, with commensurate benefits to the country, but the present trend toward different inflation-adjustment methods in each country would be arrested and reversed. The resultant uniformity of standards among countries would promote world trade and the international mobility of capital resources.

Accordingly, this research step should focus on interpretation of inflation-adjusted financial statements. This interpretation might be from the viewpoint of a) analysts in the financial community who make buy/sell decisions about corporate securities and b) managers who make operating and financing decisions based partly on the analysis of their own financial statements, but especially those managers who must interpret inflation-adjusted financial statements emanating from multiple foreign locations.

This research might focus on the four general systems of inflation accounting, as well as on the major variations proposed for each. These four are general purchasing power adjustment, current-cost accounting, exit value accounting, and combinations of these that are generally combinations of the first named two.

Although there are many research avenues to pursue in comparing the benefits of these four approaches, one of the most promising appears to be analysis of the cash flow prediction ability of each inflation accounting approach. According to one school of thought, cash flow constitutes the primal economic reality of company operations, and the benefit of any inflation accounting approach must be measured by its ability to help users predict future cash flows. Using a massive computer simulation model, this author has done extensive research in this area; most of the results of this simulation constitute a part of the author's book on current-value accounting.[5] However, the comparisons were restricted to the future cash flow prediction abilities of historical cost financial statements and financial statements prepared on the basis of only one type of current-value financial statements.[6] Approaches other than cash flow predictive ability may frutifully compare the relative benefits of different inflation accounting approaches.

Summary and Conclusions

The study *Eighty-Eight International Accounting Problems in Rank Order of Importance: A DELPHI Evaluation* should channel international accounting research priorities for the 80s. "A Concluding Note" to that study (p. 72) discusses possible extensions of the study but states, "The ultimate research payoff, of course, can only be in terms of conducting research directly on one or more of the problems identified herein as important, and this research should begin at once."

The author remains loyal to the position quoted above. In this article the five problems found to be most important by the DELPHI study have been examined. Several research projects and methodologies that are concerned with these five problems have been proposed herein; a few of those proposed closely relate to the author's own past research. Of course, without doubt a great many other worthy research projects also exist for each problem. Now is the time for accounting researchers to find solutions to these five, as well as other, international accounting problems.

Notes

1. George M. Scott, et al., "Report of the Committee on Accounting in Developing Countries," *Accounting Review, Supplement to* (1976).

2. The Recommendations to the Executive Committee of the American Accounting Association of the Committee that completed the 1976 DELPHI study included the following recommendation:

    . . . Consideration to be given . . . to establishment of regional accounting education centers which are devoted primarily to:

1. selecting outstanding candidates from adjacent countries, and
2. providing an education in accounting and related subject areas at the doctoral level which places emphasis on preparing these students for teaching careers, and
3. awarding graduates a degree or certificate which fulfills the highest academic requirements for admission to teaching careers as professors of accounting in the major educational institutions of their countries.

(These recommendations were provided only to the Executive Committee of the AAA.)

3. George M. Scott, "Currency Exchange Rates and Accounting Translation: A Mis-Marriage?" *ABACUS* (June 1975). Lane Daley and George Scott, "Measuring the Economic Effect of Exchange Rate Changes on American Companies," *Collected Papers* (Proceedings) of the 1979 American Accounting Association's Annual Meeting. Additionally, unpublished manuscripts are available on request.

4. George M. Scott, *Research Study on Current-Value Accounting Measurement and Utility* (Touche Ross Foundation, 1978).

5. Ibid.

6. This research demonstrated that, within the assumptions and limitations of the study, current-value accounting provides better information in most circumstances for predicting future cash flows from operations than does historical cost accounting.

Multinational Accounting: Some Methodological Considerations

CHARLES H. SMITH
University of Illinois at Urbana-Champaign

and

HOSSEIN SHALCHI
Simon Fraser University

During the last two decades a considerable amount of research has been conducted in the area of international accounting. This interest has resulted from the expansion in international business transactions in general, and from the growth of the multinational corporation and the internationalization of the world's stock markets more specifically.

This paper reviews the research efforts in the area of international accounting to date, and comments on the contribution of such research. A second purpose of this paper is to identify a number of problem areas that need some research attention and to suggest research methodologies that could improve the contribution of the research efforts of international accounting scholars.

International Accounting Research to Date

The international accounting research efforts to date may be classified as follows:

1. Forces influencing accounting practice.
2. The accounting profession—institutional aspects.
3. Financial accounting and auditing.
4. Accounting and economic development.
5. Management accounting.

Forces Influencing Accounting Practice

As a service function, accounting influences and is influenced by its environment. The specific manner in which accounting is practiced is, to a great extent, a function of the environment in which such practice occurs. Scholars have therefore deemed it necessary to undertake studies of the many different socio-economic environments of the world prior to making recommendations for the improvement of practice. The study of these environments has enabled researchers to identify the forces that influence the environments. Such identification has, in turn, enabled writers to identify topics and methods for research.

Several studies have given attention to the environmental factors that affect the formulation of financial accounting practices in various countries (Zeff, 1971), while others have developed more comprehensive listings of forces that influence the practice of accounting in general (Mueller, 1968, and Choi and Mueller, 1978, chap. 2).

The Accounting Profession—Institutional Aspects

Research in this area has consisted of various attempts to compare the general framework of the accounting profession in different countries, and to examine the evolution of the profession in a number of countries over time. Studies in this area have also focused on the educational and training requirements of professional accountants in different countries. The American Institute of Certified Public Accountants' study, *Professional Accounting in 30 Countries* (AICPA, 1975) is a good example of the type of study undertaken under this heading.

As a result of these studies we now have a reasonable understanding of numerous institutional aspects of the accounting profession in many countries, i.e., including major differences between countries.

Financial Accounting and Auditing

It is safe to observe that most of the research effort to date in international accounting has been in the financial accounting area. The efforts under this heading may be summarized as follows:

1. Comparative financial accounting and auditing.
2. Accounting for foreign currency translation and inflation.
3. Capital market issues.

Comparative financial accounting and auditing. The focus of these studies has been an identification, examination and comparison of the generally accepted accounting and auditing principles (including reporting requirements) in different countries and under various political systems. The survey of practices has essentially been undertaken without any rigorous analysis of the results. Thus the current state of knowledge is limited to a description of practices in different countries. The study by the AICPA (AICPA, 1975) is typical as are the publications of various international public accounting firms and of the now disbanded Accountants International Study Group.

Despite the lack of rigorous methodology and analysis, the research efforts have provided significant insight into the following matters of interest:

1. The extent of similarity in principles between countries.
2. The uniformity or diversity of standards and concepts in various countries.
3. The possible approaches that might be used to improve the accounting and auditing practices of many countries.
4. Understanding the financial statements prepared under different sets of accounting and auditing standards.

The comparative studies described above have also provided useful information for those who have conducted research on the matter of harmonization of financial accounting and auditing principles. Advocates of international harmonization point to the comparability of financial statements that will result from such harmonization (Kraayenhof, 1960; Wilkinson, 1969; Stamp, 1972), and therefore to the benefits which would accrue to those investors who do not limit themselves to the investment opportunities available in only one country.

Accounting for foreign currency translation and inflation. Literature on foreign currency translation and inflation topics may be classified as either descriptive or normative research. Descriptive studies in this area have mainly dealt with the examination and comparison of consolidation accounting practices, translation procedures, and the measurement of foreign exchange gains or losses in different countries. Even though the descriptive research in this area lacks rigorous analysis and empirical testing, it does appear that such research has been successful in identifying the issues and pointing to a number of areas in need of empirical study and conceptual development.

The normative studies in the area of currency translation and inflation have attempted to provide a theoretical foundation for dealing with the issues. A variety of alternatives have been recommended. However, as Patz (1977, p. 312) points out, the body of knowledge on the translation problem is "a massive body of opinions, methods, issues, fragmental bits of theorizing and unintegrated solutions to specific pragmatic problems, most of which were generated on an ad hoc basis." Despite the good intentions of developing a theoretical foundation for dealing with the issues, many of the studies have been procedure oriented. As a result of this orientation, basic questions such as the nature and objectives of translation have not been answered to date. Thus, it seems safe to conclude that the translation issue still lacks a rigorous, and well structured theory. Moreover, the studies to date have been based on varying assumptions and postulates which have not been subjected to empirical verification.

Capital market issues. The characteristics of capital markets vary widely from country to country, and especially between the developed and the developing countries. One group of studies on this topic has focused on a simple identification and description of the differences and similarities between various capital markets throughout the world. These studies have been successful in providing information about the nature and objectives of the capital markets as well as the sources and cost of capital in different countries.

The studies of a second category of research in this area have focused on an examination and testing of the efficient market hypothesis in relation to non-United States stock markets. The studies build on similar research undertaken on U.S. stock markets, and have therefore benefitted from the extensive theoretical and methodological developments of the U.S. studies. A state-of-the-art study by Jensen and Smith (1980) provides a broad theoretical perspective on the efficient market hypothesis in both national and international contexts. It also reviews the literature in this area and examines the methodological aspects of the research efforts performed on non-U.S. stock markets. The evidence from these studies suggests that non-U.S. stock markets do not, generally, exhibit characteristics consistent with the weak or semi-strong form of the efficient market hypothesis. This suggests, of course, that the implications of the U.S. studies for financial reporting (e.g., the market processes accounting information in an unbiased and timely manner and there exists an association between accounting information and security price behavior both in the context of return and risk measures) do not carry over for financial reporting in non-U.S. environments.

A third category of studies on capital market issues has been undertaken almost single-handedly by Choi (1973a; 1973b; 1974). The issues include the disclosure of information, determination of a firm's cost of capital, and assessment of risk. This category of studies is related to those on market efficiency, and involves a level of analysis slightly more rigorous than that of many of the descriptive studies described in subsections above and hereafter. The conclusions of this third category of studies tend not to be surprising because it is to be expected that disclosure and risk assessment issues at the international level will follow the evolutionary pattern of the U.S. The studies are, however, necessary and useful, even when undertaken with limited data bases.

Accounting and Economic Development

A number of international accounting scholars have undertaken studies on the nature of the accounting function in various (political) economic systems, e.g., market-based versus planned versus semi-planned economies. The essential hope of these studies is to describe and analyze systems in such a way as to be able to draw conclusions regarding the apparent superiority of a particular system (or parts thereof) over another. The central concern is the allocation of scarce resources within an economy, and the relationship between the micro and macro levels in economic development. Writers have suggested, for example, that the U.S. should adopt aspects of the French national planning system, and that the developing nations of the Third World could profitably adopt aspects of planned and market-based economies, as well as those who use uniform accounting systems. Studies under this heading include Campbell (1963), Enthoven (1965), Horwitz (1966), Janssen (1975), Mensah (1977), Mueller (1967), Scott (1969; 1970).

The information produced by these studies constitutes useful information for those concerned with the role of accounting information at the micro and macro levels. These studies have also suggested implications for future research. However, while some of the recommendations flowing from these studies might be intuitively acceptable to some, very little rigorous analysis and empirical evidence has been supplied in support of the recommendations. As a result, little or no hard evidence is available on the efficiency and effectiveness of the proposed alternatives.

Management Accounting

The main objective of the management accounting studies has been the improvement of the planning and control systems of multinational enterprises. Research in this area has focused on almost all aspects of MEs' financial and operational activities. These aspects include organizational control systems, budgeting, capital budgeting, tax planning, working capital management, performance evaluation, risk management (including foreign exchange risk), transfer pricing problems, and management information systems. There is evidence to suggest that basic management accounting techniques are employed on a reasonably uniform basis from country to country. However, this does not mean that all aspects of, for example, a management accounting control system for domestic operations can be duplicated for international operations. In fact, MEs have found that the application of domestic planning and control techniques to their international activities can be quite inappropriate (AAA, 1973, p. 154, and Hawkins, 1965).

As is the case with other areas of research in international accounting, most management accounting studies are descriptive in nature. Recommendations are often made as to the appropriateness of a particular alternative. However, there is little to no hard evidence that can be used to judge or validate the opinions or solutions generated on an ad hoc basis.

Research Methodologies and Topics for the Future

The main purpose of this section is to identify and discuss those research methodologies and topics that seem to be most needed in the area of international accounting. The area of study generally known as international accounting is maturing at a rather rapid rate, and it is important that the research activities of the future build upon the efforts of the past. The following subsection is therefore based on a general evaluation of the research to date.

General Recommendations on Research Methodology

While past research efforts may be categorized as 1) descriptive and descriptive/comparative, 2) analytical, and 3) empirical/verification, it is clear that the descriptive approach has been dominant. Facts, data and information have been collected (through a variety of survey techniques), described and discussed. These descriptive studies have been based on the process of induction, and have enabled the researchers to draw certain general conclusions, and to identify some implications for accounting practice and research. The descriptive studies have provided the basis for some explanation as to why things are the way they are, and, through use of the comparative method, have enabled researchers to make normative statements based on the information gathered. This particular end result is quite justified. As Haas (1969) has stated: "In sum, knowledge arises mostly out of comparison and the discovery of regularities. The greatest break-throughs in science have been made by those who saw comparability in phenomena previously thought to be unrelated" (p. 9). This has been particularly true in the social sciences.

The comparative method has not been the only basis for the analytical work conducted to date. Based on the deductive approach, writers have analyzed the facts, data, and information collected as part of the descriptive studies, and have made numerous normative statements even in the absence of a comparative analysis. The analytical or a priori approach has been applied in this manner to the study of problem areas such as translation/inflation, transfer pricing, the role of accounting information in economic development, and performance evaluation of multinational corporations. It is clear that the analytical approach is a useful methodology for analyzing certain conceptual and practical problems, especially when it is not possible to perform direct empirical tests. Such an approach plays an important role in providing a useful starting point for developing new ideas and theories. The application of analytical research is a positive step toward incorporation of the scientific approach (see discussion hereunder). With many of these problem areas we are still not certain that the results of the analyses point to the "best" solution.

As a result of the descriptive, descriptive/comparative and analytical studies we now have a reasonably good understanding of the many environmental forces confronting accounting practitioners and researchers, and have obtained significant insight into the nature of the many issues facing practitioners and researchers. This is what we are able to reasonably expect from descriptive and analytical (a priori) work. As Larson has observed:

> . . . an important function of a priori research is conceptual refinement of relatively unstructured problem areas; the objective is to render the problem susceptible to more powerful, inferentially rich research methodologies. This kind of research is frequently fragmentary and logically somewhat inarticulate; nevertheless, it serves to focus attention on the problem and provide preliminary indications of the paths of analysis which are likely to be fruitful and those which are likely to prove unrewarding. (p. 30)

The collection of information and accompanying descriptions and explanations have been a reasonable basis for making some recommendations on professional institutional matters (including education and training), financial accounting and auditing standards, the harmonization issue, and even on the appropriateness of management accounting techniques. However, despite the accomplishments to date, international accounting research is, in many respects, in its infancy when compared to the evolution that has occurred in other disciplines and in other (non-international) areas of accounting. It is possible to view the work that has been done to date as merely the foundation for the work that remains to be done. Such a conclusion is justified when one evaluates the accomplishments against the purpose of research in general and the various approaches to the development of knowledge.

A major purpose of research in general (and therefore of accounting research) is to discover new facts, advance the present state of knowledge, and to attempt to explain the behavior of certain real-world phenomena. Such explanations of real-world phenomena constitute theories. And research is the main source of theory/knowledge development. Kerlinger (1973, pp. 5, 6) discusses four general methods for acquiring knowledge: 1) the method of tenacity, 2) the method of authority, 3) the a priori method, and 4) the method of science. The first two methods are based mainly on personal beliefs, while the a priori method is based on logical reasoning. The scientific method is aimed at reducing the amount of bias that enters the process of knowledge development. It is a systematic and controlled process of knowledge development. Peirce has commented as follows on the need for a reduction of bias:

> To satisfy our doubts . . . therefore, it is necessary that a method should be found by which our beliefs may be determined by nothing human, but by some external permanency—by something upon which our thinking has no effects . . . The method must be such that the ultimate conclusion of every man shall be the same. Such is the method of science. Its fundamental hypothesis . . . is: There are real things, whose characters are entirely independent of our opinions about them . . . (in Kerlinger, 1973, p. 6)

The method of science is capable of providing better and more reliable knowledge, mainly due to its unique characteristic—self-correction (Kerlinger, 1973, p. 6). The process is empirically oriented, and involves built-in checks which reduce the impact of the investigator's personal beliefs, values, attitudes, biases and emotions. Kerlinger (1973) has defined scientific research as follows: "Scientific research is systematic, controlled, empirical, and critical investigation of hypothetical propositions about the presumed relations among natural phenomena" (p. 11).

While international accounting research to date has involved aspects of the method of science (including the empirical aspects), the studies have been mainly of a simple fact-finding and data/information collection nature. They have enabled researchers to understand and refine the issues, but have generally not been a sound enough basis for recommendations and theory development. While recommendations and normative statements have been made in the past, researchers have not been able to conclude with confidence, one way or the other, whether their recommendations really constitute the "best" alternative. We really do not know whether harmonization leads to better investment decisions nor whether a uniform accounting system facilitates national economic planning.

Other than studies such as the ones on FASB Statement No. 8 (on the translation problem) by Makin (1978) and Dukes (1978), the empirical research that has been undertaken to date has not been of the type that allows for the rigorous testing of hypotheses. We have not adopted a systematic approach to the study of international accounting issues. Analyses have not been particularly rigorous, and there has been little empirical evidence to support the validity of our recommendations (e.g., the superiority of one method over another). Concern for the careful development of theories has been at a minimum.

The call in this section is to build on the foundation of the descriptive work of the past by conducting research which provides a more objective (controlled) basis for making recommendations. This research should, to the greatest extent possible, include the four major steps of the scientific research approach: (1) identification of the problem, (2) formulation of a hypothesis, (3) deducing the empirical implications and consequences of the formulated hypothesis, and (4) testing the hypothesis by observation and experimentation (Kerlinger, 1973, pp. 11-14). While it is difficult to make normative statements based on the results of, for example, the Makin (1978) and Dukes (1978) empirical studies (on the translation problem), one cannot deny the importance of their descriptive studies. These studies reflect relatively "tight" research designs which include the use of real-world (from actual decisions) data. Hakansson (1973) has drawn attention to the need for such studies as follows: "Thus, empirical research is not only essential in the establishment of descriptive theories per se, but also in determining the descriptive fit of premises which underlie normative theories . . ." (p. 141). The point is not only that a researcher needs to develop a "tight" research design, but also that such research needs to include a well-structured theory from which hypotheses can be formulated and can then be tested empirically.

Research Topics for the Future

The recommendation of the above subsection is that there is a need for international accounting researchers to improve all phases of research methodology in order to increase the objectivity (credibility) of recommendations that are made to policy makers, e.g., accounting standard-setting bodies, and management and government decision makers. The purpose of this subsection is to draw attention to a number of problem areas that need some research attention.

The listing and discussion of topics that appear hereunder have been developed on the basis of the results of the Scott and Troberg (1980) study and our own judgment (bias!) as to a number of important issues. Scott and Troberg used the DELPHI questionnaire technique to systematically "identify the major international accounting problems," and to "rank these problems according to their importance relative to each other" (p. 2). Their list ranks thirty-one items from 1 to 30. Table 1 is made up of seventeen of the thirty-one Scott and Troberg items.

Careful examination of each of the problem descriptions in the table suggests that it is possible to develop testable hypotheses from such descriptions. The possibility exists to a greater extent for some of the topics than for others, i.e., the potential for applying the methodology described in the first section of the paper is at least partially a function of the topic itself. Some of the topics require only the application of analytical techniques to already existing data or to data that would have to be collected. It is, of course, possible that the results of the analyses could lead to the development of testable hypotheses.

The hypotheses that are developed for each of the topics should be derived from an existing theory. Researchers often neglect to relate their hypotheses to a theory, and thereby become guilty of embarking on so-called fishing expeditions. While not all research fishing expeditions are a waste of time, there can be no question about the usefulness of a theory in guiding the researcher in fruitful (research) directions. Accounting researchers tend to forget that there are numerous theories in accounting, finance, economics and psychology etc., from which testable hypotheses can be derived for accounting research.

International auditing research. Our bias in favor of auditing research is supported in the table by at least one high ranking topic, i.e., topic A-1 which is ranked third. Far more attention has been devoted at the international level to financial accounting standards than to auditing standards. In many respects this is simply not justified. Disclosure of information and harmonization of accounting standards is only one half of what is important in the area of financial reporting. The credibility (reliability) of the information is also important. It might well be asked of what benefit the harmonization of accounting standards is if the process behind the development of the numbers is not a credible one. While harmonization of auditing standards might be an appropriate long run goal, in the short run there is a need for us to determine what auditing procedures are used in various countries, and the extent to which each of these procedures is perceived as being important.

International financial accounting. The area of financial accounting standards has certainly not been neglected to date. There is, however, a need for us to move beyond the debates relating to "which standards" and the harmonization issue. The kinds of questions that have been addressed by researchers in, for example, the U.S. can also be addressed at the international level. (Much of the research methodology employed by these researchers is of the type that would enable international accounting researchers to address issues in the manner called for in the first section of this paper.) If these questions are relevant to the U.S. investor they are probably also relevant to the international investor. The time series analysis and predictive ability studies (Abdel-khalik and Thompson, 1978; Lorek, Kee and Vass, 1981; and Norton and Smith, 1979) lend themselves to being replicated. And, beyond the matter of usefulness to individual countries and the international investor, such studies are likely to produce additional insights into the more traditional issues such as harmonization.

The opportunities for replication at the international level have, of course, not gone unnoticed. Morris (1975), for example, has addressed the current value accounting issue by employing the methodology that involves the observation of security prices. And the comparative study by Davidson and Kohlmeier (1966) involved the simulation of the financial accounting standards of four European countries in order to observe the differential impact of the four countries' accounting principles. While the simulation technique is not the most rigorous analytical technique, it is certainly an improvement on the "opinion oriented" debates that have hitherto dominated decisions regarding the choice of accounting alternatives at the international level.

Capital market issues. There is a tendency for accountants to view capital market issues as part of the domain of finance and economics. It is therefore not surprising that such issues do not appear on the Scott and Troberg list.

One capital market issue of great importance to accounting's external reporting function is that of market efficiency. The Jensen and Smith (1980) synthesis of the research in this area points to the existence of market inefficiencies in non-U.S. stock markets. Jensen and Smith then go on to suggest that such inefficiencies are probably due to the different nature of capital markets in many countries. Non-U.S. markets have relatively low trading volumes, high information processing costs, and slow information flows. Needless to say, past research efforts have made considerable progress toward our understanding of the behavior of security prices in other countries. However, additional research is needed to iden-

Table 1. The Scott and Troberg Study: Seventeen of the Top One-Third Individual International Accounting Problems* In Order of Perceived Importance
(Based on a 4 point scale, 1 = extremely important,
2 = moderately important, 3 = less important, 4 = not important)

Rank	Category/Problem#	Problem	Rating in Round 3
	International Auditing Problems		
3	A-1	An auditor's report may not be easily or properly interpreted by readers in another country because it is prepared on the basis of the auditing standards and using accounting terminology of another country, or because different types of attestations are used in various countries which have different meanings.	1.68
23	A-3	It is difficult to determine the extent and competency of auditing performed by an auditor in another country, in part because of differing admissions and experience requirements for auditors.	2.11
	Exchange Rate and Transaction Accounting Problems		
1	B-1	In a world of shifting exchange rates, it is difficult to measure the economic effect of exchange rate changes on a particular company having dealings with foreign affiliates or other foreign operations, or the net effect of these rate changes on a system of interrelated companies in different countries; in some circumstances the swings in the parities of currencies are largely unrelated to the operations of affiliated companies in that country.	1.64

Rank	Category/Problem#	Problem	Rating in Round 3
8	B-6	Translation gains and losses other than on currency conversion transactions-in-process often do not reflect economic reality.	1.85
10	B-8	Too many translation approaches are now in existence around the world.	1.89
	International Tax Accounting Problems		
9	C-2	The necessity in many countries to conform financial accounting and reporting to the tax law impedes the development of sound accounting standards and affects the international comparability of the published financial statement.	1.86
	International Performance Evaluation Problems in International Operations		
30	D-5	Because the prices for which goods and services are exchanged internationally between affiliated companies are not determined by impartial markets or bargaining, distortions are introduced in financial statements which cause comparisons of foreign subsidiary performance by managers to be misleading.	2.25
30	D-6	New performance evaluation criteria and tools are needed for international operations; e.g., evaluation by comparative ratios and by value added for each overseas operation should be explored.	2.25

Rank	Category/ Problem#	Problem	Rating in Round 3
	Accounting for Inflation in International Operations		
3	F-1	Different rates and structural characteristics of inflation in different countries make it difficult to achieve comparability of financial status and results among companies in different countries for external financial reporting.	1.68
5	F-2	The lack of uniformity in approaches of inflation accounting as indicated by the emergence of different inflation accounting systems in different countries, (such as different versions of current-value accounting) further hampers comparability among unrelated companies as well as among affiliated companies in different countries.	1.74
	International Accounting Standards		
6	G-1	The lack of international accounting standards greatly diminishes the usefulness of financial statements to users in countries other than the country on whose accounting standards the statements are based.	1.81
20	G-11	There exist varying concepts and principles governing the recognition and measurement of business transactions in different countries, and there is a need for guidelines to have these concepts and their underlying practices reconciled so that adjustments can be made for the effects of differences and comparable financial information can be prepared.	2.05

Rank	Category/ Problem#	Problem	Rating in Round 3
21	G-14	Different national environments (history, culture, economic development) affect attitudes toward accounting and auditing and gathering, interpreting, and the use of accounting data; this may serve to justify completely different systems to accounting—such as an orientation to investors in some countries and an orientation of accounting as an instrument of national policy in other countries— and so may reduce progress toward international standardization of accounting.	2.08
24	G-9	The consolidation practices of groups of companies having international operations vary from one group to another, and groups headquartered in some countries do not consolidate at all.	2.13
26	G-20	The multinational enterprises' (MEs) methods of operation are much different now than when the present consolidation rules were established, suggesting the need to challenge present consolidation practices as to their suitability and investigate whether there are alternative accounting and reporting techniques to use in describing the financial activities of a ME.	2.14
	Accounting Disclosures		
13	I-1	Financial reporting and disclosure standards for international transfer prices and pricing policies are inadequate.	1.95
	Unclassified Problems		
13	J-2	There exists no comprehensive source of information about the present state of the art in international companies with respect to transfer pricing, budgeting, performance evaluation and other accounting related matters.	1.95

Source: Adapted from Scott and Troberg (1980)
*For more detailed information, see Scott and Troberg (1980, pp. 21-27).

tify market imperfections and the economic factors causing them. Also, there is a very real need to determine whether the underlying assumptions of portfolio theory and the efficient market hypothesis are applicable to countries with thin capital markets. All these matters are important to those investors who view the world in general (rather than only one country) as the market for investment opportunities.

Performance evaluation of international operations. While items D-5 and D-6 were ranked number 30 in the table, it is our judgment that these topics are important enough to justify immediate attention. There are many factors that dictate the need for adjustment of the performance measurements of foreign operations (Imdieke and Smith, 1975), and it is quite possible that the ad hoc approaches used by certain corporations are not even satisfying approaches. A number of suggestions have been made to improve this aspect of management accounting. It remains for us to determine which of the alternatives are feasible, cost efficient, and more appropriate from a decision making point of view.

Bibliography

Abdel-khalik, A. Rashad and Robert B. Thompson. "Research and Earnings Forecasts: The State of the Art." *The Accounting Journal* (Winter 1977-78): p. 180-209.
American Accounting Association. "Report of the Committee on International Accounting." Supplement to *The Accounting Review* (1973): p. 121-67.
American Institute of Certified Public Accountants. *Professional Accounting in 30 Countries.* New York, 1975.
Campbell, Robert W. *Accounting in Soviet Planning and Management.* Cambridge, Mass.: Harvard University Press, 1963.
Choi, Frederick D. S. "European Disclosure: The Competitive Disclosure Hypothesis." *Journal of International Business Studies* (Fall 1974): p. 15-23.
_____. "Financial Disclosure and Entry to the European Capital Markets." *Journal of Accounting Research* (Autumn 1973a): p. 159-75.
_____. "Financial Disclosure in Relation to a Firm's Capital Costs." *Accounting and Business Research* (Autumn 1973b): p. 282-92.
_____ and G. G. Mueller. *An Introduction to Multinational Accounting.* Englewood Cliffs, New Jersey: Prentice-Hall, Inc., 1978.
Davidson, Sidney and J. M. Kohlmeier. "A Measure of the Impact of Some Foreign Accounting Principles." *Journal of Accounting Research* (Autumn 1966): p. 183-212.
Dukes, Roland E. *An Empirical Investigation of the Effects of Statement of Financial Accounting Standards No. 8 On Security Return Behavior.* FASB, 1978.
Enthoven, Adolf J. H. "The Accountant's Function in Development." *Finance and Development* (December 1965): p. 211-16.
Fantl, Irving L. "The Case Against International Uniformity." *Management Accounting* (May 1971): p. 13-16.
Haas, Michael. "Comparison and the Development of Science." in J. Boddewyn, ed., *Comparative Management and Marketing.* Scott, Foresman and Company, 1969.
Hakansson, Nils S. "Empirical Research in Accounting, 1960-70: An Appraisal." In N.

Dopuch and L. Revsine, editors, *Accounting Research 1960-1970: A Critical Evaluation.* Center for International Education and Research in Accounting, 1973, pp. 137-73.

Hawkins, David F. "Controlling Foreign Operations." *Financial Executive* (February 1965).

Horwitz, Bertrand. *Accounting Controls and the Soviet Economic Reforms of 1966.* American Accounting Association, 1974.

Imdieke, L. and Charles H. Smith. "International Financial Control Problems." *Management International Review* 4-5(1975): p. 1-28.

Janssen, Richard F. "French Five-Year Plan, Possible Model for U.S. Misses Major Target." *The Wall Street Journal*, 12 August, 1975, pp. 1, 25.

Jensen, Herbert L. and Charles H. Smith. "The Efficient Market Hypothesis and Non-U.S. Stock Markets." Unpublished paper, 1980.

Kerlinger, Fred N. *Foundations of Behavioral Research.* Holt, Rinehart and Winston, Inc., 1973.

Kraayenhof, Jacob. "International Challenges for Accounting." *Journal of Accountancy* (January 1960): p. 34-38.

Larson, Kermit D. "A Commentary on A Priori Research in Accounting." In N. Dopuch and L. Revsine, editors, *Accounting Research 1960-1970: A Critical Evaluation.* Center for International Education and Research in Accounting, 1973, pp. 26-31.

Lorek, Kenneth S., R. Kee and W. H. Vass. "Time Series Properties of Annual Earnings Data: The State of the Art." *The Quarterly Review of Economics and Business* (Forthcoming, 1981).

Makin, John H. "Measuring the Impact of Floating and FASB 8 on Costs of Capital for Multinationals." Proceedings of Conference on the Economic Consequences of Financial Accounting Standards. FASB, 1978, pp. 1-31.

Mensah, Yaw Mireku. "Accounting Aspects of Economic Development in Ghana." In *The Multinational Corporation: Accounting and Social Implications.* Center for International Education and Research in Accounting, 1977, pp. 127-38.

Morris, R. C. "Evidence on the Impact of Inflation Accounting on Share Prices." *Accounting and Business Research* (Spring 1975): p. 82-95.

Mueller, Gerhard G. *International Accounting.* The Macmillan Company, 1967.

_____. "Accounting Principles Generally Accepted in the United States Versus Those Generally Accepted Elsewhere." *International Journal of Accounting* (Spring 1968): p. 91-103.

Norton, Curtis L. and Ralph E. Smith. "A Comparison of General Price Level and Historical Cost Financial Statements in the Prediction of Bankruptcy." *The Accounting Review* (January 1979): p. 72-87.

Patz, Dennis H. "The State of the Art in Translation Theory." *Journal of Business, Finance and Accounting* (Autumn 1977): p. 311-25.

Scott, George M. "Accounting and Economic Reform in the Soviet Union." *Abacus* (September 1969): p. 55-63.

_____. *Accounting and Developing Nations.* Graduate School of Business Administration, University of Washington, 1970.

_____ and Pontus Troberg. *Eighty-Eight International Accounting Problems in Rank Order of Importance—A DELPHI Evaluation.* AAA, 1980.

Stamp, Edward. "Uniformity in International Accounting Standards?" *Journal of Accountancy* (April, 1972): p. 64-67.

Wilkinson, Theodore L.. "International Accounting: Harmonization or Disharmony." *Columbia Journal of World Business* (March-April 1969): p. 29-36.

Zeff, Steven A. *Foreign Accounting Principles in Five Countries: A History and an Analysis of Trends.* Stipes Publishing Company, 1971.

Technical Issues in International Accounting

LEE J. SEIDLER
New York University
Bear, Stearns & Co.

International harmonization became the "Holy Grail" of accounting during the 1970s. The drive to eliminate national differences in accounting principles and practices and in auditing standards has continued into the 1980s and shows no signs of abating.

The rationale for this pursuit of international harmonization is inevitably cloaked with profound statements of high purpose. Free international capital flows are supposedly critical to the world quest for faster economic development. Since accounting is portrayed as crucial to the acceleration of international capital flows, it follows that uniform international accounting will speed world development.

It is also an article of faith that managing multinational corporations would be more efficient and less costly if the dissimilarities in local accounting practices were eliminated.

Rarely stated, but implicit in all of the arguments advanced, is the ubiquitous desire for harmony in a world that insists on muddling along in a state of confusion.

It is more likely, however, that these apparently altruistic reasons for spending so much energy in the search for international accounting harmonization cloak a substantial element of self-interest, indeed, selfishness. Internationally, big business continues to struggle with small business, with the larger tending to gradually triumph. The business of accounting is no exception. Major national accounting firms have become major international firms and they continue to grow. Since the market for accounting services is finite, large firm growth must include acquiring clients and business from smaller firms. Thus multinational accounting firms are engaged in an effort to acquire the practices of national firms in many countries.

Private business organizations, such as accounting firms, have no monopoly on selfishness. A major part of the thrust for internationally harmonious accounting standards, particularly in the area of disclosure, has come from the "third world" countries, acting through organizations such as the United Nations. Individual developing countries are frequently smaller, in terms of output and financial resources, than the multinational corporations that operate within their political boundaries. The management and accounting systems of the multinationals frequently overwhelm the ability of developing countries to control these business operations and to obtain what they believe to be their "fair share" of the spoils. The imposition of internationally consistent accounting rules and greater disclosure appears to be a device, cloaked in the desirable goal of international harmonization, which the third world nations would use to improve their leverage against the multinational giants.

"International harmonization" bears a sound of brotherhood that is difficult to oppose, in spite of the discernable self interest that underlies the movement. The search for international harmonization provides an unlimited supply of topics and titles for international meetings of accountants, permitting tax-deductible or reimbursable travel to be combined with good fellowship and good food. Indeed, so many seem to benefit from this search that one is inclined to believe that success might result in a decline in their standard of living.

There Will Not be International Harmonization

Fortunately for the peripatetic savants of the international harmonization movement, there is little chance of achieving worldwide accounting uniformity. To the contrary, current trends seem to indicate that international accountants are doing little more than piddling into the wind.

Few accountants seem to understand why the efforts at international harmonization are doomed to failure. The reasons were perhaps best summed up by one of the world's great non-accountants, V.I. Lenin. Shortly after the Russian revolution Lenin wrote:

> Accounting and control—that is the *main* thing required for "arranging" the smooth working, the correct functioning of the first phase of communist society.
>
> All citizens are transformed here into hired employees of a *single* nationwide state "syndicate." All that is required is that they should work equally, do their proper share of work, and get equally paid.
>
> The accounting and control necessary for this have been *simplified* by capitalism to the extreme and reduced to the extraordinarily simple operations. . . .
>
> When the *majority* of the people begin independently and everywhere to keep such accounts and maintain such control over the capitalists (now converted into employ-

ees) and over the intellectual gentry who preserve their capitalist habits, this control will really become universal, general, popular; and there will be no way of getting away from it, there will be "nowhere to go." *The State and the Revolution* (1917)

Lenin's point is that accounting is principally a control device. That is, accounting is used by one group to control another. Accounting is not performed because it is amusing, gratifying, or fundamentally harmonious but rather to enable some people to direct other people. Controlled groups are frequently antagonistic to their controllers and so the process by which accounting is used involves some degree of coercion. From the point of view of the controlling party, the purpose of this coercion is far more serious than some vague notion of international accounting harmonization. Consider the following examples.

Worldwide tax collections constitute the greatest source of demand for accounting services. The tax on income, both on the individual and business enterprise level, is the largest source of revenue for governments of countries with literate populations. Clearly, the collection of tax revenues, the life-blood of government, outweighs the niceties of accounting theory. Income tax evasion is frequently grounded in distortions of records or in absence of records. Therefore, tax collecting governments inevitably become involved in the bookkeeping and accounting procedures followed by individuals and companies, to provide more assurance of collecting taxes. Accountants in most countries aim at "fair presentation," or some semantic variation thereon, of financial results. Tax collectors, on the other hand, aim to collect taxes. The two goals frequently conflict. When they do, the tax collector wins.

Since tax collection systems vary widely between countries, and since governments show little sign of desiring to harmonize tax systems (except in the collection of maximum amounts from multinational corporations), there is little reason to expect that this barrier to international accounting harmonization will disappear.

Of course, governments use accounting for purposes other than tax collection. In the United States, regulation of the rates charged by permitted monopolies, such as electric utilities, is considered an important governmental function. Since it is (correctly) assumed that the regulated utilities will attempt to avoid regulation through distortion of accounting practices, government bodies (at federal and state levels) prescribe meticulously detailed accounting procedures that allow as little judgement as possible by the regulated companies. These regulated accounting codes are frequently in conflict with the "generally accepted accounting principles" promulgated by the succession of private authoritative accounting bodies in the United States. However, the power of government clearly overwhelms the private sector and, in the addendum to APB Opinion No. 2, the Accounting Principles Board made it clear that it was required to accept this government authority.

National political concerns frequently intrude on accounting with the result that accounting principles are sometimes fashioned to achieve political goals rather than those of accounting. For example, in the United States efforts by the federal government to regulate oil and gas prices while trying not to discourage the operations of oil and gas companies, led to the most acrimonious debate in U.S. accounting history. The Energy Policy and Conservation Act of 1975 called upon the SEC to request that the FASB develop uniform accounting principles for oil and gas companies. The unstated goal of this request for uniformity was to eliminate the flexibility existing in generally accepted accounting principles which permitted the companies to substantially evade accurate government evaluation of their financial positions and operating performance.

In a similar vein, economic policies of governments frequently produce accounting practices which inhibit "fair presentation," thereby increasing the level of international disharmony. For example, Sweden has for many years had a system of investment and inventory reserves which was originally enacted as investment incentives. Swedish companies are permitted accelerated depreciation far in excess of true rates of capital consumption, and are also permitted to take tax deductible reserves against inventory, depreciating their value far below reality. Indeed, in some circumstances these companies have actually been permitted to write their inventories down to negative values, thus creating the accountants' equivalent of the square root of minus one. In the early years of these practices, Swedish companies were required to record their impacts directly in their accounts, thus completely distorting the financial results. More recently, separate disclosure of the impacts of these investment incentives has been permitted. In the United States, tax laws require that taxpayers electing the LIFO inventory method (which generally saves taxes) must also use that method in reporting to shareholders and creditors. Since very few other countries permit the LIFO method, this requirement provides an obvious difference between American financial reporting and that of other countries. Understandably, few American companies would be willing to give up LIFO tax savings as their contribution to the cause of advancing international accounting harmonization.

In some instances, accountants themselves appear to have deliberately increased international disharmony. In the 1970s, multinational accounting firms were gaining a substantial foothold in the auditing of large French corporations. The movement was accelerated by the desire of several French corporations to have their shares listed on The London

Stock Exchange, and the corresponding reluctance of the exchange to accept audits by French auditors. In response, the French enacted a series of measures designed to make it far more difficult for foreigners to practice professional accounting in France, including such items as requirements that examinations be taken orally (in French) and that international firms adopt French names. The managing partner of one international accounting firm was actually convicted (but subsequently pardoned) for stealing clients.

Major Technical Issues

The preceding comments suggest that there are fundamental underlying circumstances which limit the possibility of international accounting harmonization. These forces are the dominant theme in international accounting and the relatively futile efforts of accountants will do little to overcome them.

There are also technical issues which manifest the differences in accounting between countries and which merit the attention of accounting researchers. Some of these issues actually represent differences in beliefs among accountants and thus may be susceptible to some degree of resolution. Oftentimes, the technical differences stem from the fundamental factors considered above that show little promise of being overcome. The remainder of this section describes the most serious technical issues currently dividing accountants in different countries. It is emphasized that the technical conflicts are frequently superficial manifestations of the underlying forces which prevent world accounting uniformity.

Consolidation, Translation, and Inflation

The three most significant technical problems in international accounting—consolidation, translation, and inflation—are completely interrelated and, therefore, difficult to discuss as individual items.

Although, as noted below, consolidation accounting is in different stages of development in different countries, the presentation of consolidated financial statements has increasingly been viewed as the appropriate means of showing the financial position of entities that form a single economic unit or which are under common control. When the theory of consolidation is extended to international operations, the problem of translation emerges automatically. Financial statements of entities in different countries are initially prepared in the currency of the countries in which they operate. Since amounts expressed in different currencies cannot be added together, currency translation is required.

The translation problem might not exist if the relative values of different currencies did not change. However, despite some periods of stability, changing exchange rates appear inevitable. Therefore, the question emerges as to which rate of exchange will be used to translate financial statements expressed in different currencies. Exchange rates may vary for many reasons, the most important being differing rates of inflation. Thus the three major international technical problems are interwoven. The following discussion attempts to treat them separately, but it is emphasized that this is merely for the purpose of convenience.

Translation accounting debates. It is doubtful that any reader of this publication is uninformed about the debates over translation accounting, both nationally and internationally. Theories and practice on translation or foreign exchange accounting have varied with the development of accounting sophistication, the evolution of multinational corporations, and changes in the international monetary system. While accountants in many countries are engaged in debates over translation accounting, the development of the problem in the United States and accounting responses there present the problem as well as would the experiences of any other country.

Prior to 1976, translation accounting by United States companies was, theoretically, governed by chapter 12 of ARB No. 43. The word "theoretically" is emphasized in the preceding sentence because many companies did not, in fact, follow the dictates of ARB 43.

ARB 43 is a 1953 compilation of the previous 42 Research Bulletins. The section dealing with translation accounting was originally issued in 1939 as ARB No. 4. However, the original Accounting Research Bulletin appears to have been no more than a rewrite of a committee report presented to the American Institute Accountants in 1928. That document possibly originated as an earlier draft in 1923. Thus, as late as 1975, American companies were supposed to be following a rather vague set of accounting rules written as many as fifty years earlier.

Prior to the issuance of SFAS No. 8, *Accounting for the Translation of Foreign Currency Transactions and Foreign Currency Financial Statements*, in 1976, many American companies were using whatever translation accounting method suited them.

In 1976, the FASB issued SFAS No. 8 which adopted the so-called "temporal" method translation. A slight variation on the better known monetary-nonmonetary method, SFAS No. 8 became highly controversial as soon as the first financial statements prepared under its authority were published. Leading currencies were fluctuating widely during the mid-1970s and the requirement of SFAS No. 8, that translation gains and losses be taken directly and immediately to the income statement, created a great deal of pain and anguish in many corporate headquarters. Investors were confused and were unable to understand the nature of the substantial amounts causing wide earnings fluctuations. Some companies embarked on costly hedging programs to reduce "accounting exposure" which frequently had the unfortunate result of increasing economic exposure to currency differences.

In 1980, the FASB issued an exposure draft of a possible replacement for SFAS No. 8. The exposure draft, which adopted the "all current method" of translation, also caused considerable controversy. At the time of this writing, the FASB contemplates the issuance of yet another exposure draft, hoping to refine some of the concepts expressed in the earlier document, and offers the assurance of a new standard by the end of 1982.

Dozens of articles have been written supporting or attacking the different methods of translation that were in use before SFAS No. 8, under SFAS No. 8, and that which might be used as its successor. The problem, however, does not appear to be susceptible to a single all-encompassing solution. As with other accounting problems, the individual circumstances of the multinational companies involved—and in the various countries—preclude any universally acceptable solution.

At the heart of the controversy would appear to be perceptions of the nature of foreign operations as compared to domestic operations for various companies. The United States has the world's largest domestic market. It is possible for a company to be one of the largest in the world, as is the case of American Telephone and Telegraph, having operations only in the United States. It is not unusual then, that many U.S. based companies consider the American market to be their primary concern and view foreign operation as secondary suppliers of additional business. Foreign operations may provide convenient export markets for extra production or a secondary return on technology already exploited in the U.S.

Only a small number of U.S. corporations view themselves as true multinationals, or "transnationals." That is, in only a few American corporations do operations outside the United States exist on a basis coequal to domestic.

By contrast, consider the case of Sweden. Some of the world's largest multinationals are Swedish companies. However, with a population of only seven million, Sweden is a small, developed market. The large Swedish companies operate almost entirely outside of Sweden and their principal sources of revenue are found multinationally.

As a third view, consider the situation of many Canadian companies. Canada, like Sweden, is a small market. However, Canada shares one of the longest geographic frontiers with the United States, the world's largest market. Many Canadian companies derive the majority of their revenue from foreign operations that are located almost entirely in the United States, not in a variety of nations.

Consider the implications of the translation of foreign operations for these three types of companies. For the more common, large American company, where foreign operations are essentially secondary, a translation method which takes a U.S. based perspective appears logical.

This is the perspective that was taken in SFAS No. 8. Under FASB Standard No. 8, monetary assets and liabilities of foreign operations—cash, receivables, and payables—are translated at the current rate, that is the rate of exchange in effect at the balance sheet date. However, nonmonetary assets (and liabilities, if any exist) such as inventories and fixed assets are translated under SFAS No. 8 at the so-called "historical" rate of exchange. The historical rate is the rate in effect at the time the particular item entered the foreign subsidiary's balance sheet.

The practical effect of translating at the historical rate is that inventories and fixed assets hold a constant value in U.S. dollars, regardless of changes in the exchange rate. Stripping away the elaborate theoretical rationale for this practice, the fundamental notion here is simply that the U.S. dollar is the only "real money" in the world. That is, tangible items, such as inventories and fixed assets, have a "real value" in U.S. dollars and this value is not altered by their location in a foreign country.

As a practical matter, this notion was close to reality for the first twenty-five years following World War II. During that time the U.S. dollar, aided by America's enormous prosperity, held its value while all other currencies depreciated relative to it. Indeed, during that period, there was only a single upward revaluation against the dollar, that of the German deutschmark in 1960. That revaluation was reversed six months later. Thus the assumption of an immovable dollar against which all other currencies deteriorated was logical in the circumstances of the two decades following World War II. However, by 1976 when SFAS No. 8 was issued, the dollar fluctuated both up and down against other currencies and the underlying rationale of SFAS No. 8 had disappeared.

Nevertheless, from the perspective of the many American companies that viewed their foreign operations as secondary, SFAS No. 8 remained a rational method of translation.

At the opposite extreme is the Swedish company. With its operations located around the world, the Swedish company might describe its wealth as a basket of various currencies in different jurisdictions. The underlying notion of SFAS 8, that the reporting currency (in this case the Swedish currency) is an immovable starting point, is clearly invalid. Indeed, it is difficult to intuit any rational method of translating the financial statements of the typical Swedish based multinational other than into some basic unit, such as SDR's (Special Drawing Rights) which are themselves baskets of all currencies. Stated another way it is difficult for any Swedish based multinational to realistically ascertain its wealth, expressed in terms of a single currency.

The Canadian situation provides yet another alternative. Although Canadian companies are legally and originally based in Canada, most of their operations take place in a single country—the U.S., and in a single currency—the U.S. dollar. It is questionable in this situation, whether translation is appropriate at all. If the operations of a Canadian company are, indeed, conducted principally in the United States and the wealth of those companies lies principally in the United States, what is the value of presenting financial statements in Canadian dollars? The only realistic presentation of the financial position of such an entity must be made in U.S. dollars.

Thus it can be seen that the differing perspectives of international operations lead to completely different and conflicting views of translation accounting.

Adjusting for inflation. Accountants in most major countries have considered adjusting conventional, historical cost financial statements for the effects of inflation. In many countries, some form of adjustment has been tried. However, the correction attempts have varied widely among countries and, at times, in the same country, making international comparability difficult to achieve.

Among the first to experiment with inflation correction accounting were the Dutch under the theoretical urgings of Limpberg. Best known among the companies that were influenced by Limpberg and who began to experiment with inflation accounting as early as the 1930s is N.V. Phillips Gloelampenfabrieken.

The Dutch approach was a generally economic one, not only directed toward the effects of inflation. It was hypothesized that the cost of goods sold of a company should reflect the "replacement cost" of the assets consumed in the revenue-producing process, rather than the historical cost. Although replacement cost is generally associated with the inflation problem today, Limpberg was also concerned with the impacts of technological change. That is, the development of different productive processes would change (probably lower) the replacement value of older equipment.

This theory received considerable publicity and a moderate level of application in the period after World War II. At the peak, perhaps a third of all large Dutch companies reported their financial statements on a replacement cost basis. However, that proportion is lower today.

Many Western European countries and Japan experienced very high rates of inflation in the first few years after World War II. As an encouragement to capital formation and to avoid wiping out then feeble industrial companies through excessive taxation, around 1950 France, Germany, Italy, and Japan allowed companies to apply general price indices to the cost of their fixed assets, inventories, and investments thereby adjusting the values for inflation. The companies were then permitted to depreciate, *for tax purposes*, the revalorized amounts. The "surplus" produced by revalorization was generally not taken to profit, rather it resulted in a direct credit to shareholders' equity.

The revalorizations in France had been voluntary until 1961 when the government introduced a compulsory "final revalorization." A similar method with more frequent, typically semiannual, revaluations was started in the 1960s in some Latin American countries, such as Argentina, Brazil, and Chile, that were experiencing runaway rates of inflation. These practices continue today in Latin America.

In the late 1970s Italy and Spain, both faced with high rates of inflation, again permitted companies to revalue fixed assets, inventories, and investments in the same manner.

It appears that the inflation adjustments just described were done entirely on a pragmatic basis. There is no evidence that any significant theoretical consideration was given to them. Some articles about these adjustments have appeared in academic journals, although they appear to be principally descriptive.

Spurred by increasing rates of inflation, British accountants began to consider inflation adjustments in the early 1970s. In 1975 the Sandilands Committee, a government-appointed committee, strongly recommended the adoption of replacement cost accounting for both financial reporting and tax purposes. Following review of the Sandilands recommendations by a steering group of the Institute of Chartered Accountants, an exposure draft (E.D. 18), often referred to as the Morpeth proposal, was issued in 1977. The E.D. 18, which largely followed the Sandilands Report, would have required current cost accounting—usually replacement cost—in the financial statements of all large companies. The CCA information would have replaced historical cost figures in the financial statement for fixed assets, depreciation, inventories, and cost of goods sold. E.D. 18 also called for general price level information, particularly on the impact of inflation net monetary assets, but only in a note to the statement.

However, in a unique exercise of accounting democracy, English Chartered Accountants voted, on July 6, 1977, against the implementation of E.D. 18 and cumpulsory current cost accounting. Two partners in a small firm of chartered accountants in Sussex managed to convene a special meeting of the Institute of Chartered Accountants in England & Wales at which E.D. 18 was rejected. More than 700 CAs attended the meeting and over 28,000 (of a total membership of 60,000) voted to defeat the draft by a 54 percent majority.

In November 1977 some British accountants, referred to as the Hyde group, issued new proposed guidelines for inflation accounting. Under the Hyde proposals, only cost of sales and depreciation expense would be adjusted. These two adjustments would be computed by the use of appropriate indices. However, these adjustments would not be for the entire difference between current cost and historic cost, but only for that portion of the higher cost of sales and depreciation which is equity financed. In other words, a debt to equity ratio would be computed and depreciation would then be adjusted only to the extent of the equity portion. The recommended adjustments would not appear in the income statement but would be disclosed separately. This debt-equity split follows a concept introduced by a group of German accountants several years ago, but rejected by the German government.

The Hyde proposals were substantially adopted by the ICA in "Current Cost Accounting," Statement of Standard Accounting Practice No. 16 (SSAP 16).

SSAP 16 differs from SFAS No. 33's current cost accounting in that SSAP 16 calls for both a monetary working capital adjustment and gearing adjustment.

Since the countries involved generally required that financial statements prepared for shareholders and creditors be in conformity with tax declarations, the inflation adjustments were also shown in the companies' normal financial statements.

The resulting British disclosures, still voluntary, are probably among the most sophisticated in current shareholder financial reporting. The British accepted a concept of "gearing" that apportions the expected higher replacement cost of equipment between creditors and shareholders, based on the company's present debt-to-equity ratio. The British also include an adjustment for increased working capital. The British disclosures have received considerable attention in the U.K., but it is difficult to assess the impacts they may have had on investors.

In the immediate post World War II period, American accountants devoted only sporadic attention to the problems of accounting for the impacts of inflation until the late 1970s. The most significant of these efforts was made by the AICPA in 1963, when it issued "Financial Statements for General Price-Level Changes," Statement of the Accounting Principles Board No. 3. Staff of the Accounting Research Division prepared Accounting Research Study No. 6, "Reporting the Financial Effects of Price-Level Changes'' in the same year. The general price level accounting (GPLA) advocated in APB Statement No. 3 followed the earlier ideas of several American academic accountants, including Henry W. Sweeney, who published one of the most significant works in the area, *Stabilized Accounting*, in 1936.

In 1976, the U.S. Securities and Exchange Commission issued Accounting Series Release No. 147, which called for disclosure of supplementary replacement cost information (not complete financial statements) in Forms 10-K of large, publicly held U.S. companies. The SEC's action was precipitous and uncharacteristic of the organization, which normally works through the private, authoritative accounting body. It appears that the SEC's action was initiated by John C. Burton, Chief Accountant for the SEC and former accounting professor at Columbia University, largely in response to the progress being made in the United Kingdom at the same time.

Prodded by the SEC's action, the Financial Accounting Standards Board undertook to develop a more complete inflation correction mechanism. In 1979, the FASB issued SFAS No. 33. Unable to resolve the conflict between advocates of a GPLA approach and those who preferred the SEC's replacement cost, the Board called for the use of constant dollar accounting (similar to GPLA) and current cost (similar to replacement cost). Under SFAS No. 33 large companies must provide supplementary income statements (income statement reconciliation) using both constant dollar and current cost approaches, in additon to conventional historical cost financial statements.

The long-awaited introduction of inflation correction accounting in the U.S. generated less interest and enthusiasm than was expected. Although some attention has been accorded to the results in the business media, there is little indication that investors have yet embraced the information.

A group of countries such as Canada, Australia, New Zealand, and South Africa, who typically follow U.K. and U.S. accounting closely, generally delayed their implementation of inflation correction accounting pending resolution of the disputation in the United States. SFAS No. 33 did not provide them with the anticipated guidance.

In addition to a formal method of inflation correction accounting, many countries have informal devices, usually in the tax system, that accomplish a substantial measure of inflation adjustment. For example, in the United States the LIFO inventory method provides a reasonably valid, albeit complex, method of adjusting costs of goods sold for the impacts of inflation. Several accelerated depreciation methods are used for tax purposes and, by a minority of companies, for financial reporting.

Although crude, these depreciation methods also provide a considerable measure of inflation correction to income statements.

In France the *provision pour hausses des prix* provides a tax deferral similar to LIFO, as does stock relief in the United Kingdom.

An interesting exercise in international confusion occurred in 1979 when the United Kingdom changed the rules related to stock relief. In its original version, stock relief allowed companies to tax deduct the increase in book value of inventories during the year. That amount would be returned to income six years later. Thus, there was a deferral which, if inflation continued, would probably never result in tax payments. American accountants, accounting for the operations of British subsidiaries of American companies, required the U.S. company account for stock relief as a timing difference and established a provision for deferred taxes in accordance with APB Opinion No. 11.

In 1979 the British revised the legislation, largely eliminating the possibility of the original deferrals flowing back into taxable income. Upon examination, the FASB noted that stock relief bore a great resemblance to American LIFO. The possibility exists, under LIFO, that the taxes deferred will eventually be paid, but U.S. accountants have never required a tax provision in connection with this potential liability. The British change in stock relief strongly suggested that the original American accounting for stock relief had been inconsistent with American accounting for LIFO. After some confusion, in SFAS No. 31 the FASB eliminated the need to provide deferred taxes for stock relief.

Thus, while considerable efforts throughout the world have been devoted to inflation correction accounting, there is no international consistency. Differences in history, economic trends and governmental attitudes toward business and taxation have resulted in an accounting "tower of Babel."

Inflation and translation accounting interact. The problems associated with the widely varying methods of inflation correction accounting became apparent when the FASB attempted to revise translation accounting under SFAS No. 8, during 1980-81. The all-current method proposed by the Board provides appropriate translation in many circumstances. However, when the all-current method is applied to the historical cost balance sheet of a subsidiary located in a country with high levels of inflation, bizarre results may appear.

Consider, for example, the case of an American company that built a factory in Brazil about seven years ago at a cost of Cr.5 million which was then the equivalent of U.S. $1 million. Since then, the Brazilian cruziero has depreciated against the U.S. dollar by a factor of about 10 and the exchange rate has gone from about Cr.5 to the dollar to about Cr.50 to the dollar. If the historical cruziero cost of $5 million is translated at the current rate, the translated dollar value of the plant will be only U.S. $100 thousand, rather than the original U.S. $1 million. An obvious distortion appears, due to the differential rates of inflation between the United States and Brazil.

After much deliberation, the Financial Accounting Standards Board agreed that in countries with high rates of inflation, relative to that of the U.S., an adjustment for inflation should be made to the historical cost amounts in the foreign currency financial statements before translating at the current rate.

Consolidated Financial Statements

The international differences in practices related to consolidated financial statements provide a controlled means for review of variations in international attitudes toward accounting. As a practical matter, there are few debates over the actual manner in which consolidated financial statements should be prepared. Accountants in different countries have minor disagreements, but the descriptions of the methods used to prepare consolidated financial statements, found in advanced accounting textbooks in almost any country, are similar.

Although the technical preparation of consolidated financial statements is routine, the presentation of such statements varies widely between countries. Consolidation accounting is found in its most advanced state in the United States. Indeed, the U.S. may be considered to have passed through maturity to old age. The most pressing current issues are no longer on consolidation, but on deconsolidation. That is, having achieved aggregated financial information, users of U.S. financial statements have, for the past few years, been demanding more disaggregated information. Segmented disclosure has recently been a principle issue in the U.S.

In the U.K. consolidated or "group" accounts are generally presented in a form comparable to that found in the United States. However, demands there for disaggregated information do not appear to have reached the same level as in the U.S.

In Germany, consolidated financial statements are found but the methodology is frequently abused. Japan remains virginal, so far as consolidated financial statements are involved, constantly deferring a requirement for statements that disclose the true dimensions of the "groups" that dominate the Japanese business scene.

The preceding comment about Japan suggests the fundamental issue in the development of consolidated reporting. Consolidated financial statements are essentially a form of disclosure of existing information. They do not represent any new recording or analysis of transactions or any differential accounting procedure. The separate financial statements of the various entities controlled by a parent or holding company already exist. Consolidated reporting presents those separate financial statements in a single report which may disclose significant information about the economic wealth of a parent or holding company.

The common reluctance of many people to disclose their wealth is well known. Consolidated financial statements represent a similar disclosure in their preparation and their dissemination is frequently viewed with great reluctance. Thus, absent a requirement for well prepared consolidated financial statement, enterprises in many countries continue to present parent company only financial statements, with investments in subsidiaries reflected in a manner designed to conceal the economic status of the subsidiaries and the total group.

In seeming contradiction to the immediately preceding analysis, the development of consolidated financial statements in the United States was aided by the desire of some entrepeneurs to disclose, indeed perhaps to exaggerate, the total wealth of their empires. It is said that J.P. Morgan was so proud of the giant United States Steel Company he had assembled that he insisted on the preparation and disclosure of consolidated financial statements in the company's first annual report, issued in 1903. Despite Morgan's exuberance, consolidated financial statements were not normally presented until the Securities and Exchange Commission demanded them. In an attempt to provide some insight into the organization of holding companies, the SEC required both parent company only and consolidated financial statements.

It has become clear that parent company only financial statements are of little use to investors, although they may be of interest to those studying holding companies and the pyramiding of wealth. The SEC is expected to eliminate its requirements for parent company only financial statements in the near future.

However, as noted above, investors and financial analysts have grown increasingly disenchanted with the level of aggregation inherent in financial statements. Diversified companies, in contrast to the original U.S. Steel, obtain their income from disparate sources which are affected in different ways by differing circumstances. It is difficult for a financial analyst to forecast the future operations of a diversified company if he does not know the contribution of each such operation. Financial analysts finally succeeded in getting segmented disclosure from U.S. companies, with help from the U.S. government which used the disclosure to enhance the effectiveness of anti-trust efforts.

At the opposite extreme in Japan, where the Byzantine combinations of industrial, banking, and trading operations have produced the "groups" which compete so effectively around the world, there is great reluctance to prepare consolidated statements. Periodically, Japanese authorities have required consolidated statements but, with a precision that appears to characterize Japanese operations, have consistently postponed the date or diluted the requirements.

Financial Reporting and Income Taxes

As was noted earlier, taxation of the income of business has been a major force causing the evolution of accounting throughout the world. In varying degrees, tax authorities require that financial statements prepared for conventional accounting uses reflect the same figures embodied in the tax declaration.

In Turkey the financial statements must be identical to the tax declaration. In France, an expense may not be taken in the tax declaration as a deduction unless it is also shown as an expense in the conventional financial statement.

By contrast, in the U.S. and U.K. financial reporting and tax accounting are largely divorced. In Great Britain, the tax declaration starts with the amount of income as per the conventional financial statements, but thereafter a series of adjustments may be made, such as substituting capital allowances for depreciation so that the two forms of reporting are essentially separate.

In the United States, the two income statements are prepared separately, generally without regard to each other. The only significant link between tax and financial reporting concerns the LIFO inventory method. Companies using LIFO for tax purposes are required to represent their annual, primary income statements for shareholders and creditors on a LIFO basis. This conformity has been narrowed, recently, to apply only to the income statement and to permit supplementary disclosures of FIFO results. The U.S. Treasury Department, unhappy in its role as an arbiter of financial reporting, has asked Congress to delete the conformity requirement.

A certain degree of conformity between financial statement and tax accounting is required in every country. It would be difficult to explain to the tax authorities, for example, why the amount of cash shown in the shareholders' balance sheet differs from that in the tax balance sheet.

One cannot overestimate the impact and distortions in conventional financial reporting caused by required conformity between tax and normal accounting presentations. The instinct to minimize tax payments is far stronger than beliefs in "fair presentation" or whatever other appellation is applied in each country to the goal of financial reporting. Inevitably, income will be understated, assets undervalued and liabilities overaccrued, within or outside the limits of the law, in an attempt to reduce taxes.

In countries such as Italy and Spain, where illegal tax evasion is common, the resulting distribution in financial reports makes them frequently useless. In countries where legal tax avoidance is the practice, if book tax conformity is required then financial statements reflect the same tax-oriented distortions, but to a lesser degree.

Beyond the direct distortion of financial reporting caused by tax-book conformity lies a host of other impacts. For example, in the United States it appears that the LIFO tax conformity requirement has prevented many companies from adopting that inventory method. The adoption of LIFO, which saves taxes, also results in lower reported income. It appears that many American companies, seeking higher reported earnings, have been willing to eschew real, cash tax savings in order to report higher earnings to shareholders.

Tax considerations also appear to have had an impact on the formation of accounting principles, as distinguished from accounting practice. In the United States, accountants delayed for many years attempts to impute costs to the issuance of restricted stock options to employees. U.S. government policy, during the New Deal, had been to encourage share ownership by corporate executives. As a result the Treasury Department did not tax the issuance of stock options to employees. In order to perpetuate the myth that options did not represent compensation, accountants were discouraged from issuing pronouncements that would have imputed a cost to stock options in conventional financial reporting. It was not until government policy turned against tax-free stock options that U.S. accountants moved, in APB Opinion No. 25 to impute a cost to these items.

While the mandatory linkage between accounting and tax reporting causes accounting problems, so too does the opposite situation, freedom to report transactions differently for the two purposes. One of the continuing and generally unresolved accounting problems in those countries that do not require book tax conformity has been accounting for differences between book and taxable income. When such differences are permanent, as in the case of tax-free interest received on state and local obligations in the United States, the problem is simple. However, when the differences are ones of timing, such as in the case of very rapid capital allowances in the United Kingdom as compared to conventional depreciation, a clear resolution appears to have eluded accountants.

This problem is most pronounced in countries such as Australia, Canada, New Zealand, and South Africa which tend to follow the U.S. and U.K. model of relative freedom of accounting as between financial reporting and tax considerations.

At different times, in different countries, tax timing differences have been regarded as deferred, as liabilities, or as items to be disregarded in the financial statements. At present, U.S. accounting (APB Opinion No. 11) requires a comprehensive, deferred approach. In the U.K., this approach was recently discarded in SSAP No. 19, under which liabilities for tax timing differences are established only when it is clear that they will be payable in the near future.

At the heart of the issue appears to be the question of whether individual tax timing differences should be accounted for individually or as a collective deferral. The view that results in comprehensive deferred tax accounting is that the taxes related to a specific transaction or action are only temporarily deferred. Ultimately, the transaction generating the deferral will reverse and the taxes are paid. The alternative interpretation is that in the aggregate one deferral is replaced by another and that taxes once deferred by a repetitive transaction will rarely, in fact, ever be paid.

As an example, consider a machine that is depreciated on an accelerated method for tax purposes but on a straight-line or linear basis for financial reporting. In the earlier years of the machine's life, tax depreciation will exceed book depreciation resulting in an apparent tax deferral. In the later years of the machine's life book depreciation will be greater than tax depreciation. Viewed as a single transaction, the deferral is reversed. However, in practice new machines tend to be acquired and new accelerated depreciation causes a continuing deferral. With normal replacement, aided by inflation, taxes are frequently deferred indefinitely by accelerated depreciation.

The former, individual transaction conception, presently governs U.S. accounting while the continuing deferral approach governs that of the U.K.

Employee Severance and Retirement Benefits

Relatively little attention has been accorded to the significantly international variation in accounting for employee severance and retirement benefits. There is considerable variation in the actual form of such benefits and in accounting for them.

Most countries have either government, private, or mixed pension plans for employees. In the United States, government funded social security benefits are significant but private pension plans, funded by companies, are the largest in the world. In 1980, the assets of private pension plans exceeded $350 billion. At the opposite extreme, private pension plans are insignificant in France where social security dominates the retirement scene. In Germany private pension plans coexist with a dominant social security system.

When private pension plans are of a defined contribution form there are few accounting problems. Under a defined contribution plan, employers contribute a specified amount to a pension fund which ultimately pays employees' retirement benefits. The amounts of benefits received by the employees are dependent on the contributions and the investment results of the fund. The employer has no liability to the employees beyond the original contributions.

More complicated accounting is involved in defined benefit plans. In such plans, the employer undertakes the obligation to pay a specified future benefit, thus assuming the continuing liability until the employees ultimately receive their retirement pay. The obligation to the employees is decades in the future and, since the employee group continues to turn over, is essentially a moving target. With the difficulty of predicting investment returns and rates of inflation in benefits, precise specification of the future liability is virtually impossible.

In Germany, attempts are made to estimate the future liability and amounts that have not yet been funded (unfunded pension liabilities) are carried as obligations in corporate balance sheets. In the United States although actuaries measure future obligations, the unfunded liability is yet to be placed in corporate financial statements.

The problem has a mundane sound, but the amounts involved are enormous. For example, the unfunded pension amount for General Motors Corporation at the end of 1979 was *$11.9 billion* or *more than one-half* of the company's entire shareholders' equity.

A continuing and also unresolved problem concerns severance pay. Some countries, such as Chile and Belgium, have extremely strict laws which provide for a large accumulation of severance benefits by employees. The employees who are discharged are frequently entitled to receive amounts up to several years' compensation. On the other hand, in the United States there are no requirements for severance compensation; even the traditional "two weeks notice" is at the employer's option. Practices with regard to accrual of severance pay obligations vary widely as between different countries. The situation is somewhat paradoxical since the larger the potential severance obligation, the less likely it is that employees will actually be discharged. That is, where severance pay requirements are very great, there is a strong tendency to keep even the most redundant employees on.

Other Factors

Obviously, no single article can cover all the variations in international accounting that produce unresolved technical issues. Among the other problems not described above are transfer pricing, statutory financial statement requirements, and different stages of development of capital markets.

Multinational corporations transfer large amounts of goods and services between parents and foreign subsidiaries and between foreign subsidiaries. The transfer pricing problems that are encountered in the domestic management of a multinational operation are exacerbated in the international dimension by tax considerations. Subsidiaries in different countries are taxed in differing jurisdictions. The sale of goods and services from one subsidiary to another produces taxable revenues and cost in different jurisdictions, which would be eliminated in a single country situation. Since tax rates differ between countries, there is an obvious incentive to adjust transfer prices to produce revenues in low taxing jurisdictions and costs in the high tax countries. As in many cases, the tax incentive frequently wins out over financial reporting, thus causing another distortion and problem of comparability.

In contrast to the "problems" presented in this section, the operations of the multinational corporation generally seem to provide "opportunities" to resolve international accounting problems. Multinational corporations require as uniform accounting as possible for management and control purposes. While generally conforming to widely varying local requirements, some of which were chronicled above, many multinationals also require uniform reporting within the firm. Typically, this uniform reporting closely parallels U.S. accounting practices. As a result, the multinational corporation is becoming an increasing force expanding the U.S. accounting outlook and in training accountants with this view.

Growing capital markets also appear to be a force for international accounting uniformity rather than disparity. The generally similar disclosure requirements of American and British capital markets are viewed as models for other countries. As a result, local capital market requirements tend to follow these two leaders. In addition, companies located in countries other than the U.S. and U.K. frequently wish to have their securities traded on exchanges in these two countries and therefore must conform to their accounting and disclosure requirements. The result is that many of the largest companies in countries with poor accounting prepare financial statements that conform to the highest standards of the world's most developed capital markets, thereby creating yet another force for international accounting uniformity.

Bibliography

Aron, Paul. "International Accounting and Financial Reporting." *Accountants' Handbook*, 6th edition, Lee J. Seidler, D.R. Carmichael, editors. New York: John Wiley & Sons, Inc. 1981.

deBruyne, D. "Global Standards: A Tower of Babel?" *Financial Executive* (February 1980).

Chetkovitch, Michael, and Robert Schapperle. "International Accounting Cooperation." *The SBI Journal*, Florida A&M University, 1977.

Kanaga, William S. "International Accounting: The Challenge and The Challenges." *Journal of Accountancy* (November 1980).

Lohr, Steve. "World Accounting Standards Urged." *The New York Times*, February 8, 1981, International Economic Survey, p. 24.

Mueller, G.G. "Accounting Principles Generally Accepted in the United States Versus Those Generally Accepted Elsewhere." *The International Journal of Accounting and Research* 3.2 (1968).

Previts, Gary John. "On the Subject of Methodology and Models for International Accounting." *The International Journal of Accounting and Research* 10.2 (1975).

Walker, R.G. "International Accounting Compromises: A Case of Consolidation Accounting." *Abacus* 14.2 (December 1978).

International Accounting Institutions

W. JOHN BRENNAN
University of Saskatchewan

The institutions of the internationalization of the accountancy profession have for the past few years been the focus of interest and of considerable print. The accountancy organizations have earned compliments and criticism. On the whole, the leaders of the accountancy profession are well satisfied with their efforts in this regard. The views of several of these leaders together with considerable descriptive information can be found in *The Internationalization of the Accountancy Profession* published by the Canadian Institute of Chartered Accountants in 1979, edited by the author.

This internationalization has contributed significantly to our understanding of accounting issues. Many critics suggest that little resolution of problems or differences has ensued from the process. Others hold the view that it is a matter of time and, inevitably, such effort at international harmonization will succeed. Some, from both sides, claim that pursuit of the goal of international harmonization is sufficient; in attempting to achieve resolution of differences we all gain as a result of the closer examination of the issues, the learning that occurs in the participants, and the additional research that is stimulated.

This essay will examine this internationalization with particular reference to the nature of the institutions and the nature of their activity. The objective is to suggest how the existing institutions might act to better support the goals of internationalization and to direct international accounting researchers to some areas of investigation that might prove even more productive than those previously pursued.

The institutions created *by* accountants, *for* accountants, and *of* accountants have ranged from local city and state groups to world-wide bodies. Many of these organizations are of long standing, others are very new. Over the past few years there have been a number of centenary celebrations; that of the Institute of Chartered Accountants in England and Wales involved much ceremony and was graced by the attendance of Her Majesty the Queen. As recently as 1977 in Munich, there was born a new organization, the International Federation of Accountants—a world federation of many national accountancy bodies.

National, regional and world wide bodies are the key participants in the internationalization activity. Indeed one might claim the unit of greatest importance is the national organization. These bodies have acted to form the more senior (in a geographical sense) entities while the other levels have, of course, received the press coverage. A brief look at each level is in order.

National Bodies

Institute, order, council, association, chambre are the names used to describe the organizations which reflect the views and attitudes of accountants and officers in various countries. Whatever the name, the organization usually takes the responsibility for development of accounting and auditing rules or guidelines. They also attempt to encourage liason among their members with a view to improving the impact that the professional group has in the activity of accounting.

Each accountant is a member of at least one such group. It is this group to which the individual accountant pays his primary allegiance and likely his increasingly substantial annual fees. It is to this group that the accountant looks for leadership within the domain of his professional activity.

It is no accident that it is these groups which are the instigators of formalized international accounting institutions. The world's economic activity has demanded the international outlook of its businessmen and accordingly of its accountants. The domestic accountancy bodies are bound to reflect that attitude.

Participation and interest by accountancy bodies can be directly motivated from many sources. The private nongovernmental organizations may be driven by their members who are in day to day contact with the world of international business. The essentially government controlled organizations of auditors may be encouraged by the diplomatic need to be involved in such activity; i.e., "we must not be left out, we are leaders or at least must be seen to be leaders." The net effect of these and other motives is that most accountancy bodies in the western world are now actively involved in affiliations with other accountancy bodies beyond their national borders.[1] Despite this activity it remains the national body to which the individual accountant's loyalty is tied.

Each accountant can look at the role that their national accountancy body plays in international affairs. To offer a means to focus that review a brief but closer look at a couple of examples may be in order.

The United States

The American Institute of Certified Public Accountants (AICPA) is the sole representative in world bodies on behalf of accountants in the U.S. The organization is, by activity measure, dominated by auditors but certainly encompasses all accountants in all aspects of economic activity. By this I mean not to demean the work of the American Accounting Association, the National Association of Accountants and others, but their efforts have been relatively minor in comparison to that of the AICPA.

The AICPA has for some time had a division devoted to the concerns surrounding the international activity of accountants. It was through this division that much of the support for the international accountancy institutions was generated. Their staff worked tirelessly and patiently to achieve the commitments from the U.S. and from abroad. The current senior administrator of the International Federation of Accountants, Mr. Robert Sempier, deserves specific mention in this regard.

Individual accountants in the U.S. could be said to be somewhat apathetic. The international relationships were not a grassroots issue. The senior councils of the AICPA discussed and indeed heatedly debated some international commitments. However, it is reasonable to presume that interest in the issue was centered in the senior executive offices of the top few accountancy firms. Concern but later strong support for international commitments came primarily from this source.

Because of the size of the AICPA the impact of the international liason on the organization's budget was relatively small. The exact costs are not important. It should be sufficient to indicate that only a few staff were assigned to the activity and that most of the manpower used was of the volunteer variety; senior partners of the major accountancy firms, most of whom did not even obtain compensation for out of pocket travel costs.

Some of these hard working internationalists may have adopted an outlook that centered beyond the domain and control of the AICPA but they were, and still are, in the extreme minority. Even these farsighted leaders retained a U.S.—AICPA focus to their deliberations. The vast numbers of AICPA members not so directly involved would certainly have been even more U.S. oriented. Despite the leadership role taken by the AICPA it is still safe to conclude that for its membership the national body is the relevant entity.

The United Kingdom

In the United Kingdom participation in international accounting institutions is carried out under the auspices of a coordinating body for the six major accountancy groups in the United Kingdom and Ireland. The dominant body because of its size, location, and tradition is the Institute of Chartered Accountants in England and Wales. Their Moorgate Place headquarters house the relatively few staff devoted to the international work. The Institute of Chartered Accountants of Scotland are just as committed and, in many ways, a very important influence.

The coordinating committee of the six accountancy bodies is almost equivalent to an international organization right at home. Each body has given up some of its rights and independence in the broader interest of attaining even higher goals. Despite this cooperation most organizations find it sufficiently important to be seen individually represented in many international gatherings.

Perhaps even more so in the U.K. than in the U.S. the rank and file membership of the professional bodies cherish their membership in the national organization as paramount. Leadership in international affairs has been clearly demonstrated by the profession's senior members and wide spread support has been forthcoming. However, the cost has been relatively small and in many cases has been borne not by the professional bodies but by the leading professional firms.

The Netherlands

The accountancy profession in the Netherlands is one of high repute both within and outside the country. Because of the nature of the country, international activity predominates. A very significant proportion of the total activity of the Nederlands Institut van Register Accountants (NIVRA) is devoted to international dimensions of the profession.[2] The rank and file members for geographical reasons can hardly avoid direct and frequent international contact and certainly cannot avoid the relatively high fees paid to support their organization's activity in this dimension.

The cultural setting in which NIVRA operates is considerably different than that of the U.K. and the U.S. NIVRA governs and represents accountants in the same way as does the AICPA or the ICAEW. However, NIVRA explicitly participates with a broader range of social interests in many of its regulatory or pseudo regulatory functions. The Tripartite Committee illustrates this aspect of the organization very well.

Dutch accountants have an international outlook but are still domestically oriented. Despite the significant expenditure of time and money their benefit is not seen as improved standards at home but improved standards abroad.[3] They see their effort as in a sense "foreign aid." The reaction to a proposal standard on consolidation in the U.S. and on depreciation demonstrates that they, too, saw it very much as foreign aid.

There are some nations in which the international participation is based on a need and a desire to efficiently acquire professionalism domestically. Many of the small developing nations might be cited. These countries have relied on the professional accountancy bodies of other countries to train their accountants and now are looking to the broad international forum for leadership in setting their domestic rules and standards.

Few if any nations with this attitude have been integrally involved in the internationalization movement. Many have, however, given their support, mainly moral support, to the institutions once they have been created.

The key participants have been representatives of national bodies, each with strong domestic orientation, each anxious to teach the world a better way, their way. Few have engaged in the activity in the interests of a supra national order. Lord Henry Benson was one of the few exceptions but even he was unable to persist in face of the rising tide of dissent.

Regional Bodies

The major regional organizations are the Union Européenne des Comptables Economiques et Financiers (UEC), the Conference of Asian and Pacific Accountants (CAPA) and the Interamerican Accounting Association (IAAA). A subset of CAPA with interests peculiar to its member nations is the ASEAN Federation of Accountants (AFA).

The stated objectives of these organizations have been essentially those of a national body but aimed at a regional level. The evidence of activity has varied from the biannual conferences of the IAAA to the full slate of committee efforts of the UEC.

The UEC is the exceptional regional body in that it has made significant attempts to set rules or guidelines. Despite very strong objections there has been a considerable measure of success. This success has in no small measure been aided by the existence of the European Economic Community and its resolution to harmonize laws and regulations. Progress through the UEC and the "groupe d'etude" (an association of EEC member country accounting bodies), has without a doubt been supported by the knowledge that political forces were at work which could and would force agreement.

Most of the regional bodies, including the UEC, have placed a fairly high priority in simply encouraging contact between accountants of related countries. Annual conferences are obvious examples but many bilateral, home and home, so to speak, weekend conferences are also used. These efforts generally involve only the "leaders" but now also have an increasing grassroots participation.

With the exception of the UEC and to some limited extent the AFA, the activity of these regional bodies involves relatively little technical subject encounter between accountants of different countries. The organizations have encouraged social and to some extent diplomatic contact. For this reason the individuals primarily involved have been those in leadership positions within their national body. Because their appointments emanate from that source the attitude of encounter is essentially an extension of that nation's interest.

International Bodies

The stories of the creation of the International Accounting Standards Committee (IASC) and of the International Federation of Accountants (IFAC) and predecessor groups have been told elsewhere and are referred to in other places in this volume. In total these organizations represent the efforts of accountants to broaden their focus of concern to a world level. It is these organizations that are identified as key signals of the internationalization of the profession. Understanding just what is happening in these organizations is not easy but could be indicative of future policy and possible future benefits.

The author participated as secretary of the IASC for two and one half years and has maintained some contact with participants in that organization since his departure. This participation allows more detailed analysis of the IASC and its operations than could otherwise be achieved. This review should serve as a good base for considering all world bodies and specifically, for suggestions as to how IASC might progress.

The detailed story of the creation of IASC has been well told by Lord Henry Benson[4] and John Hepworth[5] and has been updated by Alister Mason in another part of this volume. For the purpose of this article it is nevertheless necessary to specifically recall some aspects of its current and prospective organization.

The decisions of IASC are taken by a board which consists of the nominated representatives of eleven member countries. There is a proposal to expand this to thirteen countries. Nine of these countries are identified as founding members and thereby sit permanently as board members. The other board members are nominated to serve for terms of from three to five years.

Each country may appoint two individuals to represent them at board deliberations. Each country may designate a staff support person who may also participate at board meetings. The board discusses a wide range of accounting questions, deliberates on the possible solutions to accounting issues and finally decides on the precise wording of a pronouncement referred to as an International Accounting Standard.

This board is supported in its work by a number of subcommittees and a small fulltime staff. The subcommittees include representation from board member countries and nonmember countries. In the former case the individuals involved may or may not be the same individuals that participate on the board. The staff are seconded professional accountants, predominantly chosen from public practice but sometimes from education and industry. To understand just what actually occurs one must analyse the participants, the process and the outcome of IASC activity.

The participants in the IASC deliberations are appointees of the professional accountancy bodies. In some cases, e.g. NIVRA, they are simply appointed by the single accountancy body of that country. In other cases, e.g. the United Kingdom, the appointment requires some joint consultation of the relevant accountancy bodies. In the United States and Canada efforts are made to broaden the representativeness of the nominees by selecting those who could be seen to represent two constituencies at the same time. (e.g. AICPA and the Financial Executive Institute)

The sum of these appointees may reach forty accountants at any one time. This number when seen in the light of over 500,000 accountant members of constituency organizations suggests some characteristics of the individuals involved.

Committee participants are likely to be relatively senior members of their professional bodies. Certainly they are individuals who have had sufficient exposure to their professional colleagues to instill a confidence that they will appropriately represent their country in these deliberations.

Many of these individuals will have served in the senior administrative positions (e.g., president or chairman of the board) in their professional body. On some working subcommittees technical experts are appointed. In each case these individuals have already demonstrated at least nationally, but often beyond within their firms, that they are most distinguished among their accounting colleagues.

These characteristics could lead to a presumed scenario of a group of independent, stubborn, politically astute accountants, all of whom are used to being listened to instead of the reverse. All those characteristics are appropriate but there are certainly a number of compensating factors. They are above average in intelligence and on the whole could be described as clever. To survive in the professional world they must have above average ability and most certainly have a greater than average capacity for work.

As a member of the staff who served the IASC, I would rate them as among the most difficult group to teach but as perhaps the ones in which the greatest amount of learning could occur in the shortest time span. The "Ureka" process occurred regularly.

For financial and manpower resource reasons relatively few members made extensive use of technically qualified staff support. With a few notable exceptions staff were primarily diplomatic aides and the nominated representatives were relied upon to carry the technical ball.

The process at all levels of activity had a varying number of these individuals discussing technical accounting issues. Each working group always had representatives from at least three countries. The object in each case was to arrive at a position which could be presented to a larger group of similar participants until the final standard was published.

The essential task of staff and then of the committee members was first to come to an understanding of how all participants understood the problem at hand. To some extent it was definitional. For example a word like dividends has many meanings across the world. IAS 10 demonstrates the major difference.[6] Some views link dividends to an operating period (i.e., the 1978 dividends) no matter when they are paid. The other attitude identifies such payments only with the time when they are made. Clarifying such understanding is not simply translation.

Another range of problems comes from the legal systems. Tax treatments often define accounting treatments. Appreciation of this and the opposite attitude is essential, for example, if there is to be technical discussion of the topic of tax allocation.

Perhaps the most difficult aspect of all accounting issues to grapple with was the attitude of full disclosure. Attitudes emanating from an economy with large and deep equity markets were often in marked contrast to those coming from economies where the norm was closely held ownerships generally in the hands of financial institutions. Coming to a recognition of the unfortune of this underlying and frequently unstated premise was often delayed well into a project.

These issues and many more were part of each and every deliberation of an IASC committee. For the most part participants became accustomed to facing a situation where they didn't understand the other's viewpoint. This would be contrasted to the domestic rule making scene where every participant appears to presume that they, and only they, truly understand the situation. The result was very effective listening and learning occurred once misunderstanding had been noted. On the whole committee members learned much from their encounters.

The multi-step process results in a statement referred to as an International Accounting Standard. These documents are not so much monuments to the discovery of the "true" method. Rather, they are testimony to significant effort to understand all aspects of the problem. Alternatives are at least identified; some glaring gaps in national standards are often pointed out, and in some cases there is a restriction placed on the alternatives available.

The standards are not in themselves enforceable by the IASC. The standards rely on the action of a national body for acceptance.[7] Despite this restriction the influence of the standards is not limited to the enforcement route. Through the participants and indeed as a direct result of the process, the deliberations of IASC and the understanding that ensues spreads to the domestic rule making process. National rules are now being made with at least an awareness of world problems.

Informed conversations with participants suggest that a very similar situation pertains in the Federation. Participants, process, and output resemble those of IASC.

Conclusions

The general conclusion of the author is that for the internationalization of the profession to continue to prosper the basic motives and constraints upon the participants must be explicitly acknowledged. The enthusiasm for pursuit of the holy grail can drive a movement even if the nature or impact of the final goal is not clearly understood. However, once the crusaders discover they are not unified in their understanding of the quarry, and indeed they find out that finding quarry is not in their interest, the crusade is likely to dissolve. Effort should be expended to set out clearly the benefits which would ascribe to individual participants of a successful internationalization of the profession.

Researchers have unlimited opportunities to pursue the research questions of their choice. One of the purposes of this article and indeed of the whole book is to encourage such research into international accountancy topics. The specific concern in this article leads to a number of researchable questions that can be categorized under two headings: public institutions and professional firms.

Public Institutions

The IASC as an institution should be acknowledged as having a very significant teaching role. It should not be evaluated as a regulatory agency, at least not in its current form.

As a teaching vehicle it could democratize itself. The teaching function does not require the control currently exercised by the founding nations. Indeed it requires a very real sense of participation on the part of a wide cross section of the accounting world. Under the current form, this is not the case, despite recent efforts to increase "comments" from around the world.

If the regulatory function is still considered primary, then the decision making portion must explicitly involve a wider constituency. UN and OECD efforts give strong testimony that the broader constituency is essential. Current efforts by the IASC to liaise with these and other bodies might indicate a move to more of the educational role or perhaps simply a failure to specify clearly the role adopted. Research is necessary in evaluating the impact of institutions such as IASC and IFAC and indeed at all levels, regional and national as well. To know where the best future course lies for international bodies the motives of their investigators should be subjected to careful scrutiny.

Another area of research on this subject is archival. Preparation of records of what happened and how key individuals saw the events will be of lasting benefit. Many individuals were involved in the internationalization and most were senior partners of their firms. Such individuals rarely have, or take, the time to reflect on events—at least not in print. Researchers might encourage this reflection through the subject of and the methodology used in their work.

The international accountancy bodies may be excellent subjects upon which to test various positive theories of standard setting activity. To date many attempts have been made at examining the "clustering" of accounting practices. Perhaps an examination of the voting patterns by country, or even better, the attitudes and perceptions of international accounting representatives would lead to greater insights to the operation and potential contribution of such organizations.

Comparative accounting practice studies are still relevant. Examination of the links between the actual practice and the related cultural values would lead to greater understanding of the problems of harmonization. In another article in this volume Richard Burke explores the areas of cross cultural research. The concerns he expresses apply equally when applied to single culture settings.

International Professional Firms

The international professional firm of accountants has not been the focus of careful attention by researchers. Perhaps this is so because they are private organizations, in most circumstances not required to publish annual reports on their activities. However, even superficial evidence such as extent of representation on national body senior councils would suggest that the policies set by these firms are significant, even dominant influences in the very public world of accounting institutions. This is particularly the case in the international sphere. The firms themselves are perhaps the most important international accountancy institution. Their influence on accounting and auditing standards is and is likely to continue to be very large. We should know more about them—the problems they face and how these problems might be solved.

The lack of descriptive information on the international accountancy firms is apparent to all. Simply, a comparative analysis of the forms of organization adopted by those firms would provide an excellent base for future research. There are innumerable case studies to be developed from the international partnership mergers and realignments. The need for this independent analysis is anchored in the public interest argument.

These international firms provide a unique organization to look at a number of management problems. Staffing patterns and staff progression in international contexts are peculiar to accounting firms. Careful intra and inter firm comparisons may yield useful insights to international management problems.

Examination and elucidation of the firms' attempts at international harmonization of their professional standards might very well assist the broader organizations like IASC and IFAC. More information about their efforts and their success or lack of it would be useful.

There is hope and promise in the continued internationalization of the accountancy profession. To realize that future our past should be examined honestly and independently. I believe there has been a significant contribution made simply by creating the existing institutions. However, efforts must be made to identify and measure the benefits if the process is to continue. International accounting researchers have an important role to play.

Notes

1. See W. John Brennan, ed., *The Internationalization of the Accountancy Profession* (The Canadian Institute of Chartered Accountants, Toronto, 1979), appendix III for a list of members in the various international bodies.

2. Ibid, p.29.

3. Ibid, p.31.

4. Ibid, p.41.

5. Ibid, p.49.

6. International Accounting Standard 10, "Contingencies and Events Occuring After the Balance Sheet Date" (October, 1978).

7. For a description of the degrees of acceptance, see Discussion Paper, "Acceptance and Observance of International Accounting Standards" (IASC, London, 1 September 1977).

The Development of International Accounting Education

LEE H. RADEBAUGH
Brigham Young University

In 1967 at the Second International Conference on Accounting Education, Gerhard Mueller made the following observation: "If we take a somewhat long-range look (let us say about ten years into the future), I believe that most would agree that by that time the international dimension of accounting ought to be present throughout the curriculum. In other words, in 1977, our beginning textbooks should make it rather clear that the most useful type of accounting is not necessarily the same for a country just beginning its economic development process, and one which is the base of highly developed industries."[1] Mueller's prophetic statement was not simply a prediction of the future, but was also a call to the academic community to increase the international dimensions of the accounting curriculum. Although Mueller's expectations for the future have not fully materialized, the state of the art of international accounting education has made some dramatic strides.

Lee Brummet, as president of the American Accounting Association (AAA), made the following comments on the importance of internationalism in accounting education: '. . . the profession, in its development of standards and practices, must be fully aware of significant worldwide relevance and potential for consistency, articulation, or reconciliation with worldwide applications. . . . Our current international setting provides us with a basis for a kind of liberal arts education in accounting as opposed to a monolithic 'what is it and how is it done' approach."[2] Trevor Gambling stated that accounting practices in other countries are often not studied because of chauvinism and a lack of familiarity of those practices.[3] Finally, the Committee on International Accounting of the AAA concluded: ". . . the Committee believes that the Report supports the need for much more extensive education of accountants in all areas of international operations so that accountants will soon be able to take a place in the forefront of the several groups already busily engaged in rationalizing and teaching the operations of MEs [multinational enterprises]."[4]

Since the mid-1960s when the interest in international accounting began to blossom, numerous articles have been written on the importance of providing accounting students with a knowledge of the international dimensions of their discipline. As will be pointed out in more detail later in the article, however, relatively few schools made a conscious attempt to do much. The biggest catalyst for change has been the American Assembly of Collegiate Schools of Business (AACSB), the institution responsible for accrediting undergraduate and graduate schools of business.

Accreditation Standards

In 1974, the accreditation standards of the AACSB were altered to include the following statement: "The purpose of the curriculum shall be to provide for a broad education preparing the student for imaginative and responsible citizenship and leadership roles in business and society— domestic and worldwide."[5] During this same period of time in the early 1970s, a series of conferences was being held to discuss government/academic cooperation in the field of international education. These conferences eventually resulted in the creation of a Task Force on Business and International Education which submitted a report in 1977 to the Government/Academic Interface Committee for the International Education Project of the American Council on Education

The report, which was published by and is available from the American Council on Education, contains chapters on the following areas:

1. Internationalizing the Business Schools
2. Overseas Internship Programs
3. Interdisciplinary International Programs
4. International Management Development
5. Internationalization of University Studies

The following excerpt from the introduction to the report highlights some of the important findings.

The Task Force concluded that most business firms, regardless of size and type of operations, will be affected by economic and political developments on the international scene. Most businessmen will, therefore, need an ability to understand and anticipate those effects. Also, the number of American managers stationed abroad will probably not diminish during the coming decade. Several surveys have found, however, that very high percentages of individuals are still becoming presidents of multinational corporations without ever having had an international work experience, and that many managers with international responsibilities had had no international studies while at the university, and no management development programs with international content, while employed to prepare them for such international responsibilities.

There was a bifurcation of views regarding the best time to provide the international studies and training needed by future middle and top managers—in university training, or later in management development programs. There is a consensus that broad international education should be obtained while at the university and that this should be reinforced, later, with training in specific international business skills as the individual progresses through various levels of management. Yet, given that most management development programs have so little international content, and that so few middle and top managers attend the management development programs with international content, particularly as preparation for assignments where they will have international responsiblity, the burden falls ultimately upon institutions of higher education to provide the international education which will be needed.

Looking at the business schools, it was found that efforts must be made in many directions to internationalize the curriculum. This inevitably implies parallel efforts to internationalize the faculty. It was agreed that true, solid training in any of the functional fields of study in the business school should be understood to include the international dimensions of that field.

Perhaps the most astounding finding of the various surveys conducted by the Task Force was that over 75% of graduating DBA's (or PhD's in Business) have had no international business courses during their graduate studies, and that another 10% have had only one such course. Not only must this be changed, but other ways be found and utilized to provide existing faculty members with the facility to internationalize their courses, and their textbooks.

The Task Force concurs and feels that a true university education should be understood to include the international dimension. For education, in its essence and by definition, should result in the elimination of provincialism. Without this, the graduate is destined to be an uninformed citizen of the most powerful country in the world, and will be inadequately prepared to be a future manager in a high percentage of U.S. business firms.[6]

Several recommendations were made as a result of the study. The relevant one for the purpose of this article is the following:

The primary recommendation is that a joint AACSB-AIB committee be appointed to develop and direct a three-year program of summer workshops to prepare business school faculty to teach various special international business courses and to internationalize various specific functional courses. This joint committee must seek financing from both government and private sources to subsidize those workshops.[7]

In order to implement this recommendation, the AACSB, with financial support from the General Electric Company as part of its Centennial Celebration, organized a four-day plenary session in Washington, D.C. in May 1978 and a five-day workshop in each AACSB region in July 1978. The participants for each workshop were supposed to be faculty members teaching in one of the core areas of accounting, finance, marketing, and policy. The plenary session was designed to sensitize the participants to the international environment.

The five-day workshops included additional presentations from government, business, and academe as well as four half-day sessions that focused on the participants' functional areas. The purpose of the latter sessions was to generate suggestions on how the faculty could internationalize the curriculum in order to meet existing AACSB guidelines.

The accounting workshops were coordinated by Gerhard Mueller (University of Washington), with Frederick D.S. Choi (University of Hawaii), Adolph Enthoven (University of Texas at Dallas), Hanns-Martin Schoenfeld (University of Illinois), and Lee Radebaugh (Penn State University) serving as additional faculty leaders for the workshops. As a result of a grant by the Seattle office of Peat, Marwick, Mitchell & Co., all five faculty members were able to meet in Seattle to develop a philosophy and outline of the workshop sessions. The accounting group was the only one of the four disciplines able to meet in this fashion.

As a result of the Seattle meeting, the following materials were prepared for distribution to all participants in the accounting workshops:

1.   an outline of basic issues in international accounting,
2.   an annotated key item reading list,
3.   a list of suggested teaching materials for various accounting topics, such as "purpose and nature of accounting," "role of accounting in society," "environment of accounting principles," etc.,
4.   an annotated list of cases recommended for the Master's level curriculum,
5.   the May 1978 issue of the *International Accounting Forum* (the newsletter of the International Section of the American Accounting Association), and
6.   several outlines for international accounting courses.

As noted in table 1, the participation by accountants at the 1978 workshops was excellent.

The focus of the workshops for all three years was to give accounting professors some ideas on how they could include international accounting topics in the traditional accounting courses. The specific issues discussed and the pros and cons of each of the internationalization possibilities are discussed elsewhere in the paper.

Table 1.   Attendance by Discipline at the AACSB Workshops, 1978-1980

Discipline	1978		1979		1980	
	#	%	#	%	#	%
Accounting	79	32.1	45	19.5	35	25.5
Business Policy	67	27.2	64	27.7	46	33.6
Finance	36	14.6	57	24.7	27	19.7
Marketing	64	26.0	65	28.1	29	21.2
	246	99.9	231	100.0	137	100.0

In 1980, the last of these workshops was held. Several possibilities are being studied for 1981, including teaching a week-long course to faculty members to prepare them to teach a course in international accounting.

At the June 13, 1980 AACSB meeting, members voted unanimously to approve an interpretation of the Internationalization Standard. The Standards Committee and the Operational Committee had previously approved the interpretation. The interpretation reads as follows: "There is no intention that any single approach is required to satisfy the 'worldwide' dimension of the Curriculum Standard, but every student should be exposed to the international dimension through one or more elements of the curriculum." The interpretation leaves open numerous possibilities for the accounting curriculum. The major possibilities relating to accounting are: a separate course in international accounting; the international dimensions of accounting woven into the traditional financial, managerial, tax, and audit classes; or a strong accounting component in a required international business course. Each of these options will be discussed as solutions to the accreditation standard from the following perspectives: level (undergraduate and/or graduate), content, strengths, and weaknesses.

A Separate Course

Assuming that our intent is to expose *all* accounting students to international accounting, the separate course should be a required one. An elective course would not technically fulfill the requirement, but at best students would have an opportunity to take the course if they so desired. The separate course is probably the best approach from a pedagogical standpoint, because it allows the faculty member to develop a broad range of topics in greater depth than would be possible under any of the other approaches. Concepts could be taught in a more logical sequence than would otherwise be possible. Because of prerequisites, students could be kept out of the class until they have a sufficient background in their own accounting system to appreciate the issues covered in an international accounting course.

However, there are problems with an international accounting course. In many schools, there may be no room for a required course. Usually, international accounting is not considered a high priority course relative to some other aspects of accounting. In addition, it may be more difficult to find someone qualified to teach such a course. This appears to be more of a problem in the accounting area than in many others.

As early as 1966, the Committee on International Accounting of the AAA recommended ". . . the inclusion of a course or seminar on 'International Accounting' in the accounting curriculum of institutions of higher learning."[8] In spite of this recommendation, relatively few schools have taken on the challenge. In a study conducted by Terpstra in 1969, only 17 of 95 schools surveyed offered courses in international accounting.[9] In a survey of accounting department chairmen of AACSB schools conducted a few years later, only 27 of 90 schools offered course work in international accounting.[10] In a 1974 study by Daniels and Radebaugh that was a follow-up of the Terpstra study, 35 of 272 schools surveyed offered at least one course in international accounting. Unfortunately, that compared with 111 schools offering courses in international finance, 187 in international marketing, and 123 in international management.[11] In a study conducted by Burns in 1977, the number of schools offering one or more international accounting courses stood at 37, but 24 more stated that they expected to add one in the next three years.[12]

Level of Offering

The tendency has been to offer international accounting courses at the graduate level. In Burns' study, 26 of 39 courses (66.7%) were for graduate and upper-level undergraduate students. This is consistent with Mueller's contention that the course or seminar should be a graduate one so that the student would ". . . be well versed in the accounting practices and procedures of his own country and have a good understanding of accounting theories and concepts as found or referred in the current literature."[13] Rueschoff argues that the course can and should be offered very effectively at the undergraduate level.[14] Usually, such a course should be taught at the senior level after students have a sound foundation in domestic accounting concepts.

In an interesting study by Pearson, Ryans, and Hicks, three groups of accountants were surveyed to determine their attitudes on level and content of international accounting courses. These groups were Certified Management Accountants (CMA), CPAs, and academics. The CMAs represented industry, while the CPAs were from public accounting. The CMAs preferred a required course at the Master's and doctoral level, the CPAs favored incorporating international topics in existing courses, and the academics favored a separate elective international accounting course. There was a clear preference at the undergraduate level for a separate elective course or incorporation of international material in existing courses. No one really felt it necessary to have a required course at the undergraduate level.[15]

Course Content

There is probably greater variation in the course outlines of international accounting courses than in most other accounting courses. That is due primarily to a lack of universal agreement on what international accounting really is. The three main concepts most commonly mentioned are world accounting, comparative accounting, and accounting for international operations.[16] World accounting implies the study of accounting objectives, standards, and practices from the standpoint of setting uniform standards worldwide. Comparative accounting could be looked at in two different ways. One would be to examine a narrow issue (such as inflation accounting or translating foreign currency financial statements) over a broad range of countries. Another way would be to look at a broad range of issues over a few countries. The latter approach tends to be descriptive, looking at the objectives, standards, and practices of a country within its particular educational, cultural, legal, political, and economic environment. Accounting for international operations focuses on financial reporting, managerial, tax, and auditing issues peculiar to firms operating in more than one country.

  In terms of specific coverage, Dascher, Smith, and Strawser asked MNC controllers and educators to rank topics in order of importance, as noted in table 2.

  It is interesting to note that topics 2, 6, 9, and 10 by educators were price-level problems, auditing differences, developing nations, and international harmonization of financial accounting. These topics were ranked by controllers as 11, 14, 18, and 13 respectively. The controllers were obviously concerned with narrow issues affecting corporate operations rather than world and international accounting issues as defined above. This highlights a basic philosophical difference in education from the

Table 2.   Course Coverage—Practitioner versus Educator

Top Ten Topics Ranked by MNCs	Ranking by MNC	Ranking by Educator
Translation problems	1	1
Taxation	2	8
Methodological differences (inventory methods, consolidations, etc.)	3	4
Bases for financial reporting authority (APB versus company or corporations acts, etc.	4	5
Working capital management (source of funds, exchange risks, etc.)	5	13
Transfer price problems	5	7
Internal auditing (including operational auditing)	7	18
Planning and control (including performance evaluation)	8	12
Other finance aspects (banking, licensing, FDI program, etc.)	9	15
Patterns in accounting development (economic, legal, etc.)	10	3

Source: Paul E. Dascher, Charles H. Smith, and Robert H. Strawser, "Accounting Curriculum Implications of the Multinational Corporation," *International Journal of Accounting*, (Fall 1973), p. 94.

specific skills approach of interest to the controllers, to the broader almost liberal arts approach referred to by Brummet earlier in the paper.

Table 3 shows how much time was spent on certain topics in 36 international courses.

Elsewhere in her study, Burns grouped the topics into economic categories and showed that 54.3 percent of the time was spent on problems of U.S.-based multinational corporations. Most of the remaining time was spent on accounting in other industrial countries (primarily descriptive and comparative).

As can be seen, a separate course lends itself quite well to the senior undergraduate or graduate level course, and is an effective way to cover a broad range of issues in a logical sequence. However, lack of time and qualified faculty may preclude all students from being exposed to the issues.

The Integrated Approach

The integrated approach means that international accounting issues would be included in the traditional accounting courses. Some professors devote a few class sessions to international issues, whereas others prefer to dis-

Table 3.   Allocation of Time (in percents) to
International Accounting by Topic[a]

Rank by Mean Topic	Mean	Standard Deviation	Range
1. Comparative accounting principles (D)[b]	15.5	12.4	0-50
2. FASB Statement No. 8 and foreign currency translation (F)	10.9	5.9	0-30
3. Transfer pricing, foreign tax credit, and taxation of foreign source income (K)	9.5	15.4	0-95
(5)[c]	(7.1)[c]	(4.8)[c]	(0-20)[c]
4. Inflation accounting (H)	7.5	5.2	0-20
5. Financial reporting and disclosure (G)	7.4	5.0	0-20
6. Cash management and foreign-exchange management (C)	6.0	5.2	0-20
7. International accounting standards (I)	5.8	4.6	0-20
8. International accounting history and background information (B)	4.9	5.3	0-30
9. Nonaccounting business topics, including introductory background information (A)	4.9	5.2	0-20
10. Consolidations (E)	4.8	4.9	0-20
11. Other topics relating to taxation (O)	4.3	5.6	0-20
12. Other topics relating to management accounting (N)	4.1	7.6	0-50
13. Other topics relating to auditing (L)	3.7	4.1	0-20
14. Performance evaluation (J)	3.6	4.1	0-10
15. Other topics relating to social accounting (P)	3.2	11.7	0-70
(17)[d]	(1.3)[d]	(2.6)[d]	(0-10)[d]
16. Other topics relating to financial accounting (M)	2.1	3.6	0-10
17. Other topics (Q)	1.8	3.9	0-20

[a]Calculations are based on thirty-six completed questionnaires since information was not reported for three of the thirty-nine courses.
[b]The letter in parentheses following each topic indicates the order in which the topic appeared on the questionnaire.
[c]Calculations are based on thirty-five courses after deleting one international taxation course.
[d]Calculations are based on thirty-five courses after deleting one international social accounting course.

Source: Jane O. Burns, "A Study of International Accounting Education in the United States," *International Journal of Accounting*, (Fall 1979), p. 141.

cuss the issues each day depending on the topic at hand. For example, when discussing financial statement format, it would be possible to illustrate the traditional British statements where accounts are arranged in increasing liquidity. When discussing the role of the Financial Accounting Standards Board in setting standards in the U.S., one could also mention the role of tax authorities in setting book standards in Germany and

France. When mentioning the influence of the investor orientation in setting disclosure standards in the U.S., one could stress the impact of the creditor orientation in Germany and Switzerland and the government in the USSR and Peru. The possibilities are limitless as these few examples illustrate.

The benefits of this approach are obvious. All students going through the accounting program would be exposed to the international dimension of accounting, not just those fortunate enough to take an elective course. In addition, no new courses would need to be added to the curriculum. Mueller's long-range forecast in 1967 referred to earlier was that the integrated approach would and should replace separate international courses.

In spite of the pedagogical appeal of the unified approach, there are some serious problems. Because of the volume of material that already needs to be covered, it may be impossible to devote any time to international issues. This is especially true in the introductory financial course where students need to be taught fundamentals. Since the students don't know anything at all about accounting, the coverage of international topics would have to be superficial. If the students had no exposure to international business at all, the professor would have to take a little time to introduce concepts about international business which he/she has little time for. Convincing the faculty that integration is the best approach may be the most difficult problem. This would require a tremendous retooling effort on the part of most faculty. The problem is compounded by the use of graduate students to teach fundamental courses. A final problem is that current textbooks don't have the international material woven in. A separate chapter is inadequate since most faculty would be prone to leave it out.

A Required General International Business Course

The obvious solution to the AACSB accreditation standard is to have a general international business course required of all students. One would be able to build the background of international business before moving to the functional areas in the course (i.e., marketing, finance, accounting, personnel, etc.). This approach would allow a few people to specialize in international business rather than require everyone. Also, there would be no need to interfere with the content of existing core courses.

However, the major problems are: how do you fit in one more required course, and where do you find the qualified faculty? A more fundamental concern is an educational one. A solid general international business course would probably not be able to allow more than 2-3 days on each functional area. Is this enough of an exposure for students to say that they understand the international dimensions of accounting? Clearly not.

Solutions and Projections

By all indications, international business is continuing to expand and will probably do so forever. The increase in foreign investment in the U.S. means that more graduates will be working for foreign-owned firms than might have been true a decade ago, and they will probably be confronted with reports for the home office that appear to have little relevance in the U.S. Many problems that confront us in the U.S. are international in scope—such as accounting for inflation. Therefore, an understanding of other approaches to solve a common problem may help us to understand ourselves even more. The Accounting Standards Committee of the U.K. has been deeply interested in our standards on accounting for inflation and foreign currency transactions and translation. It is possible to learn from others.

It is obvious that a major hindrance to increasing the internationalization of the accounting curriculum is due to the faculty. Neither the separate nor the integrated approaches will work if there are no faculty capable of teaching the concepts. Existing faculty need to retool in order to get the job done. Georgia State University accomplished that task as a result of a grant from Touche Ross. Sub-area leaders were selected in financial, managerial, tax, and audit. They received release time to brush up on international literature and become familiar with case materials. After meeting with Touche Ross contact partners, they reviewed course outlines and developed a package of materials containing a bibliography, list of cases, copies of key readings, and suggested course outlines to be used by faculty members in each sub-area. Group meetings were held to explain the materials, and the first term of implementation was winter 1980. The project was tried again in spring 1980 after modification of the winter experience. The greatest success was at the graduate level, as expected, and the faculty felt that their overall interest in the international dimension had increased.

For faculty unable to get such grants, the road is a bit more difficult. The Education Committee of the International Section of the AAA has been involved in numerous projects since the Section's inception that are very beneficial to faculty seeking to internationalize. Among those projects are:

1. the collection of international accounting course outlines,
2. the compilation of a list of doctoral dissertations written on international accounting topics,
3. the preparation of international reading lists for the undergraduate curriculum, and
4. the completion of a study on international accounting education in the United States.

The Continuing Education Committee of the International Section put on continuing education sessions on curriculum internationalization at the 1979 and 1980 annual meetings of the AAA. Similar sessions were conducted at a few of the regional AAA meetings in 1980. It is hoped that sessions will be held at all regional AAA meetings in 1981 since the AACSB will not be holding their regional workshops.

As the quality of expertise broadens and deepens among current faculty, then graduating PhDs and DBAs will be more exposed to issues in international accounting and more inclined to include international concepts in their teaching. This is essential if international accounting is to expand at all.

Another serious drawback is the lack of good text material. Although there are several good international accounting textbooks,[17] there are no basic financial, managerial, tax, and audit textbooks with significant international materials. At least some marketing and finance textbooks have an international chapter. Advanced accounting textbooks contain a chapter on foreign currency transactions and translation as an interesting dimension of consolidations. However, that is usually the extent of the coverage. The expansion of international accounting in the traditional courses will be hampered as long as inadequate text materials continue.

The separate vs. integrated and graduate vs. undergraduate argument will probably never be resolved and will be contingent on the commitment, resources, and program structure in each school. I have taught a senior level undergraduate course for eight years, and I feel that the course has been beneficial and useful in broadening the horizons of the students. However, I still feel that such a course should be an elective.

Taking into consideration the broad educational issues of international business, I would like to see the following: a required course at the graduate and undergraduate levels that is totally or partially (½ to ⅓) devoted to the international business environment and the operations of the multinational enterprise; a conscious effort on the part of faculty to internationalize their traditional accounting courses; and, where resources allow, an elective course at the senior level and a seminar at the graduate level that are totally devoted to international accounting.

The required course would provide good exposure of international issues to *all* students. This is the best approach from an educational standpoint. Many key international business issues do not neatly fit into a functional course. The integrated suggestion is made because I believe it can be done. I have taught a basic principles of financial accounting course and have sprinkled international examples throughout the course without overwhelming the students or sacrificing basic material. My objective has been to sensitize students to international differences and help them understand how culture-bound many accounting practices are. Many schools, especially those with Schools of Accountancy offering five-year degrees, are shifting intermediate from two to three semesters in order to expand coverage and include topics in accounting theory. This would be an excellent place to internationalize the accounting curriculum. However, text material needs to be developed in this area.

Finally, my preference for a separate course will never die because the course is too much fun to teach. Realistically, the sheer volume of material to be covered in traditional courses is too great to expect much depth in the international area. For the student who is really turned on by the smattering of international accounting that he/she is exposed to elsewhere, the only satisfaction possible is from a good, solid international accounting course where the puzzle is put together.

Is there a future for education in international accounting? You bet there is. The interest is growing and so are the incentives—such as the AACSB accreditation standards. All we need now are committed faculty and better instructional materials.

Notes

1. Gerhard G. Mueller, "Curriculum Aspects of International Accounting Matters," *Proceedings*, Second International Conference on Accounting Education, (Guildhall, London, August 30-September 1, 1967), p. 41.

2. R. Lee Brummet, "Internationalism and the Future of Accounting Education," *International Journal of Accounting* 11.1 (Fall 1975):162-63.

3. Trevor Gambling, "Some Possibilities for a Course in International Accounting," a paper delivered at an accountancy seminar at the University of Illinois, March 1, 1972, p. 1.

4. American Accounting Association Committee on International Accounting, "Report of the Committee on International Accounting," Supplement to the *Accounting Review* (1973):166.

5. *AACSB Accreditation Council: Policies Procedures and Standards*, 1974, p. 26.

6. Task Force on Business and International Education, *Business and International Education*, (Washington D.C.: American Council on Education, May 1977), pp. 3-4.

7. *Ibid.*, p. 4.

8. Mueller, *op. cit.*, p. 44.

9. Vern Terpstra, *University Education For International Business* (Benton Harbor, Michigan: Association for Education in International Business, 1969).

10. Paul E. Dascher, Charles H. Smith, and Robert H. Strawser, "Accounting Curriculum Implications of the Multinational Corporation," *International Journal of Accounting* (Fall 1973):84.

11. John D. Daniels and Lee H. Radebaugh, *International Business Curriculum Survey*, (Academy of International Business, 1974). See also John D. Daniels and Lee H. Radebaugh, "The Evolvement of International Business Education," *Journal of International Business Studies* (Spring 1975):85.

12. Jane O. Burns, "A Study of International Accounting Education in the United States," *International Journal of Accounting* (Fall 1979):138.

13. Mueller, *op.cit.*, p. 42.

14. Norlin G. Rueschhoff, "The Undergraduate International Accounting Course," *The Accounting Review* (October 1972):833.

15. Michael A. Pearson, John K. Ryans and Lorraine J. Hicks, "Views of Accountants and Educators on Curriculum Internationalization," Working Paper No. 80-007, Kent State University, (January 1980), pp. 4-5.

16. For a discussion of the definition of international accounting, see Thomas R. Weirich, Clarence G. Avery, and Henry R. Anderson, "International Accounting: Varying Definitions," *International Journal of Accounting* (Fall 1971):79-87.

17. Some international accounting textbooks are: Jeffrey S. Arpan and Lee H. Radebaugh, *International Accounting and Multinational Enterprises*, (New York: Warren, Gorham and Lamont, 1981); Frederick D.S. Choi and Gerhard G. Mueller, *An Introduction to Multinational Accounting*, (Englewood Cliffs, N.J.: Prentice-Hall, Inc., 1978); Elwood L. Miller, *Accounting Problems of Multinational Enterprises*, (Lexington, Mass.: Lexington Books, 1979); Norlin G. Rueschhoff, *International Accounting and Financial Reporting*, (New York: Praeger Publishers, 1976); George C. Watt, Richard M. Hammer, and Marianne Burge, *Accounting for the Multinational Corporation*, (New York: Financial Executives Research Foundation, 1977).

Part II

Modes

Introduction

As a field of inquiry matures, two developments are readily observed. First, research contributions tend to obtain successively higher levels of abstraction. Second, research modes tend to become more systematic. Initial works in a field, for example, tend to be fairly descriptive with little attention to methods of science. Later, as the parameters of that field crystallize, contributions tend to emphasize theoretical formulations and controlled testing of hypothesized relations with the aim of explaining and predicting observed phenomena.

Utilizing the notions above, we again note that the field of multinational accounting research is still at an early stage of development; it has not reached the stage of sophisticated theory construction and verification. However, what the area lacks in development is made up for in research opportunity! The set of research questions and approaches to answering them remains open-ended with robust opportunities for accounting researchers to extend further the frontiers of this exciting new discipline.

The essays that follow exemplify promising approaches to studying the subject matter of multinational accounting. Approaches examined are behavioral, comparative, descriptive, empirical, and historical in orientation. Given the evolving nature of the field, these approaches are necessarily suggestive rather than exhaustive.

It is obvious, even to a casual observer, that people from different cultures differ in their behavior and the ways in which they perceive their social environment. The implications of cross-cultural differences for international accounting are enormous; yet, little formal attention has been devoted to this intriguing behavioral dimension. In the first essay in this section, Burke argues convincingly that much of potential interest awaits accountants in the interface between accounting, cross-cultural psychology, and sub-areas of anthropology. Insights provided by this interdisciplinary approach expand significantly the number of questions appropriate for international accounting research.

A critical analysis of comparative research is the focus of the second essay. Currently serving as director of a research center that has compiled the world's largest multinational data bank of corporate annual reports, Bavishi understandably confines his analysis to the comparative studies of multinational corporate financial reporting and disclosure. The number of research issues enumerated by Bavishi suggests that the analysis of disclosure and reporting by multinational enterprises promises to be a main-line of research activity during the 1980s.

Another major approach to international accounting research is that of description. Facts and information collected through a variety of survey techniques will make possible the level of abstraction and conceptual refinement that is required in the field. Gernon's essay provides an excellent assessment of the descriptive work that has been undertaken in the area of multinational internal performance evaluation systems. In doing so, she adds an important managerial dimension to this research framework.

In an earlier essay (in part I of this anthology), Smith and Shalchi call for more empirical research in international accounting as a basis for establishing descriptive theories and validating the "descriptive fit" of premises underlying normative theories. Dukes answers this call in his essay on foreign currency statement translations. Drawing on the subject of market price research, Dukes demonstrates that empirical research opportunities are not lacking, but neither will they lend themselves to quick solutions.

An important premise underlying the conventional accounting paradigm is that information with respect to the past is a guide to the future. In the final selection in this part, Mason demonstrates that a historical orientation can also serve as a useful research tool. In applying this approach to the evolution of international accounting standards, Mason posits a number of research challenges on a subject that may well prove to be the most critical for the field of international accounting as a whole.

The Behavioral Dimensions of International Accounting

RICHARD C. BURKE
University of Saskatchewan

The primary purpose of this essay is to explore the cross-cultural dimension as it interfaces with behavioral accounting. In order to attain this objective the concept of culture will first be addressed followed by a summary of the more persuasive arguments put forth in the social science literature as to why cross-cultural research is important to the study of human behavior. Selected areas or issues from this same body of literature that might be of interest to accountants will then be presented along with some discussion of methodological matters peculiar to cross-cultural research. With the benefit of this background, behavioral accounting studies that have addressed the issue of culture will be reviewed. Finally, a strategy will be suggested by which the behavioral dimensions of international accounting might be effectively and usefully explored. Throughout the discussion, occasional reference will be made to extant accounting research that appears particularly sensitive to cross-cultural effects.

The Concept of Culture

The concept *culture* is an illusive one. In a broad, anthropological sense it has been variously referred to as "the totality of man's learned, accumulated experience," or "those socially transmitted patterns of behavior characteristic of a particular social group." But in more precise terms, attempts at definition have merely revealed different facets of "culture" such that, even now, among anthropologists, there is no consensus.

Goodenough (1957; 1961) states that a major conceptual difficulty stems from the failure to make a crucial distinction between patterns *for* behavior and patterns *of* behavior. In one sense, culture has referred to the realm of observable phenomena—things and events "out there" in the real world. In the other, it refers to conceptual designs, or systems of shared ideas, whereby a people structure their experience or perceptions; in other words, it refers to ideas "in people's heads," not what they do or make. This division ostensibly permits the concept of culture to be dichotomized into physical and non-physical components.

Aspects of the non-physical dimensions represent for Triandis (1972) *subjective culture*, a term frequently cited in the recent literature and the one that will be used here. Defined as "a culture group's characteristic way of perceiving the man-made part of its social environment" (p. 4), this construct offers distinct operational and methodological advantages. Proposed in the form of a theoretical model, each of the hypothetical constructs that comprise it have been defined in ways that allow for cross-culturally equivalent measurement: ". . .the evidence we have so far suggest that our methods of analysis of subjective culture give us information that has both predictive and concurrent validity, is consistent with anthropological analyses and useful in understanding the way groups of people perceive their social environment" (p. 341).

Triandis elaborates on the concept as follows:

> *Subjective culture* refers to variables that are attributes of the cognitive structures of groups of people. The *analysis* of subjective culture refers to variables extracted from consistencies in their responses and results in a kind of "map" drawn by a scientist which outlines the subjective culture of a particular group. In short, when we observe consistent responses to classes of stimuli that have some quality in common, we assume that some "mediators" (attitudes, norms, values, etc.) are responsible for these consistencies. It is the cognitive structures which mediate between stimuli and responses in different cultural settings that we wish to study (1972, p. 3).

Frequent interaction is seen as both cause and effect. Living close to one another, sharing a common language and similar activities are likely to lead to high rates of interaction among peoples which in turn is likely to lead to similar norms, attitudes, and roles. "The causal chains are circular because similarities in subjective culture lead to greater satisfaction in interpersonal interaction, hence to increased frequency"(p. 4).

Subjective culture refers to cognitive structures, the processes by which man acquires, transforms, and uses information about the world. Its elements are hypothetical constructs that help us simplify our observations of human behavior. As abstractions, they do not "exist" except in the mind of the scientist (Triandis, 1972, p. 3). The construct subjective culture—or any definition of culture—is also a generalization. No two people from the same culture share identical mental configurations; each constructs his own on the basis of experience. Subjective culture, therefore, is, in this sense, a common denominator, a theory developed by a scientist that attempts to account for the tendency of members of a culture to behave the way they do.

The Need for Cross-Cultural Research

In response to the question "Why do cross-cultural psychology?" Berry provided a number of reasons:

> Cross-cultural psychology seeks to comprehend the systematic covariation between cultural and behavioral variables. Included within the term *cultural* are ecological and societal variables, and within the term *behavioral* are inferred variables. Thus the purpose is to understand how two systems, at the levels of group- and individual-analyses, relate to each other. Ideally, of course, more than covariation is sought; under some conditions *causal* relations may be inferred as well.

But as Berry goes on to point out, the more popular and necessary motivation behind the recent interest in cross-cultural research is the desire to test the generality of psychological laws. Prior to 1970, most attempts to understand the determinants of human behavior had a distinctly ethnocentric bias. Psychological theories merely "pretended to be universal" but almost all were figments of Euro-American imagination (Triandis, 1980a, p. 53). Since then, the recognition that generalizations which seek explanation are impossible without comparison in different settings for most people (Köbben, 1970, p. 586), led to the present effort to establish which aspects of psychological theorizing are truly universal, which may be modified by cultural variables, and which may be valid only in a particular culture or geographic area. Two distinct trends have emerged: one is the effort to assess the generality of theories originating in Western industrialized cultures; the second consists of attempts to formulate approaches specifically designed to account for cross-cultural differences and similarities (Jahoda, 1980).

Much of the rationale behind the surge of interest in cross-cultural research could also be applied to accounting. Are there patterns of differences in the ways in which people from different cultures react to the accounting process? If one considers the three perspectives in behavioral accounting which can be applied—the influence of the accountant's technical function on behavior (e.g. the behavioral effects of an audit), the behavior of accountants themselves (e.g. how they make decisions about materiality), and the influence of accounting information on those receiving the information (Hofstedt and Kinard, 1970, p. 43)—the principles of reinforcement alone suggest that some behavioral patterns are likely to be molded by culture. Behaviors that are rewarded will tend to prevail; those that are not will tend to be extinguished. To the international accountant this issue is of obvious importance. If research should fail to support this impression, that is, if it should be found that the principles of reinforcement in an accounting context are pan-cultural, this too would be good to know.

In a general pragmatic sense, therefore, the justification for conducting cross-cultural behavioral research in accounting is to answer the question whether the findings of behavioral researchers in one culture can be transformed with or without modification for effective use in another. Only empirical research can answer this question. Social scientists from other fields have rarely engaged in research where accounting provided the stimuli and there is no evidence to indicate that this situation will change. On the other hand, much of their research has a definite relevance as will be shown in the following section.

The Search for Cross-Cultural Differences

During the period when cross-cultural research began to expand, the major emphasis was on the search for differences (Cole and Scribner, 1974, p. 12). This section presents a brief discussion of some findings from this line of inquiry that may be germane to behavioral accounting research.

Language and Meaning

Language "is at one and the same time a vital social force and an individual tool of communication and thought; it is, so to speak, on both sides of the culture-cognition relationship" (Cole and Scribner, 1974, p. 8). Given that accounting may—with a little imagination—be regarded as the "language of business," the concept of linguistic relativity (also known as the Whorfian hypothesis) may contain some research implications.

Linguistic relativity: Could man's thought processes and subsequent behavior be affected by the language he uses? Some social scientists have argued that they are, but to what extent is a matter of considerable controversy. Originating in the last century, Sapir, in 1929, extended the notion of linguistic relativity by putting forth the hypotheses that "we see and hear and otherwise experience very largely as we do because the language habits of our community predispose certain choices of interpretation" (Mandelbaum, 1949, p. 162). In 1940, Whorf advanced these ideas. In its most severe form, the Whorfian hypothesis has been interpreted as claiming that we live in the world around us principally as language presents it. Language is not simply a system for reproducing ideas; it actually guides our mental activities, defines our experience and shapes our ideas.

While Whorf may not have agreed with such a strict interpretation, others have. The point remains that if these claims are true, then language must play a very significant role in the totality of culture.

Sapir's and Whorf's arguments have been a source of fascination and debate for a generation but so far little has been resolved (Howell and Vetter, 1976, p. 360). While it is probable that most scholars would reject the idea that language imposes inescapable and rigid constraints on cognitive processes, few would be likely to allow linguistic relatively no role whatsoever (Cole and Scribner, 1974, p. 59). Recently, Lucy and Shweder (1979) introduced new evidence regarding the role of language as a factor in human color memory. They conclude, based on their empirical work, that "language appears to be a probable vehicle for human color memory, and the views developed by Whorf are not jeopardized by the findings of any color research to date" (p. 604).

If the characteristics of a language have some determining influences on cognitive processes and, thereby behavior, what implications might this have for accounting? That different "accounting languages" codify and categorize differently is easily seen and that such differences might direct perception and thought into certain habitual channels, or have a significant impact on our thinking in other ways, is hardly startling. The Acheson (1972) study described later shows clearly how this can occur. But at a more subtle level, are there cognitive and behavioral group effects of having the same accounting language merely expressed in a different tongue? Some cross-cultural research suggests such a possibility.

Dimensions of affective meaning: The Whorfian hypothesis includes in language both its structural and semantic aspects. While the latter consist of a self-contained system of meanings inseparable from structure, the two have been studied more or less independently of each other. In particular, Osgood and his associates have developed another approach to the relationship between language and thinking by focusing on the *connotational* dimensions of people's cognitive maps by means of the semantic differential (Osgood, May, and Miron, 1975; Osgood, 1977).

This research appears to have developed a powerful argument for the fundamental similarity of affective meaning systems across the 21 language/culture communities studied. Factor analysis based on the scale means disclosed the first three factors—evaluation, potency, and activity—to be the same as those obtained in earlier studies with English-speaking Americans. Osgood et al. (1975, p. 189) conclude that human beings, "no matter where they live or what language they speak, apparently abstract about the same properties of things for making comparisons, and they order these different modes of qualifying in roughly the same way in importance."

Apart from these common elements of affective meaning systems, numerous differences were also encountered, "particularly in the meaning of concepts" (1975, p. 191). Osgood et al. used these differences to develop semantic profiles of the cultures surveyed which were compiled in an *Atlas of Affective Meanings*. "A potential gold mine of information about subjective culture" (p. 271), this atlas can "serve as a source of verbal materials having known affective properties for use in many types of cross-cultural psycholinguistic experiments — experiments on human cognition, perception, learning, and so forth" (p. 192).

A limitation—recognized by Osgood and his associates—lies in the "horizontal" approach utilized in this research. A horizontal approach is confined to a particular level of representativeness across a variety of cultures, while the focus of a vertical study is on several different levels within the same culture (Jahoda, 1980, p. 92). Ideally, any global study of human culture should maximize depth and breadth simultaneously.

A number of accounting studies on affective meaning have already been conducted using the semantic differential (e.g. Haried, 1972, 1973; Oliver, 1973, 1974). In addition, Haried (1973) used—and found to be more sensitive for identifying differences in the meaning of accounting terms—the antecedent-consequent method developed by Triandis (1972) for the analysis of subjective culture. Using different American interest groups, both researchers found potential semantic problems existing in accounting communication. This raises an interesting question from an international accounting point of view. If "vertical" differences have been found intraculturally, is it not likely that horizontal differences may be found across cultures either at the level of terms employed in financial statements or with respect to underlying accounting concepts? Research using both these methods could make a valuable contribution to the facilitation of accounting communication across cultural boundaries. It might even, eventually, result in an "atlas" of affective meanings.

Culture and Communication

While the parallel drawn earlier between accounting and language can only be carried so far, there is little doubt that the means by which communication affects, and is affected by, the behavior of individuals in organizations is a legitimate concern for accountants (Becker, 1968; Hofstedt and Kinard, 1970). Not only is it vital at the financial accounting level but it is at the very center of management control systems. The semantic research previously mentioned deals with one aspect of communication but a number of accounting studies using different approaches have focused on other ramifications. Schiff and Lewin (1970), for instance, have shown how poor communication coupled with related misunderstandings can result in the manipulation of budgetary data by managers.

Apart from those already discussed, cross-cultural studies on aspects of communication of relevance to accounting are few in number but what there is does not provide "systematic evidence for the universality or boundary conditions of theories formulated in the United States" (Davidson and Thomson, 1980, p. 45). Thus, according to Whittaker and Meade (1967), prior to 1967, "barely a handful" of experimental investigations of source credibility and the persuasive effects of communication had been conducted in a cross-cultural setting but since then a number of studies require the qualification of some Western findings. For example, it has been shown that oral as opposed to written communications, male as opposed to female sources of communication, can differ significantly in effectiveness from one culture to another. Wright and Phillips (1979) have examined cross-cultural differences in the assessment and communication of uncertainty. Their evidence suggests that significant qualitative differences do exist.

These and other findings serve to illustrate the potential impact of cross-cultural research on communication theory. Theorizing at the level of international accounting should not blindly assume the generalizability of Western findings.

Motivations, Norms, and Attitudes

In 1971, an American Accounting Association Committee noted that the implications of motivation theory for accounting are perhaps greater than those of any other behavioral area. It was argued that since a major purpose of managerial planning and control systems is to motivate performance and since organizational goals and accomplishments are often stated in accounting terms and individual performance is often evaluated by accounting measures, an understanding of the motivational effects of accounting systems and reports is vital. Hence, answers are needed to questions such as "Are accounting indicators of performance effective in motivating individuals to accomplish the goals of the organization?"; "Do they assist individuals in achieving maximum fulfillment of their job-related needs, particularly when they are making their maximum contribution to the organization?" (p. 255).

It is possible to examine these and related questions within the context of contemporary motivation theory. Maslow's (1954) theory of personality and motivation, Herzberg's (1966) "motivation-hygiene" theory, and

McClelland's (1961) achievement motivation theory have been used in the business and accounting literature for this purpose. For example, Lawler and Rhode (1976) found that intrinsic factors that lead to self-actualization are frequently more important motivational factors than are extrinsic rewards such as money. More recently, the application of contingency theory (Lawrence and Lorsch, 1969), which views the functioning of organizations in relation to the needs of their particular members and the external environmental pressures facing them, has been growing in importance.

However, much of the supporting evidence behind this research has relied on assumptions that do not allow for an interplay of cultural influences. These assumptions have recently been questioned by cross-cultural findings. For example, Jahoda (1980) claims that while the causal web leading to high achievement motivation is a very complex one in Western society, its character is substantially different in non-Western society. Triandis (1980b, p. 49) reports that achievement and affiliation tend to be negatively correlated in the West but positively correlated in Japan.

The point is that cross-cultural research has shown that not all of the key elements of contemporary motivation theory may be universal. Societies differ not only as to the motivational patterns that are frequent in them but also as to their norms and attitudes, all of which interact at the cross-cultural level. Organizational psychology in particular has demonstrated intercultural differences that have relevance for behavior in organizations: the problems of motivating members differ from one society to another; prevailing needs for achievement, affiliation, security, and self-actualization vary as do norms about social control and the attitudes of people toward authority (Tannenbaum, 1980). Even a quick perusal of the literature in this area will clearly demonstrate the dangers of assuming the generality of behavioral accounting findings on motivation.

Perception and Cognition

Psychological research related to various dimensions of decision making behavior has greatly increased our understanding of individual behavior in organizations. In recent years a number of accounting investigators have borrowed from, and effectively extended, this body of knowledge. Throughout this endeavor, questions concerning perception and cognition have played a central role. As used in psychology the term *perception* generally refers to processes by which people organize and experience information that is primarily of sensory origin while *cognition* typically includes mental processes such as memory, classification, reasoning, and judgment. Although frequently treated separately in the psychology literature, the two are closely related.

From an international accounting point of view, an interesting issue is whether cultural experience affects the stimuli we select for attention. For example, are we predisposed by culture to attend to those stimuli with which we are most familiar? Research by Berry (1969) on culture and selective perception suggests that we are. Also, under some conditions, the selective organization of perception can be used as an aid in the satisfaction of needs. In other words, we see what we want to see and what we want often has a cultural orientation.

Studies on the antecedents of cognitive style (Witkin and Berry, 1975) have demonstrated the cross-cultural generality of original Western findings on socialization factors contributing to the development of differentiation i. e., the ability to differentiate and organize features of the environment and to distinguish between phenomena that are internal to one's self and those external to it. Results indicate that just as child-rearing practices which encourage obedience in the child and conformance to parental authority are associated with the development of less differentiated functioning, the same tendency appears in societies which place a strong stress on conformity, where authorities in the social, religious, and political domains carry great influence and where adherence to the prescriptions of these authorities is expected. On the other hand, both families and societies which place less stress on conformity and are loose in their organization tend to foster the development of greater differentiation.

The work of researchers such as Preale, Amir, and Sharan (1970) and Wright and Phillips (1979) appears to support this view. On the whole, evidence suggests that the ability to cope with complexity is likely to be more prevalent among people in economically advanced countries than in the less advanced ones (Tannenbaum, 1980; p. 296). Berry (1975) developed a highly elaborate model that attempts to synthesize both anthropological and psychological perspectives in this area.

These and other studies question the cross-cultural generality of existing findings reported in the cognitive complexity/cognitive style accounting literature. The same might be suspected of some other human information processing models used in behavioral accounting research. For example, Segall, Campbell, and Herskovits (1966) in a study of "enduring cross-cultural virtue" (Lonner and Triandis, 1980, p. 5) demonstrated cultural differences in perception which the authors attributed to the concept of "ecological cue validity" which is an aspect of Brunswick's (1956) notion of "probabilistic functionalism." Other accounting studies on perception may also be culturally sensitive: for example, research on perceptions of auditor independence (Lavin, 1976, 1977; Imhoff, 1978; Firth, 1980); accounting interest groups' differential perceptions of innovations (Hicks, 1978).

Based on these and other findings from cross-cultural research, it would appear that there is sufficient evidence in the literature to suggest that there are distinct benefits, both theoretical and practical, to be obtained from testing the universality of behavioral accounting models and other behavioral findings. However, doing so in a methodologically defensible manner is another matter.

Methodological Issues

Studies dealing with the culture/person interaction face all of the methodological problems of research conducted in a homogeneous culture plus many additional ones. A reasonably broad overview of methodological issues peculiar to cross-cultural research can be obtained by considering three major issues: experimentation, the emic-etic controversy and sampling and translation problems.

Experimentation

Cross-cultural psychologists have traditionally had a preference for experiments and the manipulation of variables, the primary aim being the prediction of the particular choices members of a culture will make in response to certain stimuli. The effective use of this method requires standardization of research procedures in such a manner that operationally equivalent observations can be selected and compared.

In a cross-cultural setting, the experiment presents very special difficulties. Since "culture" essentially cannot be manipulated, we must resort to quasi-experimental designs exploiting natural variations. Also, there is a strong likelihood that the culture variable will interact with the experimental treatment which, in turn, may seriously threaten the internal validity of the study. For example, the meaning of the experimental task and/or the research setting may vary from culture to culture; instructions may be interpreted in different ways; or the researcher may evoke different reactions. Other problems center on possible cultural differences in motivation and on the empirically demonstrated tendency of some culture groups to behave in different ways, e.g., to make fewer extreme judgments. Overcoming these difficulties requires careful planning, which assumes, of course, that the researcher is fully aware of their existence (which in turn requires that he has a "theory" about them).

Recognition of these problems has had at least two very noticeable effects. First, strategies of data collection have been expanded in recent years. This can be clearly seen from articles such as Longabaugh's (1980) on the direct observation of behavior under natural conditions, Pareek and Rao's (1980) on cross-cultural surveys and interviewing, and Bochner's (1980) unobtrusive methods in cross-cultural experimentation. Many of these developments are along anthropological lines. Second, attempts have been made to counter experimental difficulties with new techniques. These devices have included attempts to use culture-free "compensation checks" to assess, for instance, whether the task that is communicated is the same as the task that is responded to (Cambell, 1964), as well as a variety of multitrait, multimeasure approaches.

Emics, Etics, and Theories

A major debate with both serious theoretical and methodological implications has centered on the well-known contrast between *emic* and *etic* orientations in cross-cultural research. The essence of the emic idea is that cultures can only be understood in their own terms. Individual traits among different cultures have different histories and different "cultural meanings"; hence, they are not the same and cannot be compared. A strict interpretation of such cultural relativism—and one still subscribed to by many anthropologists—is that cross-cultural psychological comparisons are meaningless. In contrast, the etic view attempts to study behavior across many cultures from an "outside" or universal perspective. As such, etics represent culture-free aspects that, if not universal, must at least, by definition, operate in more than one cultural unit.

Methodologically the problem for cross-culture behavioral research is to avoid the pitfall of using the emic concepts of one culture to explain characteristics of another; that is, to avoid imposing an artificial etic and thus lose the meaningful emic aspects of another culture. Prior to the 1970s, most cross-culture research was guilty of such ethnocentrism; tests or procedures developed in a Euro-American context were translated for use in other parts of the globe with little concern for appropriateness (Triandis, 1980a, p. 35).

In order to define an emic concept adequately, it is necessary to be aware of all its relevant etic components. Thus one of the challenging elements in cross-culture research is that we must think panculturally; we must learn to view the same data from both points of view. For most of us this is not as easy as it may sound. Most of us function in what some have viewed as a "single experimental treatment;" we are unable to remove our own cultural screens which constantly, and unavoidably, filter our perceptions of the world. However, Davidson, Jaccard, Triandis, Morales, and Diaz-Guerrero (1976) have proposed a number of solutions to the emic-etic dilemma. One approach is to start with a construct that appears to have universal status and to develop emic ways to measure it.

Representing a third level of abstraction—etics being more abstract than emics—is Naroll's (1971) concept of *theorics* (discussed by Berry, 1980). Used as a means by which the social scientist can interpret and explain emic variations and etic constancies, theorics play a vital role in theory construction.

Sampling and Translation

As with all research, what constitutes a "proper" sample depends upon the purpose at hand. But, as Brislin et al. (1973, p. 21) point out, plausible rival hypotheses due to sampling arise any time comparisons are made between cultures since any differences found may be attributable to different selection methods or qualities of the samples rather than to the culture variable. Random sampling may not be a solution here and may well add to, rather than lessen, the difficulties of interpretation. Nonrandom samples intelligently selected are likely to produce more meaningful results.

As would be expected, translation from one language to another poses another serious obstacle. However, the decentering technique proposed by Werner and Campbell (1970) is recognized as having made a major contribution in this area. Basically, decentering involves generation items in each culture involved in a study and then, in each case, modifying them to suit the other cultures. The end result of this process is that the final instrument is no less suitable in one culture than in the others. Brislin et al. (1973, pp. 37-44) provide a good overview of this technique.

Previous Accounting Research

In what appears to be the only anthropological study dealing with accounting, Acheson (1972) explored the degree to which accounting systems influence perceptions of business opportunities in Cuanajo, a Tarascan village in Mexico. Comparison of the local view of business entry possibilities derived from the native system of accounts with more formal accounting methods led him to conclude that the native accounting system, by encouraging the collection of very different kinds of data, strongly influenced the perception of opportunities and played a critical role in influencing business decisions.

Chevalier (1977) conducted an experimental study to test whether the same accounting information may be perceived differently by different cultural groups. Using French Canadians and English Canadians as subjects, he found that the two groups did not differ in their perception of the importance of published financial information in making investment decisions. However, part of the research design included providing subjects with additional information not presently available in published financial statements—data on human resources, earnings forecasts, and management philosophy. While both groups perceived this unpublished information as important in their decision making, the French Canadian subjects attached a significantly higher degree of importance. Chevalier concluded that "while the results do not provide conclusive evidence against the proposition that financial information users have universal needs, they nevertheless indicate the need for further research" (p. 49).

In what may be likened to a fishing expedition, Burke (1980) attempted to test the hypothesis that the nationality of the user of an accounting report does not significantly affect his or her decision making behavior. Over 100 graduate students studying in business schools in England, Switzerland and the United States participated. Subjects were grouped on the basis of nationality into three classes: those from the United States (U.S.), those from the United Kingdom (U.K.), and the remainder were classified as "other."

The research design involved four experimental treatments which were obtained by combining two conditions (one positive, one negative) of nonaccounting information—represented by a president's letter—with two conditions of financial statement information (again one positive, one negative). Each subject was randomly assigned one of the experimental treatments and was asked to predict future earnings per share (EPS) numbers.

While the research plan was considerably more complex—for example, an attempt was made to apply Heider's (1958) theory of the balanced state of cognitions—and a number of interesting cross-cultural results were obtained, perhaps the most interesting concerned the conditions under which the president's letter had some impact. When the accounting information was positive, the nonaccounting information had little effect on the EPS predictions of all groups. However, when the accounting information was negative, the "other" subjects' (but not those from the U.K. nor the U.S.) decisions were materially affected by the tone of the letter (p < .01). What is perhaps even more interesting is that the "other" subjects were apparently unaware that they were so affected. In response to a direct (post EPS prediction) question on this issue, members of this group claimed to have attached the same level of importance to the letter regardless of whether they had received negative or positive accounting information. On the basis of this and other results the hypothesis could not be supported.

A number of accounting studies that have considered the cultural dimension are of interest here. Jaggi's (1975) study of managerial value orientations indicates that the reliability of financial statements in many countries is a reflection of cultural values. His conclusion, along with those of others, that the procedures for the development of accounting principles should be modified to suit different cultural environments is obviously an important one. The research of Frank (1979) and Nair and Frank (1980) established a clear association between economic and cultural variables and the classification of countries into groups based on their accounting practices. Because of the differences, the authors conclude that it may be more difficult for policy makers to achieve harmonization of accounting practices than was previously realized. Along similar lines, McComb (1979, p. 14) argues that international harmonization of accounting will not result from the mere imposition of uniform accounting practices but from an awareness of the cultural and societal reasons responsible for present differences.

A Strategy

How might accountants grapple with the complexities of doing cross-cultural research? Experience has shown that there are no simple solutions. Merely attempting to modify our measuring instruments is quite likely to produce a morass reminiscent of the helter-skelter, hit-or-miss approach characteristic of early work in cross-cultural psychology. What is needed is a planned approach that will circumvent the complexities as much as possible. The purpose of this section is to suggest such a strategy.

A three-stage approach within a general framework would probably be the most practical route. In order to facilitate achieving the primary purpose of analyzing subjective cultures, namely, the development of general laws that predict, Triandis (1972) suggested that the search for such laws should be carried out at four levels of abstraction. At the most general level there would be laws that are valid across all culture groups; at the next level there would be laws that apply only within particular types of cultures; at the third, would be laws that depend on cultural and demographic characteristics; and at the most specific level would be empirical generalizations that apply to extremely specific subgroups (pp. 5-6). An attempt to elucidate the applicability of various generalizations along these lines provides a general framework that might best serve the interests of behavioral research in international accounting.

Within that framework, the introductory phase of a research plan might well benefit from an examination of the extent to which *similarities* in accounting behavior transcend cultures rather than from a search for interesting cross-cultural differences. While such a suggestion may appear trivial, it rests upon a number of assumptions which have become generally accepted only in relatively recent times—recall the emic/etic controversy discussed earlier. There are also two basic arguments that lend support: 1) such a strategy offers a number of methodological advantages; 2) this is the direction in which cross-cultural psychology is heading.

Methodologically, according to Triandis, Malpass, and Davidson (1972, p. 14), studies that attempt to provide the cross-cultural generality of a relationship or phenomenon "can be done with relatively loose methodology, since if the finding is obtained in spite of differences in the stimuli, responses and people, it must be a strong finding." On the other hand, attempts to show differences "require extremely stringent controls and a multimethod approach, since there are many competing hypotheses that can account for the observed differences."

Furthermore, it is worth noting that many of the methodological difficulties that torment the cross-cultural psychologist may not be as serious an obstacle to the accounting researcher. As accountants, we may be more concerned with comprehending the systematic covariation between cultural and behavioral variables, i.e., with predictive ability, and less so with causal relations or what our tests are really measuring. For example, to borrow an illustration from psychology, so long as intelligence tests are treated *solely* in terms of their ability to predict future school performance, arguments about the nature of the test need not arise. But as soon as we wish to know what intelligence tests *really* measure, then we enter into an area of seemingly endless arguments and ambiguity. Questions of validity comprise the core of much methodological controversy in cross-cultural psychology. To a practical field like accounting, however, solutions to problems of this kind are less urgent and are not as constrained by the absence of theoretical formulations underlying the research.

Apart from the supposition that etic measurements are possible, the search for cross-cultural generalities must also assume away the dilemma associated with culture change. Since the cultures of the world are in a constant state of metamorphosis, the search for universals in subjective culture assumes a structural invariance that transcends time, i.e., that the same essential social as well as psychological structures persist as cultures evolve (Lonner, 1980b, p. 144). While not all social scientists share this view (those that subscribe to a strict form of cultural relativism would not), it would seem that most cross-cultural psychologists now believe that the establishment of universally valid psychological laws is a worthwhile goal. A discussion of this entire issue together with an analysis of the empirical evidence is provided in a recent review by Lonner (1980b), but this trend can be readily discerned from research conducted over the last ten years. Osgood's studies on the cross-cultural universals of affective meaning and Chomsky's (1972) "psychic unit of mankind" argument in linguistics—that at a very basic level, man's capacity for language is grounded in his biological make-up—have provided a major impetus.

An exploration for level two generalizations would seem to be a reasonable starting point. A concerted set of studies concerning a limited but vital set of issues might be undertaken with standardized instruments and common research designs in carefully selected countries. As research progresses, the search for similarities may well disclose differences. At one level we might find identity, at another wide variability. If so, replications and a structured quest for further differences would naturally evolve. This might be viewed as a second phase in an ongoing research strategy while the search for theorics would be the third, and final, stage.

These second and third stages would involve many of the methodological technicalities alluded to earlier. While these cannot be even summarized here, four points merit a brief mention. First, studies involving just two cultures have distinct limitations. There is no intermediate position in such a case and it is for that reason that Campbell (1964, p. 333) noted that "no two naturally occurring things are comparable." But when three or more cultures are involved, two or more degrees of freedom are available, and similarities and differences can be discerned. A second point is that when several researchers—preferably with different cultural backgrounds—collaborate on a study, there is less likelihood that an ethnocentric framework will be artificially imposed. Third, in the area of theory building, the best method, according to Brislin et al. (1973, p. 7), is to find cultures that are high, medium and low on a trait and then to discover the reasons for the difference.

The final point is that in the search for differences, an unusual amount of methodological rigor is required. Competing hypotheses to those being researched must be systematically eliminated at the design stage of a study. A number of useful controls and multitrait, multimeasure approaches to overcome bias are suggested in the literature. Irwin, Klein, Engle, Yarbrough, and Nerlove (1977) and others have discussed the problem of establishing validity in cross-cultural measurements. Other devices abound. One that this writer found useful was the inclusion of semantic differential type judgments to explicitly measure the meaning of the task during an experiment. In an experimental setting, a rule of thumb well worth remembering is that the more structured the stimulus pattern, the less it is amenable to perceptual distortion. This point is singularly important in cross-cultural research.

Conclusions

At no point throughout this discussion was it possible to provide convincing evidence that "culture" is a factor that can be safely ignored in behavioral accounting research. On the contrary, what evidence does exist would suggest the opposite. Psychological investigations over the last ten years clearly demonstrate the importance of this variable. Whether these findings carry over in important ways into that subset of behavioral research we associate with accounting remains to be seen. In the meanwhile, there seems little choice but to conclude that claims made to the effect that culture is not an important parameter of accounting behavior should be recognized for what they are, namely, assumptions—and highly tenuous ones at that—rather than empirically tested facts.

If, in the future, we learn to analyze and measure accurately how the elements of subjective culture impact on accounting concerns, we may be able to arrive at a reasonably satisfactory resolution of this issue. If research should demonstrate that culture is not a material factor this would certainly simplify matters. Allowing for other environmental differences, the benefits of our findings in any country could then be effectively transferred across cultural boundaries. On the other hand, if future research should demonstrate important differences, and if we learn about the consequences of these differences, we may be able, based on advances in technology and the ability of accountants to design their systems to influence behavior, to incorporate modifications such that cultural influences may help rather than hinder the goals for which these systems are intended. Such knowledge may also facilitate the training of accountants from one country to interact more effectively with accountants in another.

A final point is worth mentioning. It may be wise, as Lambert (1980, p. 28) observed, "for those who do cross-cultural research to gird themselves to be patient in the face of criticism even when that criticism is occasionally unwarranted." Due to the almost limitless subtleties of cultural diversity and in light of the methodological difficulties that are inherently involved in this type of research such criticism, even if "occasionally unwarranted," is bound to occur.

Bibliography

Acheson, J. "Accounting Concepts and Economic Opportunities in a Tarascan Village: Emic and Etic Views." *Human Organization* (Spring 1972): 83-91.

Barrett, G., and B. Bass. "Cross-Cultural Issues in Industrial and Organizational Psychology." In M. Dunnette (ed.), *Handbook of Industrial and Organizational Psychology,* Chicago: Rand McNally, 1976, pp. 1639-86.

Becker, S. W. "Discussion of the Effect of Frequency of Feedback on Attitude and Performance," *Empirical Research in Accounting: Selected Studies, 1967,* Institute of Professional Accounting, Graduate School of Business, University of Chicago, 1968.

Berry, J. "An Ecological Approach to Cross- Cultural Psychology," *Netherlands Journal of Psychology* 30, (1975): p. 51-84.

Berry, J. and P. Dasen (eds.), *Culture and Cognition: Readings in Cross-Cultural Psychology,* New York: Metheun, 1974.

Bochner, S., "Unobstrusive Measures in Cross-Cultural Experimentation," in H. Triandis and J. Berry (eds.), *Handbook of Cross-Cultural Psychology,* Vol. 2, Boston: Allyn and Bacon, 1980, pp. 319-88.

Bourguignon, E. *Psychological Anthropology,* New York: Holt, Rinehart and Winston, 1979.

Brislin, R., W. Lonner and R. Thorndike, *Cross-Cultural Research Methods,* New York: Wiley, 1973.

Brunswick, E. *Perception and the Representative Design of Experiments,* Berkeley, California: The University of California Press, 1956.

Burke, R. C. "Some Parameters of Financial Analysis Behavior: An International Comparison Under Experimental Conditions," 1980, Working Paper 80-16, College of Commerce, University of Saskatchewan.

Byrne, D. *The Attraction Paradigm,* New York: Academic, 1971.

Campbell, D. "Blind Variation and Selective Retention in Creative Thought as in Other Knowledge Processes," *Psychological Review* 67 (1960): p. 380-400.

—————. "Distinguishing Differences in Perception from Failures of Communication in Cross- Cultural Studies." In F. Northrop and H. Livinston (eds.), *Cross-Cultural Understanding: Epistemology in Anthropology,* New York: Harper and Row, 1964.

Chevalier, G. "Should Accounting Practices Be Universal?" *CA Magazine* (Canada) (July 1977): p. 47-50.

Chomsky, N. *Language and Mind,* enlarged edition, New York: Harcourt, Brace, Jovanovich, 1972.

Cole, M., and S. Scribner. *Culture and Thought,* New York: Wiley, 1974.

Davidson, A., J. Jaccard, J. Triandis, H. Morales, and R. Diaz-Guerrero. "Cross-Cultural Model Testing: Toward a Solution of the Emic-Etic Dilemma," *International Journal of Psychology* 11 (1976): p. 1-13.

Davidson, A., and E. Thomson. "Cross-Cultural Studies on Attitudes and Beliefs." In H. Triandis and R. Brislin (eds.), *Handbook of Cross-Cultural Psychology,* Vol. 5, Boston: Allyn and Bacon, 1980, pp. 25-72.

Diaz-Guerrero, R. *The Psychology of the Mexican,* Austin, Texas: University of Texas Press, 1975.

Driver, M., and T. Mock, "Human Information Processing, Decision Style Theory, and Accounting Information Systems," *The Accounting Review* (July 1975): p. 490-508.

Eckensberger, L., W. Lonner, and Y. Poortinga, *Cross-Cultural Contributions to Psychology,* Lisse, Netherlands: Swets and Zeitlinger, 1979.

Ember, C. "Cross-Cultural Cognitive Studies," *Annual Review of Anthropology,* 6 (1977): p. 33-56.

Firth, M. "Perceptions of Auditor Independence and Official Ethical Guidelines," *The Accounting Review* (July 1980): p. 451-466.

Frank, W. "An Empirical Analysis of International Accounting Practices," *Journal of Accounting Research* (Autumn 1979).

Goodenough, W. "Comment on Cultural Evolution," *Daedalus* 90 (1961): p. 521-28.

—————, "Cultural Anthropology and Linguistics." In P. Garvin (ed.), *Report of the*

Seventh Annual Round Table Meeting on Linguistics and Language Study, Washington, D. C. : Georgetown University Monograph Series on Language and Linguistics, 9, 1957.

Haried, A. "The Semantic Dimensions of Financial Statements," *Journal of Accounting Research* (Autumn 1972): p. 376-91.

_____ , "Measurement of Meaning in Financial Reports," *Journal of Accounting Research* (Spring 1973): p. 117-45.

Herzberg, F. *Work and the Nature of Man,* Cleveland, Ohio: World Publishing Co., 1966.

Hicks, J. "An Examination of Accounting Interest Groups' Differential Perceptions of Innovations," *The Accounting Review* (April 1978): p. 371-88.

Hofstedt, T., and J. Kinard, "A Strategy for Behavioral Accounting Research," *The Accounting Review* (January 1970): p. 38-54.

Howell, R., and H. Vetter, *Language in Behavior,* New York: Human Sciences Press, 1976.

Imhoff, E. "Employment Effects on Auditor Independence," *The Accounting Review,* (October 1978): p. 869-81.

Irvine S., and W. Carroll, "Testing and Assessment Across Cultures: Issues in Methodology and Theory." In H. Triandis and J. Berry (eds.), *Handbook of Cross-Cultural Psychology,* Vol. 2, Boston: Allyn and Bacon, 1980, p. 181-244.

Irwin, M., R. Klein, P. Engle, C. Yarbrough, and S. Nerlove, "The Problem of Establishing Validity in Cross-Cultural Measurements", *Annals of the New York Academy of Sciences* 285 (1977): p. 308-25.

Jaggi, B. "The Impact of the Cultural Environment on Financial Disclosure," *The International Journal of Accounting, Education and Research* (January 1975): p. 75-84.

Jahoda, G. "Theoretical and Systematic Approaches in Cross-Cultural Psychology." In H. Triandis and W. Lambert (eds.), *Handbook of Cross-Cultural Psychology*, Vol. 1, Boston: Allyn and Bacon, 1980, pp. 69-142.

Klineberg, O. "Historical Perspectives: Cross-Cultural Psychology Before 1960." In H. Triandis and W. Lambert (eds.), *Handbook of Cross-Cultural Psychology,* Vol. 1, Boston: Allyn and Bacon, 1980, pp. 31-68.

Köbben, A. "Comparativists and Non-Comparativists in Anthropology." In R. Naroll and R. Cohen (eds.), *A Handbook of Method in Cultural Anthropology,* New York: Natural History Press, 1970, pp. 581-96.

Lambert, W. "Introduction to Perspectives." In H. Triandis and W. Lambert (eds.), *Handbook of Cross-Cultural Psychology,* Vol. 1, Boston: Allyn and Bacon, 1980, pp. 15-30.

Lavin, D. "Some Effects of the Perceived Independence of the Auditor," *Accounting, Organizations and Society,* 2.3(1977): 237-44.

_____ . "Perceptions of the Independence of the Auditor," *The Accounting Review* (January 1976): pp. 41-50.

Lawler, E., and J. Rhode, *Information and Control in Organizations,* Pacific Palisades, California: Goodyear, 1976.

Lawrence, P., and J. Lorsch. *Organization and Environment,* Homewood, Illinois: Irwin, 1969.

Longabaugh, R. "The Systematic Observation of Behavior in Naturalistic Settings." In H. Triandis and J. Berry (eds.), *Handbook of Cross-Cultural Psychology,* Vol. 2, Boston: Allyn and Bacon, 1980, pp. 57-126.

Lonner, W. "A Decade of Cross-Cultural Psychology," *Journal of Cross-Cultural Psychology* 11.1 (March 1980a): 2-34.

_____ , "The Search for Psychological Universals." In H. Triandis and W. Lambert (eds.), *Handbook of Cross-Cultural Psychology,* Vol. 1, Boston: Allyn and Bacon, 1980b, pp. 143-204.

Lonner, W., and H. Triandis, "Introduction to Basic Processes." In H. Triandis and W.

Lonner (eds.), *Handbook of Cross-Cultural Psychology,* Vol. 3, Boston: Allyn and Bacon, 1980, pp. 1-20.

Lucy, J., and R. Shweder, "Whorf and His Critics: Linguistic and Nonlinguistic Influences on Color Memory," *American Anthropologist* 81.3 (September 1979): p. 581-615.

Mandelbaum, D. *Selected Writings of Edward Sapir,* Berkeley, California: University of California Press, 1949.

Marsella, A., R. Tharp, and T. Ciborowski (eds.), *Perspectives on Cross-Cultural Psychology,* New York: Academic, 1979.

Maslow, A. *Motivation and Personality,* New York: Harper and Row, 1954.

McClelland, D. *The Achieving Society,* New York: Litton, 1961.

McComb, D. "International Harmonization of Accounting: A Cultural Dimension," *International Journal of Accounting Education and Research* 14 (Spring 1979): p. 1-16.

Nair, R., and W. Frank, "The Impact of Disclosure and Measurement Practices on International Accounting Classifications," *The Accounting Review* (July 1980): p. 426-50.

Oliver, B. "A Look at the Semantic Differential as a Tool to Assist Faculty Teaching Evaluations," *Decision Sciences* (October 1973): p. 549-58.

_____. "The Semantic Differential: A Device for Measuring the Interprofessional Communication of Selected Accounting Concepts," *Journal of Accounting Research* (Autumn 1974): p. 299-316.

Osgood, C. "Objective Indicators in Subjective Culture." In L. Adler (ed.), *Issues in Cross-Cultural Research. Annals of the New York Academy of Sciences,* 285, 1977, pp. 435-50.

Osgood, C., W. May, and M. Miron, *Cross-Cultural Universals of Affective Meaning,* Urbana: University of Illinois Press, 1975.

Pareek, U., and T. Rao. "Cross-Cultural Surveys and Interviewing." In H. Triandis and J. Berry (eds.), *Handbook of Cross-Cultural Psychology,* Vol.2, Boston: Allyn and Bacon, 1980, pp. 127-80.

Preale, I., Y. Amir, and S. Sharan, "Perceptual Articulation and Task Effectiveness in Several Israel Subcultures," *Journal of Personality and Social Psychology* 15 (1970): p. 190-95.

Sapir, E. *Language,* New York: Harcourt Brace, 1921.

Schiff, M., and A. Lewin, "The Impact of People on Budgets," *The Accounting Review* (April 1970): p. 259-68.

Segall, M. *Cross-Cultural Psychology: Human Behavior in Global Perspective,* Belmont, California: Wadsworth, 1979.

Segall, M., D. Campbell, and M. Herskovits, *The Influence of Culture on Visual Perception,* Indianapolis: Bobbs-Merrill, 1966.

Spindler, G. (ed.), *The Making of Psychological Anthropology,* Berkeley: University of California Press, 1978.

Tannenbaum, A. "Organizational Psychology." In H. Triandis and R. Brislin (eds.), *Handbook of Cross-Cultural Psychology,* Vol. 5, Boston: Allyn and Bacon, 1980, pp. 281-334.

Triandis, H. *The Analysis of Subjective Culture,* New York: Wiley, 1972.

_____. "Introduction to Handbook of Cross-Cultural Psychology." In H. Triandis and W. Lambert *(eds.),* Handbook of Cross-Cultural Psychology, Vol. 1, Boston: Allyn and Bacon, 1980a, pp. 1-14.

_____, "Reflections on Trends in Cross-Cultural Psychology," *Journal of Cross-Cultural Psychology,* 11.1 (March 1980b): p. 35-58.

Triandis, H., R. Malpass, and A. Davidson, "Cross-Cultural Psychology," *The Biennial Review of Anthropology,* (1972): p. 1-84.

Tyler, S. *Cognitive Anthropology,* New York: Holt, Rinehart and Winston, 1969.

Werner, E. *Cross-Cultural Child Development: A View from the Planet Earth,* Belmont, California: Wadsworth, 1979.

Werner, O., and D. Campbell, "Translating, Working Through Interpreters and the Problem of Decentering." In R. Naroll and R. Cohen (eds.), *A Handbook of Method in Cultural Anthropology,* New York: Natural History Press, 1970, pp. 398-420.

Whorf, B. "Language, Thought and Reality," *Technology Review* 42 (1940): p. 229-31; 247-48.

Witkin, H. "A Cognitive Style Approach to Cross-Cultural Research," *International Journal of Psychology* 2 (1967): p. 233-50.

Witkin, H., and J. Berry, "Psychological Differentiation in Cross-Cultural Perspective," *Journal of Cross-Cultural Psychology* 6 (1975): p. 4-86.

Whittaker, J., and R. Meade, "Sex of the Communicator as a Variable in Source Credibility," *Journal of Social Psychology* 72 (1967): p. 27-34.

Wright, G., and L. Phillips, *Probablistic Thinking in Cross-Cultural Perspective,* Uxbridge, Middlesex: Brunel Institute of Organization and Social Studies, Brunel University, 1979.

Transnational Reporting and Disclosure

VINOD B. BAVISHI
University of Connecticut

Introduction

A review of the annual reports of a sample of domestic firms quickly indicates that the extent of disclosure varies from company to company. These differences are multiplied when examining reports from an international sample. In general, variations in disclosure practices of multinational corporations (MNCs) are substantial.

Once the domain of domestic shareholders and creditors, annual reports and other corporate data published by MNCs increasingly are being scrutinized by host governments and the public at large, including organized labor and public-interest groups. Owing to differences in multinational reporting practices, a number of international and regional organizations have assumed the task of remedying what they perceive to be gaps in multinational reporting and disclosure. Competing with private accounting institutions, disclosure proposals of the United Nations Commission on Transnational Corporations, the Organization for Economic Cooperation and Development, and the European Economic Community are often overlapping and insensitive to business needs. This is particularly the case in the area of "soft" nonfinancial data. This essay restricts its analysis to disclosure and reporting by multinational corporations and is motivated by a desire to further the analysis of international disclosure practices. Its purposes are: first, to summarize recent studies which examine international disclosure practices; second, to evaluate these research studies in critical fashion; and third, to raise a number of research questions and thereby suggest directions for further inquiry.

Summary of Recent Research

A summary of eight research articles/monographs, gleaned from the literature of the past ten years, is provided here. The selection is not intended to be all inclusive. Our objective is simply to provide a general overview of research done to date on international disclosures.

Table 1 summarizes the research objectives, methodology, and conclusions of each of these studies.

Evaluation of Recent Research

Before identifying areas for improvement, let us note, in all fairness to the studies analyzed, several difficulties inherent in transnational disclosure research.

First and foremost, researchers face the difficulty of the absence of an international set of generally-accepted accounting principles. To assess current disclosure practices by multinationals, one needs a reference list of disclosure items for comparison purposes.

Another problem which has plagued researchers in the past is that financial reports of foreign multinationals were not easily available. For example, 10-K's of U.S. firms are available in microfiche form in university libraries across the U.S. Only one or two university locations, however, have collections of foreign annual reports.

Given these difficulties, the following commentary provides a list of general limitations for consideration by future researchers. Common limitations relate to samples studied, data analysis, construction of disclosure indexes, causal variables explaining disclosure trends, and disclosure media employed.

All of the studies examined refer to disclosure practices of large industrial corporations based in developed countries. Several important groups of companies were excluded; namely, multinationals in service industries, multinationals based in third world countries, and government-owned multinationals. Also, disclosure issues relating to smaller multinationals may be considerably different than those associated with larger companies.

Extant disclosure studies also suffer from limited data analysis. Studies conducted to date have analyzed disclosure practices more or less by country and/or by industry only. Little analysis has been done in terms of the association between the extent of disclosure and a reporting company's characteristics. Features such as the degree of multinationality, company size, the presence or absence of foreign-denominated debt, reg-

Table 1. Transnational Reporting and Disclosures: Summary of Research

Author, Title and Publication	Research Objectives	Research Methodology	Conclusions
1. Choi, Frederick D.S., "Financial Disclosure and Entry to the European Capital Market," *Journal of Accounting Research*, Autumn 1973, pp. 159-75.	• Assess the relationship between disclosure and capital market entry.	• 18 eurobond participant firms (non-U.S. and non-U.K. based) and a control group of 18 nonparticipants selected from Fortune's 1971 list of non-U.S. companies. • 5 years annual reports spanning the years prior to and subsequent to entry. Disclosure Index constructed comprising 36 items—both narrative and financial in nature.	• Experimental firms examined significantly improved their financial disclosure upon entry into the European capital market.
2. Barrett, M. Edgar, "Financial Reporting Practices: Disclosure and Comprehensiveness in an International Setting," *Journal of Accounting Research*, Spring 1976, pp. 10-26.	• Overall extent of financial disclosure. • Degree of comprehensiveness of firms' financial statements.	• Annual Reports for 1963-72 of 103 large firms in total, consisted of 15 firms located in U.S., Japan, U.K., France, W. Germany, and Sweden and thirteen firms located in the Netherlands. • Seventeen items of information were selected to compute disclosure index.	• Overall level of corporations' financial disclosure steadily improved from 1963 to 1972. • Wide level of variance was observed between U.S. and U.K. firms vs. firms from other countries in the sample.

Table 1, continued

Author, Title and Publication	Research Objectives	Research Methodology	Conclusions
3. Barrett, M. Edgar, "The Extent of Disclosure in Annual Reports of Large Companies in 7 Countries," *International Journal of Accounting*, Spring 1977, pp. 1-24.	• Determine whether financial disclosure in foreign company annual reports is significantly different than found in U.S. annual reports.	• Same as above.	• Extent of financial disclosure in the annual reports of major publicly-held U.S. corporations was greater than that found in other countries in the sample. • U.S. annual reports were not uniformly better than those of other five countries in terms of specific categories of disclosure.
4. Gray, S. J., "Segment Reporting and the EEC Multinationals," *Journal of Accounting Research*, Autumn 1978, pp. 242-53.	• Examine segment reporting in EEC countries to determine actual practice and differences in disclosure between companies based in EEC countries.	• Annual reports for 1972-73 of the 100 largest industrial multinationals based in the EEC and listed on stock exchanges in 1973 were used. • Eight items of information of segmental disclosures were used.	• Overall level of disclosure was low except sales by business or geographic areas. • Statistically significant differences existed in the extent of disclosure between U.K. and continental EEC companies.
5. Gray, S. J., "Managerial Forecasts and European Multinational Company," *Journal of International*	• Establish extent of disclosure of forecasts in practice and ascertain differences in disclosure between compa-	• Same as above in terms of sample size and years. • Three items of information were used.	• The overall level of disclosure of forecasts would seem to be low and largely of a qualitative nature.

Author, Title and Publication	Research Objectives	Research Methodology	Conclusions
Business Studies, Fall 1978, pp. 21-32.	nies based in the different countries.		• While there are some inter-country differences in the European context, these do not, in general, provide support for the hypothesis that the extent of disclosure is correlated with national equity market efficiency.
6. Lafferty, Michael, *World Accounting Survey*, Financial Times, London 1980.	• Provide a measure of the quality of information found in the annual reports of MNCs and make recommendations.	• 1979 annual reports of 200 companies based primarily in developed countries were used. • 100 point scale was used to measure the quality of information in annual reports. • The pronouncements and proposals of national and international standard groups were used as international yardsticks of accounting and non-financial information.	• The practice of consolidation is widespread throughout the sample companies, but great diversity in consolidation methods was observed. • The quality of segmental data was considered poor. • Nonfinancial disclosure was found to be more patchy and varied than financial disclosure. • Approximately one-third of the survey companies publish their annual reports three months after the year-end date.

Author, Title and Publication	Research Objectives	Research Methodology	Conclusions
7. Lees, Francis A., "*Reporting Transnational Business Operations*," The Conference Board, New York 1980.	• Identify items of information that financial analysts deem important and show the extent to which large U.S.-based multinationals supply the information that is sought.	• Annual reports (1978 or 1979) and Form 10-Ks of 218 U.S.-based multinationals were used. • Questionnaire responses from 75 financial analysts in the New York City area were used to identify the relative importance of 40 disclosure items. A scoring system of 100 points was derived based on actual reporting practices and relative weights given by financial analysts.	• Disclosure by major U.S. MNCs has improved, but there is a gap between the amount of information sought by financial analysts and that which is actually provided.
8. Bavishi, Vinod B., and Wyman, Harold E., "Foreign Operations Disclosures by U.S. Based MNC's—are they adequate?," *The International Journal of Accounting*, Fall 1980, pp. 153-68.	• Contrast foreign operations disclosures required in the U.S. and proposed by international accounting standard setters • Determine foreign operations disclosure practices of U.S.-based multinational corporations	• 1978 annual reports of 296 U.S.-based multinationals were used. • Ten information items of geographical disclosures were reviewed.	• The tendency to use a few broad geographic areas for reporting foreign sales, assets and income was found. • Market price was the most popular basis for transfer pricing. • Few firms reported voluntary information relating to foreign operations. • Differences exist between foreign operations disclosures required by national accounting standards and those proposed by the international organizations.

istration on foreign stock exchanges, number of shareholders, distribution of ownership, and level of profitability are examples in this regard.

Several researchers constructed an index to measure the quality of disclosure. Such an index provided a tool for disclosure comparisons between countries, years, and industries. Several questions, however, can be raised regarding the validity of prior disclosure indexes.

Information items and their relative importance used in the construction of disclosure indices in most instances were based on work done earlier using U.S. analysts as a validation base. On this score, several questions merit answers. Do international users have the same needs for information as do U.S. investors? Would disclosure items of interest change over time? Is different information needed from foreign compared to domestic companies?

How should actual disclosure practices be scored? Should disclosure items be weighted equally or ranked on a scale from say 1 to 5?

Can a subjective evaluation of non-financial disclosures be reflected in such an index? If so, how?

Is there a method of assuring against penalizing a company for not disclosing items which are simply not applicable to it?

It is generally asserted that multinational corporations have shown improvement over time in the area of disclosure. Reasons underlying this phenomenon have seldom been identified, however. For example, the extent of improvement attributed to external factors such as national accounting standards, changes in business and political risks, and the increasing use of international capital markets were not studied or explained.

It is generally agreed that the most important medium of external financial disclosure is the annual financial statement. Most studies reviewed here relied upon annual disclosures in the form of financial statements provided to shareholders. In recent years, however, additional disclosures are being called for through quarterly reports, government filings in the home country (such as Form 10K in the U.S.), government filings in host countries, proxy statements, and registration statements associated with new offerings of securities. Unfortunately, none of the studies examined here attempted to examine the cost/benefit tradeoff associated with these alternative avenues of disclosure.

Suggestions for Future Research

In recent years, emphasis in the area of disclosure research has been on explaining differences in disclosure practices between countries. A less-explored research dimension is the relationship between corporate financial disclosure and firm characteristics as well as the impact of such disclosures on capital markets. It is hoped that our earlier discussion will provide a basis for improving research methodologies utilized in future inquiries into the nature of international disclosures.

In terms of specific suggestions, a natural avenue of further research would be studies aimed at reporting populations not addressed by studies reviewed here. Such populations would include multinationals in service industries, international companies from third world countries, state-owned enterprises and smaller sized reporting entities.

A study or studies examining the relationship between increased corporate disclosure and the concommitant reactions of capital market participants would be a useful addition to the literature. The following questions might serve as a focus for such research. Thus, do firms disclosing more information experience a lower cost of capital compared to firms disclosing less information? Is the information value of foreign firms' financial statements more than that of domestic firms? The rationale here is that the quantity of information available to investors concerning domestic firms is far greater than the case of foreign firms. Do investors located in different countries impound consistently the earnings information contained in foreign financial statements for multinationals listed on multiple stock exchanges?

Studies examining the association between extent of disclosure and firm characteristics would be useful. Variables such as firm size, degree of multinationality, profitability, number of shareholders, size of foreign currency denominated debt levels, and registration on overseas exchanges appear to be possible explanatory variables.

In recent years, there has been increased discussion in academic, government, and business circles on quantifying the cost of regulation. Although financial executives, in concept at least, are in favor of providing more information about foreign operations to statement users, the cost of providing added information is a constraining factor. The following research questions need to be addressed in this area: What are the cost components of external reporting for multinational corporations? What is the total cost of complying with external financial reporting requirements for multinational corporations?

Because of the attention being accorded foreign operations disclosures, construction of disclosure indexes for multinational corporations in reporting their foreign operations would facilitate monitoring of changes in disclosures over time. A number of avenues may be pursued in constructing such a disclosure index.

A study of user's needs would be a first task. A cross-national group of investors, analysts, and creditors, with experience in evaluating international investments, could be queried for identification of disclosure items and its relative importance. Disclosure standards of international organizations could also be used as yardsticks to measure the extent of disclosure. Finally, in order to avoid counting those disclosure items which are not applicable to a particular firm, an applicable disclosure score could be computed for each firm by including only items applicable to that firm. Then, actual scores could be compared against applicable disclosure scores. The percentage relationship between actual score versus applicable score could then be used for comparative purposes.

Summary and Conclusions

The purpose of this review of recent research on international disclosure has been: first, to summarize and assess research done to date; and second, to suggest directions for future research by raising a number of unanswered questions.

Eight research articles/monographs selected from the literature of the past decade were summarized. Generalized evaluative comments dealing with research methodology followed.

The review concludes by identifying specific areas for further research. Most prominent, in this writer's opinion, are: 1) measurement of relationships between disclosures and the preferences of capital market participants; 2) analysis of cost/benefit of international disclosures; and 3) construction of foreign operations disclosure indexes.

Internal Performance Evaluation of the Foreign Operations of the Multinational Corporation

HELEN MORSICATO GERNON
University of Oregon

Using information to evaluate the performance of multinational corporation (MNC) foreign subsidiaries and managers is a critical international accounting issue. There is a paucity of adequate performance evaluation systems and those that do exist have developed in a rather haphazard fashion. The issue of translating foreign-currency information to parent-currency complicates the matter; however, translation is an integral part of the problem and must be included in any discussion of MNC internal performance evaluation systems.

The purpose of this paper is two-fold. First, a general discussion of the development of MNC performance evaluation systems is presented. Then, the current issues in this area are discussed, followed by suggested topics for future and continued research.

MNC Performance Evaluation Systems

Performance evaluation may be defined as the periodic surveillance of financial interests to ensure that the objectives of the enterprise are being accomplished to the fullest (Choi and Mueller, 1978, p. 266). The performance evaluation system of an enterprise is an integral part of the financial control system. An effective performance evaluation system requires a reporting system which gathers information on the actual results of a corporation's financial interests. These actual results are generally compared to a firm-determined standard to pinpoint deviations so that corrective actions may be instituted.

This section discusses the development of MNC financial control systems with an emphasis on internal performance evaluation. A summary of the results of previous research studies is included.

The Concept of Control and the MNC

Control may be defined to include planning, implementing, evaluating, and correcting performance by use of feedback so that corporate goals may be attained (Horngren, 1977, p. 6). The control function in the MNC will differ depending upon the type of attitude taken by the corporate management toward multinational business policies. Perlmutter (1969, pp. 11-13) has sorted these business policies into three classifications: 1) ethnocentric (home-country oriented); 2) polycentric (host-country oriented); and 3) geocentric (world oriented).

The ethnocentric attitude is one in which home-country standards are thought to be superior and therefore are applied world-wide. The polycentric attitude begins with the assumption that host-country cultures are different. Therefore, the local affiliate operates quite autonomously, and the evaluation and control functions are determined locally. The goal of the geocentric approach toward corporate functions is to consider the foreign subsidiaries as part of a whole whose focus is on worldwide objectives as well as local contribution with its unique competence. To accomplish the geocentric goal, corporate managers try to establish standards for evaluation and control which are both universal and local.

The attitude of corporate management affects the location of decision making. If an MNC headquarters allows decisions to be made at the foreign subsidiary level, the corporation will be considered decentralized. If decisions which affect the foreign subsidiaries are made at management headquarters, then the corporation is considered centralized. Generally, companies do not make all decisions at one location or the other, but aim for a collaborative approach between headquarters and several levels within the organization. However, it is not uncommon for a corporation to appear relatively more centralized than decentralized or vice-versa. This degree of centralization or decentralization ultimately affects the control function of an MNC which in turn affects planning decisions and evaluation of performance (Daniels, Ogram, and Radebaugh, 1976, p. 487).

> A major distinction between domestic and multinational planning focuses on this issue of organizational form of operations and points out the dichotomy present in the two approaches. Domestic operations are usually decentralized as profit centers that are oriented toward short-term planning by the profit center for the profit center. The planning process of the multinational company carries a strong dual orientation. Not only are plans used locally, but they are used by headquarters in an attempt to coordinate on a worldwide basis. This allows the company to achieve both its comparative advantage and many of its objectives. The organization here is centralized in contrast to the decentralization of the domestic operations. The changed emphasis on the planning process results in planning and evaluation conflicts, and further complicates an already difficult process (Scott, 1972, p. 68).

Robbins and Stobaugh (1973a, p. 46) have found that the control of the financial function within the MNC evolves around both the degree of foreign experience which the firm has had and the size of the firm's foreign operations. Size is defined in terms of the annual sales of the foreign units as follows:

Small—less than $100 million
Medium—from $100 to $500 million
Large—over $500 million.

Three phases of the evolutionary process are described by Robbins and Stobaugh. The first phase, known as ignoring the system's potential, involves a lack of foreign experience by the headquarters' management, a relative and absolute small scale of foreign operations, and a resulting financial control system which does not operate in a coordinated manner. Each foreign subsidiary operates independently while improving its own performance possibly at the expense of the total profits of the firm.

Phase two is depicted by a strong central staff which makes most of the financial decisions for the system of foreign subsidiaries with the goal of worldwide optimization. During this phase the foreign operations are increasing in relative importance and the corporate managers are gaining experience and insight as to the profit opportunities which may be earned from intercompany financial connections.

The third phase, compromising with complexity, finds the head-quarter's powerful corporate staff formulating guidelines for the foreign subsidiaries to follow because operations have grown too complex and large in number for corporate management to make a separate decision on each financial transaction between affiliates in the system. The subsidiaries are once again operating in a decentralized fashion; however, their decisions are controlled by a "rule book" issued by headquarters.

Robbins and Stobaugh (1973a, p. 151) point out that the MNC's foreign experience and size characteristics, which determine whether the firm is operating in Phase I, II, or III of the evolving financial function, also affect the techniques to evaluate the performance of foreign subsidiaries.

A small firm operating in Phase I is reported to evaluate the performance of a foreign subsidiary very informally. Budget preparation in the foreign operations is far less sophisticated than it is domestically. Decision making is decentralized with authority and responsibility for decisions delegated to the subsidiary managers.

The medium-size MNC is characterized by centralized decision making and tight supervision over the foreign operations. Rate-of-return is commonly used as an indicator of performance along with a formal budget.

The large enterprise also uses rate-of-return and formal budgets as two very rigid indicators of performance. Generally, the evaluation process in this size entity revolves around procedures, directives, and corporate standards. It is very common for the large firm to employ a number of worldwide and regional comparative measures.

In summary the control function of an enterprise involves the planning, implementation, evaluation, and correction of the performance of its operations. The attitude of the corporate management toward business policies determines whether an MNC will be ethnocentrically, polycentrically or geocentrically oriented toward the control function. The attitude toward the control function affects the location of decision making and the degree of centralization or decentralization to be allowed by the corporate management. The question of centralization or decentralization of foreign operations is also determined by the size of foreign operations and the amount of experience the firm has had with the foreign environment. The evolution of the MNC financial function and system of performance evaluation may also be linked to these different phases of foreign experience and size of foreign operations.

Exporting the Domestic Control System

A large majority of U.S. companies use the same system to control foreign operations that they use to control domestic interests. The most common elements of the control system that are exported internationally are the financial, budgetary, and statistical control techniques. There is a strong tendency to impose the methods developed for appraising domestic operations upon foreign operations. It is also common to find that the home office top management plays an important part in the control process.

Hawkins (1965, pp. 26-29) relates four reasons why most multinational corporations export their financial, budgetary, and statistical control techniques. The first reason is that the financial, budgetary, and statistical aspects of the system do not represent a critical problem until the operation is a going concern. Second, the installation of the established domestic system overseas is much cheaper than designing an entire system for the international organization. Third, corporate accounting groups require that all the corporation's operating groups use similar reporting forms for financial and operating data. Fourth, the domestic executives in control of the new foreign operations are more comfortable and already familiar with the domestic control system and prefer to use it internationally.

Hawkins explains that the exported versions of the domestic control system are seldom as successful or as effective internationally as they are domestically. This breakdown occurs because the domestic and foreign operations differ in three fundamental areas. These areas include the mix and relative importance of their long-range objectives; their organizational structure, manning, practices and policies; and the character of the environmental factors relevant to the success of the respective operations. These points will be considered in turn.

Often the objectives that have been established for domestic operations differ significantly from the goals established for international operations. Organizational differences between domestic and foreign operations will lessen the efficiency of the domestic financial, budgetary, and statistical control techniques exported for use overseas. For various legal, political, and economic reasons, corporations rarely duplicate their domestic organizational structure overseas. Decision making in the international organization tends to be more centralized than in the domestic organization. The foreign operations also have less lateral communication within the field management organization and follow different employee promotion and compensation policies.

Due to environmental differences, the methods used for evaluating the success of foreign operations often differ from the methods used by domestic operations. Superimposing a domestic control system established in one environment on an operation in a different environment with different objectives usually results in a breakdown of the system.

Likewise, the exportation of domestic standards for overseas evaluation is seldom appropriate. Due to the differences in the overseas company's market opportunities, investment in facilities, overhead costs, and exposure to risk, there is a need for the development of performance standards that are peculiar to the foreign investment.

As a result of corporate exportation practices, the financial control systems in use by foreign operations tend to communicate distorted pictures of the corporate objectives to the overseas organization; motivate the overseas organization away from top management's desired objectives; and provide inappropriate standards to appraise the performance of the overseas organization.

Description of MNC Internal Performance Evaluation Systems:
Prior Studies

The Committee on International Accounting of the American Accounting Association provides a list of observed approaches to the evaluation of entity resource utilization and managerial performance at the general management level of divisions or subsidiaries. This list includes the following:

1. No formal evaluation of operations exists: the general manager's performance evaluation for salary, bonus, and promotion purposes is entirely subjective on the basis of personality and other personal traits. This approach cannot be considered desirable and typically is not found in domestic operations; however, it is rather more frequently encountered in evaluation of foreign subsidiaries and their managers;

2. Operating results are evaluated in absolute terms which are generally profit or return-on-investment (ROI). Here, a subjective evaluation is made about what is good performance and the general manager is rewarded accordingly. This approach also includes a large subjective element and is found only where more sophisticated approaches have not been developed;

3. Operating results of the entity are compared to operating results of other entities in the same family; resource utilization and the entity general manager are both evaluated on this basis since an identity is assumed to exist between the two for evaluation purposes. This approach is called "the comparison of entities" approach, and it has merit where the most important environmental variables are much the same for the entities compared;

4. Operating results are evaluated relative to operating results for the same entity in preceding periods and an identity between the general manager and the entity is assumed. This approach is called the "temporal comparison." A major problem here is that an improvement over a preceding period's poor results still may not represent good performance in absolute terms; and

5. Operating results are evaluated on the basis of how closely they conform to planned operating results. While this is potentially an excellent evaluation approach, in practice the evaluation is often less than satisfactory. For example, performance is often based on actual compared to budget for only key factors such as profit and ROI, the constituents of which may not be entirely controllable by the general manager. Another common problem with this approach is that the plan becomes obsolete because of factors beyond the general manager's control and the plan is not revised in consideration of this. With this approach too, an identity is generally assumed between operating results and the general manager's performance. (Committee on International Accounting, 1974, p. 252)

Note that none of these approaches makes a clear distinction between the performance of the entity and the performance of the manager, although such distinctions could and should exist. All of the approaches, except the first, use a form of net income as an indicator of success.

Several studies concerned with evaluation and control techniques of the MNC provide evidence that this list of techniques established by the Committee on International Accounting is correct. A summary of the results of each study follows.

Mauriel. Mauriel conducted a study to examine the nature, scope, and effectiveness of multinational performance evaluation and control systems. He found that the fifteen giant multinational companies (sales of over $5 billion) that he interviewed placed heavy emphasis on financial controls. They also required their subsidiaries to use standard domestic budgeting and financial planning techniques. These firms used the profit or investment center concept with increasing emphasis on return-on-investment as a performance measure. Mauriel also found that currency differences require a careful approach to interpreting the meaning of the overseas division's balance sheet and earnings statement. In most instances, the foreign manager was given little control over many decisions made by the parent company that would ultimately affect his operating results. Mauriel also observed a lack of understanding of and concern for the impact of currency fluctuations on performance evaluation systems (Mauriel, 1969, p. 36).

McInnes. McInnes's research entailed a survey of thirty moderately sized multinationals (sales in the $100-$300 million range). This study focused on the design of financial reporting systems between corporate headquarters and foreign affiliates, and the use by corporate executives of reported financial data in the evaluation of its foreign operations (1969, p. 12). The research findings strongly supported the notion that there is very little difference in the design and implementation of financial reporting systems for foreign and domestic operations. Table 1 provides McInnes's tabulation of the control techniques used most frequently in foreign and domestic performance evaluation.

McInnes also found that 17 percent of the corporations required their subsidiaries to report only local-currency information; U.S. dollar information was required from 30 percent; both U.S. dollar and local-currency reports were required from 50 percent; and for 3 percent of the firms, the requirement depended upon the country involved.

Financial Executives Research Foundation. The Financial Executives Research Foundation sponsored a study on the financial control of multinational operations which was designed to codify those methods of financial control currently used by multinational companies. The study carefully reviewed the procedures used by thirty-four multinational corporations. Each corporation had members in the Financial Executives Institute, and each published separate figures in their annual reports for at least some aspect of their foreign operations. As many as 94 percent of the companies held their subsidiaries responsible for profit performance and used this as a measure of performance evaluation (Bursk, Dearden, Hawkins, and

Table 1. Most Useful Financial Control Techniques Used in
Evaluating Operations

| | Foreign | | Domestic | |
	Frequency of Mention	Weighted[a]	Frequency of Mention	Weighted
Return-on-Investment	21	50	19	48
Comparison with Plan	17	42	19	48
Comparison with History	11	20	10	17
Analysis of Income Statement	9	16	7	13
Analysis of Balance Sheet	—	—	5	6

Source: McInnes, 1971
[a]This is a weighted average of the three control techniques which were stated by each firm as the most useful for evaluation.

Longstreet, 1971, p. 25). Profit as compared to a profit budget was the principal measure of profitability with return-on-investment (ROI) mentioned next. Another conclusion was that an MNC control system should measure how well the foreign subsidiary manager has managed his operations in light of environmental peculiarities and foreign-currency fluctuations.

Robbins and Stobaugh. The evaluation practices used by the MNC in evaluating foreign operations were studied by Robbins and Stobaugh in 1973. Financial executives of thirty-nine MNCs were interviewed, and the published records of an additional 150 MNCs were studied. They found that foreign and domestic subsidiaries were evaluated on the same basis and that the basic measure of performance was a form of return-on-investment with budgets used for supplemental information. The corporations reported that no separation between the evaluation of the subsidiary and manager was recognized. Local-currency financial information was required by 44 percent of the firms, U.S. dollar information by 44 percent, and both types were required by 12 percent (1973b).

Morsicato. Morsicato examined the use of U.S.-dollar and local-currency information by international division executives (IDEs) in the chemical industry in evaluating the internal performance of their foreign managers (1980b). Seventy U.S.-based MNCs with subsidiaries operating abroad participated in the first phase of this field study by completing a mailed questionnaire. Thirty-three of these participants were involved in the second phase consisting of personal interviews.

The questionnaire yielded the information necessary to document the financial measures currently used by MNCs to evaluate the performance of subsidiary managers. Table 2 summarizes the financial measures used as indicators of internal performance evaluation. Profit, return-on-investment, budget compared to actual profits, and budget compared to actual sales are the measures used most frequently after translation in U.S. dollars. Budget compared to actual profits, budget compared to actual sales, and profit are those used most frequently before translation in local currency.

The MNCs studied use more U.S. dollar information than local currency information when internally evaluating their foreign operations, although the majority of the IDEs think that local currency financial state-

Table 2.   Financial Measures Used as Indicators of Internal
Performance Evaluation

After Translation in U.S. Dollars (Percent[a])	Before Translation in Local Currency (Percent)	Financial Measures
81.4	70.0	Profit
80.0	52.9	Return-on-investment (assets)
78.6	72.9	Budget compared to actual profits
72.9	72.9	Budget compared to actual sales
65.7	35.7	Cash-flow potential from foreign subsidiary to U.S. operations
43.6	31.4	Return-on-equity
45.7	38.6	Budget compared to actual return-on-investment
34.3	30.0	Ratios
21.4	18.6	Residual income
12.9	11.3	Others

[a] These figures represent the percent of the total seventy corporations which report using each particular measure.

ments provide better information than U.S. dollars for the evaluation of subsidiaries and managers.

A majority of the corporations use the same basic techniques to evaluate subsidiary performance as they use to evaluate manager performance. Likewise, a majority of corporations apply the same performance evaluation techniques domestically as they do abroad.

These studies demonstrate the following: 1) there was and is now little apparent difference between the performance evaluation systems employed for domestic and foreign operations; 2) there is no consistency or uniformity when considering the issue of separating the manager's performance from that of the subsidiary; 3) most corporations use a subset of return-on-investment, budgeting, and comparisons when evaluating the performance of foreign operations; and 4) corporations were U.S. dollar-oriented in 1969, more aware of local-currency information in 1971, split between using U.S. dollar or local-currency information in 1970 and 1973, and are now recognizing the value of using local currency for evaluating the performance of their foreign operations.

MNC Performance Evaluation: Today and Tomorrow

Several of the current issues and topics needing further research relative to the quality of information used by management for decision making stem from prior research studies. Other areas of interest in this field have developed as the MNC has evolved. Each of these areas of concern is pursued in this section.

MNC Recognition of Operating Environment

One of the purposes of the Morsicato study (1980b) was to determine whether there is a relationship between the foreign operating environment of a subsidiary and the measures used by a corporation to evaluate that subsidiary's performance. This aspect of the study focused on whether or not a corporation's system of internal performance evaluation is designed to reflect environmental differences (for example, cultural, legal, political, and economic). Whether a firm modifies the performance evaluation system in accordance with changes which have occurred in a specific environment was also investigated.

The results of the Morsicato study indicated that, in general, the firms are not systematically designing performance evaluation systems that recognize environmental differences. Two philosophies of performance evaluation were identified from the overall responses of the IDEs. The first is an inflexible philosophy with established policies which should be used worldwide without exception. The second is a flexible philosophy established by subjectively considering the important elements of each geographic area which may change as conditions change. Corporations are practicing both philosophies and incorporating combinations of the two into their operations.

The corporations exhibited a variety of behavior toward specific geographic differences, problems, and peculiarities. No patterns in this behavior were evident from the data collected. Coping with the environment appears to be almost firm specific; therefore, it was difficult to generalize and/or report results based upon the corporation's behavior as a group.

These results indicated that MNCs perceive the need to incorporate environmental peculiarities into their control systems. However, at this time, no feasible method of accomplishing this task has been developed. Morsicato and Diamond (1980) have suggested that the Farmer-Richman Model be integrated into the development of performance evaluation standards for the managers of MNCs. The result of this integration makes it possible to systematically incorporate environmental factors into the evaluation of managerial performance. Further efforts in this area are critically needed to enhance the validity of MNC performance evaluation systems.

The Use of Local Currency Information

If a subsidiary operates within a country with a stable currency, an evaluation of the subsidiary's performance in either U.S. dollars or local currency should be meaningful. It is, however, important to internally evaluate foreign operations in local currency when the currency is unstable because of the distortions that occur in translating financial and comparative information into U.S. dollars. Today's foreign environment is plagued by highly and frequently fluctuating currencies; therefore, a foreign subsidiary's performance is more clearly reflected by its local currency operating results.

Profit, return-on-investment, and cash flow in U.S. dollars retain validity when used to evaluate the value of the subsidiary to the enterprise as a whole. These particular financial measures should not be applied during the evaluation of a subsidiary manager. Subsidiary managers should be evaluated on meeting primary goals in local currency, i.e., annual profits and sales.

Comparisons of the past, present, and future operations of a subsidiary are far more meaningful and valid if calculated in local currency. Comparing either the U.S. dollar or local currency results of subsidiaries operating in different environments is not a worthwhile endeavor. In order to achieve a meaningful comparison, the environmental peculiarities of each different operating environment would have to be isolated and weighted (see Morsicato and Diamond, 1980).

Past studies indicate that corporations recognize the value of using local currency for evaluating the performance of their foreign operations. However, currently there is a problem with universally employing local currency information. Many high echelon managers do not understand how to interpret subsidiary results reported in local currency. These managers also have difficulty understanding and interpreting the effect that foreign exchange gains and losses have on the overall enterprise results. Decision making by boards of directors and management headquarters is generally based upon U.S. dollar information. If one level of management bases decisions upon U.S. dollar information and another level upon local currency information, problems with goal congruency and optimization of resources may result. Further attempts toward developing goal congruent MNC performance evaluation systems are needed.

Translation

If U.S. dollar information is to be used for internally evaluating the performance of foreign operations, then the current rate method should be used for translating the information from local currency to U.S. dollars. Translation of the subsidiary's financial statements would then be from the local perspective which recognizes that the transactions actually occurred in the local currency by retaining the foreign currency as the unit of measure. When internally evaluating the performance of foreign operations, the foreign statements provide the most meaningful presentation of a subsidiary's activities. Translation of these statements should not affect the relationships within them.

The current rate method translates all assets, liabilities, revenues, and expenses at the current rate of exchange. Throughout the translation process operating relationships and income statement ratios remain intact, i.e., relationships that exist in local currency will also exist after the statements are translated to U.S. dollars. If the exchange rate changes during the period, then the corresponding translation gain or loss is recognized as occurring in the same period. The current rate method provides translated financial statements that are more similar to local currency financial statements than any other method. Using local currency information to evaluate foreign operations adds support to the arguments for using the current rate method of translation. Both produce an evaluation that augments the local perspective of the foreign subsidiary and manager.

Many U.S. managers cannot interpret operating results presented in local currency. Foreign subsidiary financial statements translated at the current rate provide the manager with the same perspective as local currency, while not requiring him to deal with local currency. This allows headquarters to review foreign managerial decisions from the perspective of the foreign manager, because the foreign currency is retained as the unit of measure.

The local perspective recognizes that foreign operations are functioning in different countries with different economic environments, and may have operating relationships with the parent that differ from domestic subsidiaries. This perspective also recognizes that the local currency financial statements of a foreign subsidiary represent the most meaningful presentation of the subsidiary's activities. A valid evaluation of these activities can only be accomplished by acknowledging that the foreign subsidiary is a separate unit that operates in a foreign currency.

The Financial Accounting Standards Board is now reviewing FASB No. 8 on translation and is advocating the use of the current rate method for external financial reporting. A change to the current rate method for both internal and external reporting purposes is expected should the FASB require use of current exchange rates.

Separation of Subsidiary and Manager Performance

It is very difficult to meaningfully evaluate the operating performance of a foreign subsidiary manager without first considering all of the uncontrollable costs which have been allocated to his operation. Allocating uncontrollable items to the subsidiary is necessary when determining the subsidiary's contribution to total operations. Use of a company-wide standard ROI is possibly acceptable when evaluating subsidiary performance but it is not an acceptable practice when evaluating the performance of the subsidiary manager. Evaluating a foreign subsidiary as an independent profit center is questionable; however, evaluating the subsidiary manager as though he operates a profit center is out of the question.

The evaluation of the subsidiary should be separate from the evaluation of the subsidiary manager. The manager's evaluation should involve a degree of subjectivity that allows for the consideration of environmental peculiarities and the specific objectives of the manager being evaluated. Responsibility for results that are beyond his control should not be delegated to the manager. Objective measures of performance may be used to evaluate the subsidiary as an investment.

The manager should be evaluated in local currency before nonoperating items, i. e., interest, taxes, exchange gains and losses, etc. This policy evaluates the manager based upon the operations that he actually controls. The subsidiary may then be evaluated in U.S. dollars after allocation of uncontrollable costs.

The development of flexible performance evaluation models which are capable of incorporating factors peculiar to an MNC for the separate evaluation of subsidiary and manager is needed by multinational corporations. The ultimate goal of research in this area is the development of such models. These reporting systems should be designed to give proper credit in an interactive environment to the subsidiary manager for his contributions to performance of the subsidiary.

Summary

The development of MNC performance evaluation systems is a critical multinational accounting issue. The importance of adequate performance evaluation techniques for appraising international operations takes on an added perspective when one considers that international resource allocation decisions are based upon these evaluations (Hopwood, 1972). An extension of this argument is to say that performance evaluation techniques employed by an MNC will have international economic impact.

This paper explored the development of MNC performance evaluation systems and documented the results of prior studies in this area. Several variables that influence the internal performance evaluation of foreign subsidiaries and managers were identified. Relationships among these variables were identified and recommendations for further research were suggested. These recommendations included designing performance evaluation systems that 1) recognize the peculiarities of the operating environment, 2) utilize local currency information, 3) utilize the current rate method of translation, and 4) separate subsidiary and manager performance.

Bibliography

Bursk, Edward C.; Dearden, John; Hawkins, David F.; and Longstreet, Vector M. *Financial Control of Multinational Operations*. New York: Financial Executives Research Foundation, 1971.

Choi, Frederick D. S., and Mueller, Gerhard G. *An Introduction to Multinational Accounting*. Englewood Cliffs, New Jersey: Prentice-Hall, Inc., 1978.

Committee on International Accounting. "Report of the Committee on International Accounting." *The Accounting Review,* Supplement to 48 (1973): 120-35.

Daniels, John D.; Ogram, Ernest W.; and Radebaugh, Lee H. *International Business: Environments and Operations*. Reading, Mass.: Addison-Wesley Publishing Company, 1976.

Diamond, Michael A. and Morsicato, Helen G. "An Approach to 'Environmentalizing'

MNE Performance Evaluation Systems." *International Journal of Accounting Education and Research* 16 (Fall 1980): 247-66.

Hawkins, D. F. "Controlling Foreign Operations." *Financial Executive* 33 (February 1965): 25-32.

Hopwood, Anthony G. "Empirical Study of the Role of Accounting Data in Performance Evaluation." *Empirical Research in Accounting* (1972): 156-93.

Horngren, Charles. *Cost Accounting: A Managerial Emphasis.* Englewood Cliffs, New Jersey: Prentice-Hall, Inc., 1977.

McInnes, J. M. "Financial Control Systems for Multinational Operations: An Empirical Investigation." *Journal of International Business Studies* 2 (Fall 1971): 11-28.

Mauriel, John J. "Evaluation and Control of Overseas Operations." *Management Accounting* (March 1969): 35-41.

Morsicato, Helen G. "Effect of FASB NO. 8 on MNE Performance Evaluation." Unpublished article presented at AAA Annual Meeting, August 1980a.

_____.*Currency Translation and Performance Evaluation in Multinationals.* Ann Arbor, Michigan: UMI Research Press, 1980b.

Perlmutter, H. "The Tortuous Evolution of the Multinational Company." *Columbia Journal of World Business* 4 (January-February 1969): 9-18.

Robbins, Sidney M., and Stobaugh, Robert B. *Money in the Multinational Enterprise.* New York: Basic Books, Inc., 1973a.

_____. "The Bent Measuring Stick for Foreign Subsidiaries." *Harvard Business Review* (September-October 1973b): 80-88.

Scott, George M. "Financial Control in Multinational Enterprises: The New Challenge to Accountants." *International Journal of Accounting Education and Research* 7 (Spring 1972): 55-68.

Foreign Currency Financial Statement Translation: A Review of the Evidence on Security Market Responses to Statement No. 8

ROLAND E. DUKES
University of Washington

Introduction

The issuance and implementation of *Statement of Financial Accounting Standards No. 8*, "Accounting for the Translation of Foreign Currency Transactions and Foreign Currency Financial Statements," (hereafter FAS 8) has resulted in the most extensive and prolonged discussion of merits and demerits of any of the first forty Statements the Financial Accounting Standards Board (FASB) has issued. Moreover, the end is not in sight. In August 1980 the FASB circulated a new Exposure Draft of a proposed revision to FAS 8 entitled "Foreign Currency Translation," yet there does not appear to be overwhelming acceptance of the proposed new rules.

The purpose of this paper is threefold: 1) to summarize, critique, and synthesize the results of a number of studies that have investigated the impact of FAS 8 on the security returns of multinational firms; 2) to summarize the proposed revision to FAS 8 and discuss some of the research questions that arise with the new solution; and 3) to outline what appear to be important research opportunities in this area. In a sense, the overall objective of this paper is to summarize what is known about the effects of FAS 8 on market agents' behavior and to suggest what needs to be done to resolve this continuing controversial issue.

Review of Empirical Evidence

A number of studies have investigated the relationship between the issuance and initial implementation of FAS 8 and possible security market effects for affected multinational firms. Before reviewing the studies, consider why an effect on security return might or might not be expected.

effects for affected multinational firms. Before reviewing the studies, consider why an effect on security return might or might not be expected.

The issue of whether a mandated accounting policy change should be expected to affect security returns is not easily answered. At one level, the accounting change by itself does not alter any cash flows of the firm, thus the economic value of the common shares should not be affected. However, there are several reasons why security returns might be affected. First, the accounting change may induce changes in decision-making behavior by management, and these changes in turn alter the future cash flows of the firm. Second, the accounting change may result in new disclosures regarding the firm, which could in turn result in a new security market equilibrium. Third, some have argued that the accounting change required by FAS 8 increases the fluctuations in reported earnings, and that security market agents will respond (negatively) to these FAS 8 induced variations in reported earnings. Finally, the reporting change may sufficiently alter the financial statements such that the firm is in technical default on a debt covenant or otherwise violate some contractual arrangement it has entered into, thus again inducing a security market response.

More detailed arguments could be made, but the above briefly summarizes the opposing perspectives on why security market effects may or may not be observed with the issuance and implementation of FAS 8. The null hypothesis in the studies summarized here is that security returns of multinationals are unaffected by FAS 8. Finding a security market effect would require further investigation as to the underlying cause of the effect.

Dukes (1978)

The primary issue addressed is whether the common stock security returns of firms required to comply with FAS 8 have been affected by the issuance and implementation of the Statement in any statistically significant manner. Common stock security returns are defined as the change in share price between the beginning and end of a period plus dividends received during that period, all divided by the common stock share price at the beginning of the period (adjusted for stock splits and stock dividends, where necessary). The test periods studied begin in January 1975 with the issuance of the FASB *Exposure Draft,* "Accounting for the Translation of Foreign Currency Transactions and Foreign Currency Financial Statements" [FASB, 1974], and extend through two to three years following this date during which FAS 8 was being implemented. Both the issuance of the Exposure Draft and its implementation are treated as events which could provide a response by the securities market. Two separate periods prior to FAS 8 are also investigated for the purpose of validating the research methods employed.

The first method of analysis was a comparison of the security returns of a sample of 479 multinational firms with a control sample of domestic firms. The empirical results are that the security return behavior or portfolios of multinational firms is *not* significantly different from the return behavior of comparable portfolios of domestic firms. The mean difference between the monthly returns of six portfolios of affected (multinational) firms and the monthly returns of portfolios of six unaffected (domestic) firms of equal relative risk was not statistically different from zero for the three test periods studied. The six portfolios of multinational firms were constructed such that each portfolio contained firms using the same method of accounting for multinational operations prior to FAS 8 (see table 1). The three time periods studied were: 1) January 1968 through December 1969, a period of relative stability in foreign exchange markets; 2) January 1970 through December 1974, a period of considerable change and variability in foreign exchange markets; and 3) the primary test period, January 1975 through December 1976, during which Statement No. 8 was issued and initially implemented.

The basic test procedure followed in all of the portfolio level analysis is similar to that of Gonedes (1978) and is described as follows:

1.   For each firm in each accounting method group (hereafter group) and for both the information and control samples, relative risk (beta) is estimated for three separate 60-month periods using the market model and ordinary least squares regression. The three periods over which betas were estimated were: period one, January 1963 through December 1967; period two, January 1965 through December 1969; and, period three, January 1970 through December 1974.

2.   For each group in both samples and in each of the three test periods, firms are ranked from lowest to highest according to the estimated beta, and the top (bottom) one-half are used to form a low (high) beta portfolio with equal weighting of the included securities.

3.   For each group in both samples and in each of three test periods, the high and low beta portfolios are combined with weights such that a group portfolio is formed which has an estimated beta equal to one:

Group beta $= 1.0 = [x \cdot \text{low beta}] + [(1-x) \cdot \text{high beta}]$
     where:

          x = weight of low beta portfolio and
          $(1-x)$ = weight of high beta portfolio.

Table 1.   Summary of Pre-FASB-8
Accounting Methods Group Classifications

Group	Description	Number of Firms
1	Translation method: Current/Noncurrent Foreign currency gains/losses recognized immediately	150
2	Translation method: Current/Noncurrent Foreign currency gains/losses deferred	87
3	Translation method: Monetary/Nonmonetary Foreign currency gain/losses recognized immediately	57
4	Translation method: Monetary/Nonmonetary Foreign currency gains/losses deferred	39
5	Translation method: Hybrid-Current rates for all current assets (incl. inventory) and all liabilities, historical rates for noncurrent assets Foreign currency gains/losses recognized immediately	83
6	Translation method: (Same as 5) Foreign Currency gain/ losses deferred	63
		479

4.   The monthly return of each portfolio is computed for the period of interest subsequent to the portfolio formation dates. The portfolio for the three periods were formed as of the following dates: (1) January 1968, (2) January 1970, and (3) January 1975. Monthly returns for the portfolios were computed over the three periods: (1) January 1968 through December 1969, the 24-month stable foreign

exchange market period; (2) January 1970 through December 1974, the 60-month transition period in forcign currency markets; and (3) January 1975 through December 1976, the 24-month period after the Exposure Draft on foreign currency translation (which eventually was adopted as FAS 8).

5.   For each month in each test period, the difference between the monthly return of an information sample portfolio and the monthly return of the comparable control sample portfolio is calculated. Given that relative risk is the only parameter affecting equilibrium expected portfolio returns (and the estimated relative risk for all groups has been set equal to one), the differences calculated above are expected to be zero. If, on the other hand, multinational firms are adversely affected by FAS 8, the differences in returns (information sample less control sample) are expected to be negative in period three. The monthly return differences in periods one and two, however, are prior to FAS 8 and are, therefore, not expected to be affected by it. In these periods, the differences are not expected to be statistically different from zero. If they are found to be statistically different from zero, it would then appear that there are other differences between the information sample and control sample firms.

6.   The specific null hypothesis being tested is that, collectively, the mean monthly differences over the test period for the six comparisons are equal to zero. Since this is a multivariate analysis, the Hotelling T^2 test is the appropriate test statistic to use. This test allows any one of the six groups, or any weighted combination of them, to reject the null hypothesis that the mean differences are equal to zero. For a discussion of this test, see Bolch and Huang [1974].

Table 2 presents results of the Hotelling T^2 test for periods one, two, and three. When the null hypothesis is true, the T^2 statistic can be transformed to the central F statistic with (P, N-P) degrees of freedom, where P equals the number of portfolios (P=6) and N is the number of monthly observations on each portfolio (N=24 or 60). In each table, the T^2 statistic is converted to an F statistic, and critical values of F for various levels of significance are given. The null hypothesis (that the difference between the portfolio returns of all six groups is equal to zero) is rejected if the calculated F statistic is greater than the critical value shown at the chosen level of significance.

The null cannot be rejected even at the 0.10 level in any of the three test periods. That is, none of the three test periods have mean differences

Table 2. Hotelling T² Test Results

Group	Pre-FASB Statement No. 8 Accounting Method	Difference in Returns (Information Group Less Control Group) Mean	Standard Deviation	T²	F*
A: FOR PERIOD ONE					
1	C/NC—Immediate Recognition	−0.00143	0.01612		
2	C/NC—Deferral	−0.00401	0.01485		
3	M/NM—Immediate Recognition	0.00298	0.01870		
4	M/NM—Deferral	0.00266	0.02222		
5	Hybrid—Immediate Recognition	−0.00357	0.02010		
6	Hybrid—Deferral	0.00232	0.02574	9.41	1.23
B: FOR PERIOD TWO					
1	C/NC—Immediate Recognition	0.00158	0.01404		
2	C/NC—Deferral	0.00240	0.01362		
3	M/NM—Immediate Recognition	−0.00023	0.02160		
4	M/NM—Deferral	0.00050	0.02769		
5	Hybrid—Immediate Recognition	−0.00239	0.01586		
6	Hybrid—Deferral	0.00296	0.01862	5.88	0.90
C: FOR PERIOD THREE					
1	C/NC—Immediate Recognition	−0.00191	.018705		
2	C/NC—Deferral	−0.00324	.017865		
3	M/NM—Immediate Recognition	−0.00262	.019683		
4	M/NM—Deferral	0.00057	.032296		
5	Hybrid—Immediate Recognition	0.00280	.018790		
6	Hybrid—Deferral	−0.00542	.026291	6.33	0.83

*$F = T^2 [(N-P)/P(N-1)]$, where N = number of observations for estimation (N = 24) and P = number of portfolios (P = 6). Selected fractiles for the F distribution are:

Level of Significance	(Panels A and C) Value of F (6,18)	(Panel B) Value of F (6, 55)
0.25	1.45	1.35
0.10	2.20	1.88
0.05	2.66	2.27
0.01	4.01	3.15

in monthly portfolio returns significantly different from zero. Given these results for periods one and two, confidence is gained that the control sample is appropriate to use as a standard for period three.

The period three results in table 2 show that the null hypothesis of no difference cannot be rejected at conventional levels of significance. Even at the 0.25 level of significance, where there is a relatively high (0.25) probability of rejecting the null even though it is true, none of the return differences are large enough to reject the null hypothesis. In short, the above analysis does not reveal statistically significant differences in returns between any of the multinational portfolios and their comparison control sample portfolios for any of the three periods examined.

Shank, Dillard, and Murdock (1979)

Shank, Dillard, and Murdock (1979) (SDM) investigate the impact of FAS 8 in two areas. First, they use a field interview and questionnaire methodology to query management regarding possible effects FAS 8 may have had on capital investment, financing, and operating decisions. Second, the impact on the stock market is investigated, using a somewhat different methodology and different sample than Dukes.

In analyzing the possible impact of FAS 8 on management actions, SDM develop a limited non-random sample of 25 large, affected multinational firms, including four major banks.

Shank, Dillard, and Murdock report finding considerable impact on management actions resulting from FAS 8. Key conclusions include: (a) a majority of the firms investigated have changed the proportions of local currency debt and home country debt in their capital structures to reduce exposure to translation adjustments under FAS 8, (b) a majority of the firms have entered forward markets to cover translation exposures under FAS 8, and (c) a vast majority of the firms believe the financial cost of implementing FAS 8 has been significant in terms of increased reporting and analysis costs (SDM, pp. 3-4).

In studying potential securities markets effects of FAS 8, SDM use a somewhat different sample and a different methodology than Dukes. With regard to sample, SDM identify multinational firms classified into four possible groups:

I) FAS 8 required changes of translation method (from current/non-current to temporal) and of deferral practice (118 firms, hereafter group I). Note this group meets the same criteria as Dukes' group 2.

II) FAS 8 required a change of translation method only. All firms were using a current/noncurrent method of translation prior FAS 8 and were recognizing immediately exchange gains and losses (221 firms, hereafter group II). Note this group meets the same criteria of Dukes' group 1.

III) FAS 8 required a change of deferral practices only. While it is not explicitly stated in SDM, apparently this group was using the temporal method but were deferring exchange gains and losses (64 firms, hereafter group III). Note this group meets the same reporting criteria as Dukes' group 4.

IV) FAS 8 did not require a change of either translation method or of deferral practices. This is the control sample for SDM (108 firms, hereafter group IV). Note this group meets the same criteria as Dukes' group 3.

Firms in groups I, II, and III are "matched"with a firm in the control group IV, where matching was on the basis of a) industry, b) approximate size, and c) "general risk class." Good matches were not always possible on all the matching variables, thus SDM run two sets of tests, one with "excellent" matches, and a second set of tests with "excellent" and "good" matches combined. Given the limited size of group IV, it would appear that a control firm (from group IV) could be matched with more than one experimental firm (all the firms in group I, II, or III).

SDM proceed to test for differences in stock market response, measured several alternative ways, between the three affected groups (I, II, and III) aggregated into portfolios, and the unaffected, matched portfolios composed of firms from group IV. The first test examines for changes in systematic risk or beta around the issuance of FAS 8. Betas are computed, using the single index market model, for all firms over two twenty-four month periods. The first period includes calendar years 1974 and 1975 and is considered a pre-FAS 8 period. The second period includes calendar years 1976 and 1977 and is considered to be a post-FAS 8 period. SDM argue that if the mandated change in reporting for multinational operations increased the markets' assessment of systematic risk, the portfolio beta for the affected firms should increase while the unaffected (control) groups would not change. The SDM results are presented in table 3. Note that all the portfolio betas increase from before to after FAS 8, including all six control portfolios. SDM do not test whether this increase is significant, but it would appear to be highly significant except for the group 3 control portfolio. Assuming that whatever is the cause of the overall increase in beta is not acting differently on affected (experimental) and control forms, SDM proceed to test whether the increase for the experimental firms is more than that for the control firms. They find the differential increase not significant at the 5% level of significance.

Tests are also performed on the change in variance in the estimates of betas pre and post-FAS 8. It is argued that the change of accounting methods might induce a higher level of disagreement about the beta level and thus increase the dispersion in the distribution of estimates of systematic risk. Again, a persistent increase in sample variance is observed from the pre to post period for both experimental and control groups. Again, however, the differential increase between the experimental and control groups are not significant. SDM conclude that "the results are not strong enough to support the hypothesis that [FAS 8] resulted in significant increases in the perceived riskiness of the firms" and "the results do not support the hypothesis that [FAS 8] reduced the level of consensus in the market about the riskiness of the firms affected."

Table 3.   Changes in Beta Around the Issuance of FAS 8

	Group 1 Change of Method and Deferral		Group 2 Change of Deferral only		Group 3 Change of Method only	
	Experimental	Control	Experimental	Control	Experimental	Control
EXCELLENT MATCHES						
1) Before	.860	.905	.950	.906	.931	.972
2) After	1.037	1.124	1.244	1.015	1.174	1.026
3) Difference over time (2-1)	.177	.219	.294	.109	.243	.054
4) Comparative Difference (Experimental minus Control)	−.042		.185		.189	
EXCELLENT AND GOOD MATCHES						
1) Before	.806	.868	.896	.891	.923	.925
2) After	.976	1.024	1.159	1.121	1.185	1.004
3) Difference (2-1)	.170	.156	.263	.230	.262	.079
4) Comparative Difference (Experimental minus Control)	.014		.033		.183	

Source: Shank, Dillard and Murdock (1979).

Tests are also conducted by SDM regarding differences in risk adjusted rates of return. The test methodology here is very similar to Dukes. Portfolios for both experimental and control firms are constructed such that all portfolios have a beta equal to one. Given that expected returns are equal, differences between experimental and control portfolio actual returns are expected to be zero. On the basis of test results, SDM conclude "the data do not indicate that the rate of return earned by the affected firms in the months surrounding the release of FAS 8 was any less, after allowing for systematic risk, than the rate of return earned by comparable firms not affected by the Statement."

In a fourth area of investigation, SDM examine for possible impact of the issuance of FAS 8 on price-earnings ratio (P/E). P/Es are calculated for each firm at four points in time: a) November 30, 1975, after the public release of the Statement but before its implementation; b) March 1, 1976 during its initial stages of implementation; c) March 1, 1977 and; d) February 1, 1978. SDM do not perform any statistical tests on these data "because of the intrinsic 'softness' of P/E values." They observe that the P/E values decline for both experimental and control portfolios from the first to the last date. SDM note that while all multinationals have experienced falling P/Es over the period, "the P/Es for those firms affected by [FAS 8] do not decline noticeably more than the P/Es for the firm not affected by it."

Dukes and Pfeiffer (1979)

In a follow up study to Dukes (1978), Dukes and Pfeiffer (1979) (DP) investigated the information content of the "exchange gain or loss" item found in financial statements of multinationals complying with FAS 8. They note that the same "accounting exposure under FAS 8 may be related to drastically different economic exposures for different firms." For example, product exporters/importers with small investments in long lived assets in foreign countries face a much different situation than firms with production facilities in foreign countries. Given FAS 8, however, it is quite possible for them to report the same exchange gain or loss. DP present some preliminary evidence on the market response to the exchange gain and loss numbers reported in compliance with FAS 8.

Data on exchange gains or losses reported in 1976 financial statements were collected for 214 firms. For 1976 and for the sample studied, the median effect of exchange gain or loss was a loss equal to seven-tenths of one percent of operating income. This was surprisingly low, given 1976 was a year of considerable fluctuations in foreign exchange rates.

Given the small size of the exchange effect, DP rank the firms on the size of the exchange effect deflated by operating income. Two portfolios are then constructed, one with one half of the firms with the most positive exchange effects and a second with the firms with the most negative effect. Each portfolio is constructed such that it has a beta equal to one, hence expected returns for the portfolios are equal. The difference in portfolio returns (the Exchange Losses Portfolio minus the Exchange Gains Portfolio) are observed over the period January 1976 through June 1977. The period includes the period over which the exchange effect is realized and is reported in financial statements. The results are that over the eighteen month period the cumulative difference in returns is -5.0 per cent. This is the direction one would expect if the exchange gain or loss signal possessed information content; however, the difference is not statistically significant.

More research needs to be conducted on this issue. Dukes and Pfeiffer look at only one year of data, and in that year the exchange effect seems small. Also, control for other information signals such as changes in earnings before exchange effects needs to be exercised. Finally, firms might be classified into groups a priori based on an analysis of their economic exposure, testing these groups separately for information content. Much remains to be done here.

Proposed New Standard and Related Research Issues

In January 1979 the FASB added to its agenda a project to reconsider Statement No. 8. In August 1980 the board issued an Exposure Draft of a proposed statement that would supersede Statement No. 8.

The proposed statement would require the use of current exchange rates to translate all of a foreign entity's assets and liabilities into a reporting currency. The translation of inventories and plant assets are the primary items affected, as these items would have been translated at historical rates under Statement No. 8. The effect of this change is to increase the accounting measure of net asset exposure.

A second major difference between Statement No. 8 and the proposed Statement is that gains and losses arising from the translation of a foreign entity's assets and liabilities will not be included in determining net income for the period. Rather, the translation adjustment would be disclosed and accumulated in a separate component of stockholders' equity until substantial or complete liquidation occurs, or until permanent impairment of the restated net investment in the foreign entity is determined.

These two changes will significantly alter the translation adjustment that will be computed by most firms, and, perhaps more important, will greatly reduce the impact on the income statement of the translation adjustment by taking it directly to stockholders' equity. For most multinational firms it is likely that these changes will have a material effect on their financial statements. Assuming this to be the case, several research issues arise.

Of immediate interest is whether market agents responded to the proposed changes by altering the return and risk expectations for multinational firms. This would suggest an events type study where security returns of multinationals are investigated around the announcement date of the proposed Statement and around the announcement date of the final Statement once it is issued.

Of equal or even greater interest would be documenting changes in management decision-making caused by the accounting policy change. In particular, a replication of an Evans, Folks, and Jilling (1978) type study would be useful once the proposed standards were implemented. There are a number of possible reasons management's behavior may change with the new standard, and a researcher would want to attempt to identify the underlying motivations for the changed behavior. For example, the accounting changes might impact upon the restrictiveness of debt covenants, in which case management may alter its behavior to maintain flexibility. Alternatively, management may alter decisions because of the impact on earnings and their concern for how market agents interpret reported earnings, or because of effects of the change on executive compensation. A market effects study cannot address these issues as well as a study of decision making on a firm by firm basis.

Modification of reporting requirements for multinational firms might be addressed using the "reversal" methodology of Noreen and Sepe (1980) and of Smith (1980). The notion is that when a policy establishing body reverses an earlier decision, affected parties will likewise reverse the actions taken in response to the initial policy decision. While the proposed standard does not exactly reverse FAS 8, it is a major modification and does essentially reverse some of the income statement effects of FAS 8. The proposed standard effectively requires the deferral of translation gains and losses, whereas FAS 8 required immediate recognition in the income statement of this item. Thus the reversal methodology would appear to have some applicability to this issue.

There are likely to be other interesting questions that arise as the proposed standard is itself modified and approved in final form. Also, the interaction of standards, such as FAS 33 (Financial Reporting and Changing Prices), with multinational accounting issues is likely to lead to additional research issues.

Other Research Questions

The impact of foreign operations on U.S. based firms' overall operations is growing increasingly important. As a result, accounting rules used to measure foreign operations also become important.

A number of research areas present themselves as a result of the above phenomena. One important area of research in the future will be continuing to gather empirical evidence on the reaction of various parties to the imposition of alternative accounting policies. Such research efforts presume, of course, that the evidence gathered is of value to at least some interested parties. The usual justification for such studies is that policy makers should be interested in understanding the economic consequences of their actions. The empirical research is not undertaken, however, with the expectation that it will lead to policy recommendations per se.

Another important and continuing area of research has to do with understanding the optimal operating behavior of enterprises in an international environment. Given different markets, production factors, tax incentives, and rates of economic growth and inflation, among other influences, the optimal financing and production strategies for a multinational firm are not obvious. International economists are addressing these issues, but as of now our understanding of optimal firm strategies in an international setting lags far behind our understanding of these issues in a single country setting.

Without a well developed normative framework in which to view the firm, accounting policies are difficult to evaluate. For example, if it is not possible to be precise in defining economic exposure in an international setting, then it is not possible to evaluate various measures of exposure as defined in an accounting system. This seems to be the major problem in evaluating the alternative foreign currency translation methods currently being considered by the FASB. Moreover, the economic exposure may be different for two firms with identical foreign asset and liability positions because of different markets for products and services. The result is that there is a wide divergence of opinion among managers regarding the preferred accounting measurement method. It appears that different methods may be theoretically preferable for firms with different operating characteristics. Thus another problem would be to specify under what firm operating conditions one accounting method is preferred to another. More specifically, is it possible to identify some firm characteristics which lead to generalization regarding preferred multinational accounting measurement rules? Until these questions are answered it is likely that controversy will continue to surround the issue of accounting for multinational operations.

Foreign exchange rates have behaved much differently during the past decade *vis à vis* the decade of the sixties. What effect, if any, has this change in the international monetary system had on management decision making? It would appear that there have been real changes in the economic environment in which the multinational firm exists. It should be possible to identify subsequent consequences of these changes and then proceed to gain insights into the factors which influence decision making in a multinational setting. Again, gaining a greater understanding of the framework in which managers of multinational firms make decisions is likely to lead to insights regarding the preference for one accounting method over another in a given economic setting.

Finally, and not directly related to FAS 8, the new proposed standard modifying FAS 8 represents the first major revision the FASB has made of its own accord to any of its Statements. Such an action opens up a whole series of research questions. Can the key factors which influenced the decision to revise be identified? Going one step further, can we identify what factors or influences are predictive of a policy revision? Along another dimension, what effect has this revision had on the power and authority of the FASB to issue pronouncements and to have them accepted by the affected parties? Some argue that the revision will enhance the board's credibility in the view of both financial report preparers and users; others see the revision as a weakness, reflecting the board's inability to obtain acceptance for reasonable standards that have undesirable effects on the reporting from the perspective of report preparers.

Issues in multinational accounting have become very complex and difficult for the FASB to resolve. It is an area fertile for research. The resolution of the issues is likely to come slowly, and the accounting researcher has an important role to play in assisting the policy maker to obtain answers to many unresolved issues.

Bibliography

Bolch, B. W., and C. J. Huang, *Multivariate Statistical Methods for Business and Economics*. Englewood Cliffs, New Jersey: Prentice-Hall, Inc., 1974.

Dukes, R. E. *An Empirical Investigation of the Effects of Statement of Financial Accounting Standards No. 8 on Security Return Behavior*. Financial Accounting Standards Board, 1978.

Dukes, R. E. "Forecasting Exchange Gains (Losses) and Security Market Response to FASB Statement No. 8," In *Exchange Risk and Exposure*, R. Levich and C. Wihlborg, eds. Lexington, Mass.: D.C. Heath and Co., 1980, pp. 177-94.

Dukes, R. E., and G. Pfeiffer, "The Information Content of Exchange Gain and Loss Signals: Some Preliminary Evidence," Cornell University Working Paper, March 1979.

Evans, T. G., W. R. Folks, and M. Jilling, *The Impact of Financial Accounting Standards*

No. 8 on the Foreign Exchange Risk Management Practices of American Multinationals: An Economic Impact Study. Financial Accounting Standards Board, 1978.

Financial Accounting Standards Board, *Statement of Financial Accounting Standards No. 1*, "Disclosure of Foreign Currency Translation Information," FASB, December 1973.

_____. *Statement of Financial Accounting Standards No. 8*, "Accounting for the Translation of Foreign Currency Transactions and Foreign Currency Financial Statements," FASB, October 1975.

_____. *Proposed Statement of Financial Accounting Standards*, "Foreign Currency Translation," FASB, August 1980.

Gonedes, N. J. "Corporate Signaling, External Accounting, and Capital Market Equilibrium: Evidence on Dividends, Income, and Extraordinary Items," *Journal of Accounting Research* (Spring 1978):p. 26-79.

Griffin, P.A. "What Harm Has FASB 8 Actually Done?" *Harvard Business Review* (July-August 1979): p. 8-18.

Noreen, E., and J. Sepe, "Market Reaction to Accounting Policy Deliberations: The Inflation Accounting Case," *The Accounting Review* (April 1980).

Smith, A. "The SEC 'Reversal' of FASB Statement No. 19: An Investigation of Information Effects," University of Chicago Working Paper, December 1980.

Shank, J. K., J. F. Dillard, and R. J. Murdock, *Assessing the Economic Impact of FASB 8*, Financial Executives Research Foundation, 1979.

The Evolution of International Accounting Standards

ALISTER K. MASON
Deloitte, Haskins & Sells

This essay focuses on the institutional responses that have been made to the need for international accounting standards. It dwells at some length on aspects of the International Accounting Standards Committee's formation, projects, willingness to adapt, and problems of getting international standards accepted. The activities of three other bodies—the Organization for Economic Cooperation and Development, the United Nations, and the European Economic Community—in the area of international accounting standards are also summarized. Throughout this discussion, points regarding possible future developments are made.

Steps towards the establishment of international auditing standards are not covered. However, it is noteworthy that one of the most active committees of the International Federation of Accountants (established in 1977 to harmonize auditing standards) is the International Auditing Practices Committee, which operates in much the same way as the IASC—although its pronouncements are called International Auditing Guidelines, not Standards.

A concluding section offers some thoughts about future directions.

Accountants International Study Group

One of the earliest proponents of international accounting standards was Jacob Kraayenhof, President of the Seventh International Congress of Accountants which was held in Amsterdam in 1957. While much has happened since Kraayenhof spoke on the urgency of international accounting cooperation and standarization,[1] initial progress was slow. It was not until 1966 that words gave way to action. That was the year in which

Sir Henry Benson was President of the Institute of Chartered Accountants in England and Wales. While attending the annual meetings of the Canadian Institute of Chartered Accountants (CICA) and the AICPA, he raised with his presidential counterparts the possiblity of forming a three-nation group to study accounting and auditing requirements and practices. These discussions led to the formation of the Accountants International Study Group (AISG).

The AISG's terms of reference were as follows: "To institute comparative studies as to accounting thought and practice in participating countries, to make reports from time to time, which, subject to the prior approval of the sponsoring Institutes, would be issued to members of those Institutes." The Group had an eleven year life, during which time twenty studies on accounting and auditing topics were issued. These studies, and their dates of publication, have been listed elsewhere,[2] and so they need not be listed here.

The studies are all comparative, and while conclusions were reached, these were not binding on the sponsoring institutes (which were, in addition to the three bodies mentioned above, The Institute of Chartered Accountants of Scotland and The Institute of Chartered Accountants in Ireland). However, a few of the studies had an impact on national standards subsequently issued in the three nations, and they became a useful reference source. Even more important, perhaps, was the fact that they demonstrated the possiblities and benefits of international cooperation.

New national pronouncements and the evolution of practice are gradually rendering the AISG studies somewhat obsolete, particularly those published in the early years. However, two which were published in 1975 should have continuing interest:

International Financial Reporting focuses on the problems encountered in trying to communicate clearly with financial statement users in other countries, where there are differences in accounting principles or auditing standards. It recommends that both "primary" and "secondary" financial statements be officially recognized, and suggests ways of clarifying the auditor's report and the summary of accounting policies. In reviewing this study Mueller wrote: "*International Financial Reporting* is a truly pioneering piece of work, since there exists virtually no literature on this specific topic and since the recommendations put forward are original with the AISG."[3]

Comparative Glossary of Accounting Terms in Canada, the United Kingdom and the United States is a reference work which assists readers in one of the three nations in understanding the accounting literature of the other two. The 160 terms and concepts covered fall into three categories:

(a)   where the word or phrase is in general use by accountants in the three nations but has different meanings in one country from another;

(b)   where the word or phrase is in use in one country but not another; and

(c)   where another word or phrase is used having the same or similar meaning.

International Accounting Standards Committee (IASC)

The first steps towards the IASC's formation were taken in 1972 at the Tenth International Congress in Sydney where senior officers of the AISG's member bodies met to consider the possibility of forming a more broadly-based committee—and one that would not simply write studies, but would establish international standards. The driving force behind this meeting, and the events which followed, was once again Sir Henry Benson.

Without Sir Henry's vision and vigour it is highly unlikely that the discussions at that Sydney meeting would have progressed, in nine short months, to the signature (on June 29, 1973) of an "Agreement and Constitution" by representives of leading accounting bodies from nine countries: Australia, Canada, France, Germany, Japan, Mexico, the Netherlands, the U.K., and the U.S. In signing the agreement, these bodies, which became the founder members of the IASC, undertook:

(a)   to establish and maintain an International Accounting Standards Committee, with the membership and powers set out below, whose function will be to formulate and publish in the public interest, basic standards to be observed in the presentation of audited accounts and financial statements and to promote their worldwide acceptance and observance;

(b)   to support the standards promulgated by the Committee;

(c)   to use their best endeavours:

(i)   to ensure that published accounts comply with these standards or that there is disclosure of the extent to which they do not and to persuade governments, the authorities controlling securities markets and the industrial and business community that published accounts should comply with these standards;

(ii)   to ensure that the auditors satisfy themselves that the accounts comply with these standards. If the accounts do not comply with these standards the audit report should either refer to the disclosure of non-compliance in the accounts, or should state the extent to which they do not comply;

(iii)   to ensure that, as soon as practicable, appropriate action is taken in respect of auditors whose audit reports do not meet the requirements of (ii) above;

(d)   to seek to secure similar general acceptance and observance of these standards internationally. (Source: *Preface to Statements of International Accounting Standards.*)

The constitution provided for the admission of other bodies as associate members, who were prepared to sign the above agreement, and were able to satisfy the founder members regarding their potential to contribute to the IASC's work. Numerous bodies were admitted, and by the time of the Eleventh International Congress, the founder and associate member bodies totalled fifty-three, from forty-two different countries, which together represented more than 400,000 individual accountants.

Under the chairmanship of Sir Henry the IASC started issuing a steady stream of exposure drafts, which after comment and amendment were published as International Accounting Standards (IASs). The schedule of IASC projects finalized and in process, set out under the next heading, indicates the output under Sir Henry and his successors.

The second Chairman of the IASC was Joseph Cummings, of the U.S., whose term of office ran from mid-1976 to mid-1978. He was succeeded by an Australian, John Hepworth, and in 1980 the first chairman whose home language was not English took office: J.A. Burggraaff, of the Netherlands. By the time Mr. Burggraaff assumed his duties the total membership had advanced to fifty-nine bodies, representing forty-five countries.

IASC Projects Finalized and in Process

The status of the various IASC projects, up to and including decisions made at the November 1980 meeting, was as follows:

International Accounting Standards Issued	*Date of Issue*
IAS 1—Disclosure of Accounting Policies	Jan. 1975
IAS 2—Valuation and Presentation of Inventories in the Context of the Historical Cost System	Oct. 1975
IAS 3—Consolidated Financial Statements	June 1976
IAS 4—Depreciation Accounting	Oct. 1976
IAS 5—Information to be Disclosed in Financial Statements	Oct. 1976
IAS 6—Accounting Responses to Changing Prices	June 1977
IAS 7—Statement of Changes in Financial Position	Oct. 1977
IAS 8—Unusual and Prior Period Items and Changes in Accounting Policies	Feb. 1978
IAS 9—Accounting for Research and Development Activities	July 1978
IAS 10—Contingencies and Events Occurring After the Balance Sheet Date	Oct. 1978

IAS 11—Accounting for Construction Contracts   March 1979
IAS 12—Accounting for Taxes on Income   July 1979
IAS 13—Presentation of Current Assets and
    Current Liabilities   Nov. 1979

Discussion Papers Issued

Treatment of Changing Prices in Financial
Statements: A Summary of Proposals   March 1977
Disclosures in Financial Statements of Banks   March 1980

Exposure Drafts Issued or Approved for Issue

E11—Accounting for Foreign Transactions and
    Translation of Foreign Financial Statements
    (Revised ED to be issued in 1981)   Dec. 1977
E15—Reporting Financial Information by Segment   March 1980
E16—Accounting for Retirement Benefits in the
    Financial Statements of Employers   April 1980
E17—Information Reflecting the Effects of Changing
    Prices   August 1980
E18—Accounting for Property, Plant and Equipment
    in the Context of the Historical Cost System   August 1980
E19—Accounting for Leases   Oct. 1980
E20—Revenue Recognition   April 1981

Projects at Earlier Stages

Accounting for Business Combinations
Accounting for Government Grants
Accounting for the Capitalisation of Finance Costs
Related Party Transactions

The thirteen IASs completed to date are summarized from the perspective of the main alternatives provided:

1. Five IASs are concerned exclusively with disclosure; the other eight cover both "measurement" (used in this paper to mean affecting the calculation of net income) and disclosure. Only one disclosure requirement provides an alternative—the changing prices information called for by IAS 6.

2. One IAS setting measurement standards—IAS 10—provides no alternatives. The other seven provide alternatives as follows:
    • Some flexibility in applying the basic principles of a) inventory valuation, b) the allocation of the cost of depreciable assets over

their useful lives, and c) computing tax expense (but not in the basic principles themselves)—IASs 2, 4, and 12 respectively.
- Small amount of flexibility in determining whether two specific types of company should be consolidated—IAS 3.
- Alternative provided in one of three basic principles (reporting of prior period items and the amount of adjustments resulting from accounting policy changes)—IAS 8.
- Alternative provided in accounting for those development expenses which meet five specified criteria—IAS 9.
- Percentage-of-completion method, rather than completed-contract method, permitted where specified conditions in a construction contract are satisfied—IAS 11.

3.   In each case where an alternative is provided for, the method followed is required to be disclosed—and in some cases the reason for following a particular method has to be disclosed too.

This brief summary suggests that the IASs are not as "loose" as some have protrayed them. Where alternatives have been provided, the choice is between methods or practices which have the support of respected national standard-setting bodies: practices which many accountants consider clearly undesirable, such as arbitrary write-downs of inventories to create secret reserves, are not permitted. Adherence to the IAS would therefore lead to a significant improvement in countries where such undesirable practices are presently followed.

As a practical matter, the IASC cannot take a position that is incompatible with a national pronouncement in one of the countries whose support is vital to the international acceptance of an IAS on that topic. On a continuing basis, therefore, we may expect to see IASs which are worded sufficiently broadly to be compatible with the position taken by the FASB and the standard-setting bodies of certain other influential countries.[4] While national standards on some topics, e.g., foreign currency translation, appear to be moving closer together, on others they regrettably seem to be diverging, e.g., accounting for income taxes.[5]

In concluding this section, it should be observed that none of the IASs have yet been superseded, although the exposure draft "Information Reflecting the Effects of Changing Prices" is intended to supersede IAS 6. However, the intent has always been that, as the years go by, existing IASs will be "tightened and strengthened."[6] Presumably, one of the ways of strengthening them will be to reduce, wherever possible, the situations where alternatives are provided.

Changes in IASC Policies and Procedures

The IASC has been criticized for not being responsive to suggestions for change. The record, however, shows that from its earliest days it was willing to consider such suggestions, and to respond by making changes that it considered practical and/or appropriate.

Changes Made Prior to Amendment of Agreement and Constitution

During the period, up to October 1977, in which the initial Agreement/Constitution were in effect, the following changes were made:

1. By the end of 1974 it had become apparent that having four meetings of the IASC per annum would result in too great an output of IASs and exposure drafts. The meetings were therefore cut back to three per annum.

2. The period provided for comment on the first three exposure drafts was four months. Some of the member bodies apparently found it difficult to submit comments in that period, particularly where the comments were to be formulated by a committee, or where more than one exposure draft was out for comment at the same time. Accordingly, the period was extended, and now generally ranges from five to seven months, depending on the complexity of the topic and the number of drafts out at the same time.

3. When the first two IASs were issued, no information on the comments made by exposure draft respondents, or on the changes made as a result of comments received, was published. Starting with IAS 3, however, such information has generally been provided in *IASC News*.

4. The steering committees assigned to each project were initially comprised of representatives appointed by founder members, with no associate member bodies being represented. However, starting with the project that led to IAS 6 (on which work started in mid-1974), most of the steering committees included one associate member representative.

5. Initially, except for an industrialist from the Netherlands and a Japanese academic, all the representatives appointed by the founder members to the IASC were either in public practice or were executives of the member accounting bodies. There is now a trend to-

wards appointing other representatives holding industrial or commercial positions.

Changes Incorporated in Amended Agreement/Constitution

The new Agreement/Constitution, which was approved on October 10, 1977, incorporated a number of changes. The more substantive were:

1. Under the initial Agreement there were Founder Members, being professional bodies from the nine countries which originally signed the Agreement, and Associate Members, being bodies from other countries which applied for membership and were accepted. Under the amended Agreement the Associate Members become "members," and the IASC's business is conducted by a board comprising representatives of the founder member bodies and of two member bodies. (These additional two representatives presently come from Nigeria and South Africa; their terms expire in 1982.)

2. The initial Agreement/Constitution required auditors to disclose, in their reports, any departures from IASs, regardless of whether the departure was disclosed in the financial statements. Auditors are now only required to disclose those departures from IASs which are not disclosed in the statements.

3. The initial definition of "financial statements" made specific reference to just two statements: balance sheets and income statements. The new definition also refers to statements of changes in financial position—presumably to reflect the fact that IAS 7 now requires that such a statement be presented as a basic financial statement.

4. The Constitution previously required all exposure drafts to include "the arguments for and against the adoption of a particular standard." This was not carried forward to the new Constitution. This deletion would seem to be undesirable, as a closely-reasoned standard would be much more persuasive than a series of unsupported statements. In adapting an IAS for local publication, each country would have to develop a separate rationale (a needless duplication of effort and one that raises the possiblity of significantly different reasoning supporting the same standards.

Recent and Proposed Changes

During 1978 the IASC's Board adopted the practice of making available to members who are not represented on the board copies of proposed exposure drafts before they are approved for release. This gives these members an opportunity of providing substantive comments at an early stage. These members were already expected to participate in the procedures for developing IASs in the following ways: a) suggesting projects for study; b) preparing summaries of practice in their country; c) submitting relevant publications; d) publishing and distributing approved exposure drafts; e) collecting and summarizing comments on exposure drafts; and f) publishing and distributing approved IASs.

Some of the member bodies also have to translate exposure drafts and IASs from English to the local language.

A second new practice instituted by the board in 1978 was to start providing member bodies, at their request, with a specific individual contact on the board through whom comments on any IASC matter may be made.

At its June 1980 meeting the board decided to broaden its base along two lines: 1) By approaching international organizations of business, labor, stock exchanges, financial analysts, and banks with the request to cooperate (in a manner still to be agreed upon); 2) By expanding the board to thirteen seats, with the hope that the two additional seats will be filled by developing countries.

Acceptance of IASC Standards

National support of IASC pronouncements has not been uniform. Thomas has summarized the approaches as follows:

> Some accountancy bodies have declared to their members that international accounting standards are to be accorded the same status as domestic accounting standards. Each IAS is accompanied by an explanation of the relationship between the international standard and any domestic standard dealing with the same subject.
>
> Other accountancy bodies have issued statements declaring support for the concept of international standards and strongly encouraging their members to accept them. Some of these bodies indicate the extent to which an international standard differs from the related domestic standard. They often offer to review, or encourage the relevant body to review, the basis of the domestic standard, with the objective of eliminating any differences.
>
> There are some member countries, however, that have not yet presented any formal statement of the status of IASs to the members of the accountancy profession.[7]

Difficulty in implementing the requirement that *all* enterprises adhere to—or identify deviations from—IASs is well recognized. Nevertheless, it is widely felt that conformity with IASs is particularly relevant for public companies which have foreign shareholders or creditors. In Canada the *CICA Handbook* encourages this by stating that "For companies that report in an international environment . . . it is desirable that they disclose conformity with or identify deviations from International Accounting Standards. . . ." (Paragraph 1501.05). However, according to the CICA's biennial survey of the financial statements of 325 large companies, none made such disclosure.[8]

To ascertain U.S. practice the author conducted a NAARS (National Automated Accounting Research System) search of the "Fortune 500" companies' financial statements for years ended between July 1978 and June 1980; this revealed no references to the IASC or its Standards. In the U.K. IASs are given slightly more recognition: while none of the fifteen property companies covered by the 1979 edition of *Survey of Published Accounts* provided depreciation on freehold or long leasehold properties, only three referred to non-compliance with IAS 4.[9]

International surveys also reveal few references to the IASC. A Financial Times survey of the annual reports of 100 major European companies states that ". . . references to IASC are few and far between."[10] (However, the Swedish company Sandvik provides a detailed explanation of the seven respects in which its accounts do not comply with IASs.) A subsequent Financial Times survey covering more countries revealed much the same situation.[11]

The IASC believes that more references to its standards in annual reports will increase their authority and influence. Accordingly, some member bodies are now urging larger companies in their countries to refer to IASs. For example, in November 1980 member bodies in Canada wrote to the 300 largest companies quoted on the Toronto Stock Exchange, urging them to include a reference such as: "The accompanying financial statements are prepared in accordance with accounting principles generally accepted in Canada and conform in all material respects to International Accounting Standards."[12]

Actions Taken by OECD and UN

One of the reasons why the IASC may now be particularly concerned about increasing the authority and influence of IASs is that both the Organization for Economic Cooperation and Development (OECD) and the United Nations are taking steps to establish international standards of accounting disclosure—and perhaps accounting measurement too.

OECD Actions

The members of the OECD are twenty-four non-Communist countries in Europe, Asia, North America, and Australia which are relatively well industrialized. In 1976 the governments of these countries jointly issued a "Declaration on International Investment and Multinational Enterprises." Annexed to this declaration was a series of "Guidelines for Multinational Enterprises," one section of which was entitled "Disclosures of Information."[13] This urged the disclosure in annual financial statements of several items, including the names and percentage ownership of the main affiliates, the policies followed in respect to intra-group pricing, and the segmentation of sales by both geographical area and major lines of business.

Observance of these guidelines by multinational companies is voluntary unless they are enforced by the OECD member countries. Some nations have taken steps to encourage companies based in their countries to observe them: in the U.S., for example, Messrs. Kissinger (Secretary of State), Simon (Secretary of the Treasury), and Richardson (Secretary of Commerce) wrote in August 1976 to the chief executive officers of 800 large U.S. corporations commending the guidelines to their attention. (A NAARS search of the "Fortune 500" companies' financial statements for years ended between July 1978 and June 1980 revealed no references to the OECD's guidelines, but it is possible that the companies were nevertheless complying with them—many of the guidelines being in conformity with U.S. GAAP.) However, it is clear that some European companies are attempting to follow the guidelines.[14]

In July 1978, the OECD established an Ad Hoc Working Group on Accounting Standards to review existing harmonization efforts and to ascertain the desirability of greater OECD involvement in this area. On the basis of its 1980 survey, *Accounting Practices in OECD Member Countries,* the working group argued that greater OECD involvement in accounting harmonization efforts was warranted.

While the OECD does not intend to form a new international standard-setting body, accounting measurement rules may very well be added to its present guidelines. Furthermore, in clarifying the matters to be disclosed under the existing guidelines, there is the danger that definitions contrary to those embodied in IASs or national standards will be developed.

United Nations

The interest of the UN in accounting was stimulated in 1974, when a report by the Group of Eminent Persons commissioned to study *The Impact of Multinational Corporations on Development and on International Relations*[15] was published. This report's prime conclusion was that a "Commission on Multinational Corporations" should be established (p.52), which would be served by an "Information and Research Centre on Multinational Corporations" (p.54). Of particular importance for accountants, however, was the recommendation that "an expert group on international accounting standards should be convened, under the auspices of the Commission on Multinational Corporations" (p.95).

This "Group of Experts" was formed in 1976 with the prime purpose of recommending: ". . . a list of minimum items, together with their definitions, that should be included in reports by transnational corporations and their affiliates, taking into account the recommendations of various groups concerned with the subject-matter."[16]

The Groups of Experts' report includes a 34-page list of recommended disclosures: i) by the "enterprise as a whole," i.e., consolidated data; and ii) by individual member companies, including the parent company. The majority of the disclosures for these two classes are in the realm of financial information, but certain nonfinancial disclosures are also recommended. There was, however, one recommendation that went far beyond disclosure: that the financial statements of all subsidiaries should be consolidated, and all associated companies are to be accounted for by the equity method—two of the most far-reaching recommendations on *measurement* that could be made. These, like the disclosure recommendations, were stated in the form of unsupported assertions, unencumbered by analysis or reasoning.

Following publication of this report the UN's Commission on Transnational Corporations was directed to take steps to promote its recommendations. The Commission concluded that a working group be established by the Economic and Social Council, which (after some disagreements about the group's composition) formed an "Ad Hoc Intergovernmental Working Group of Experts on International Standards of Accounting and Reporting." Thirty-four countries are members of this ad hoc group: some, like Egypt, Morocco, Swaziland, and Tunisia, have not been noted in the past for their participation in international accounting activities, but many of the countries that have are members. The Group is required, among other charges, to take into account the earlier Group of Experts' report; to consult the international accounting bodies which it deems appropriate on matters pertaining to the development of international standards; and to concentrate on formulating priorities, taking into account the needs of home and host countries, particularly those of developing countries.

The Ad Hoc Group had its first meeting in February 1980, and its second nine months later—to which the IASC was asked to submit a report on its progress, plans, and problems. It is too soon to tell what the Group's impact is likely to be, whether it will attempt to duplicate the

IASC's work, and how much it will be influenced by political considerations.

European Economic Community (EEC)

An important development for accountants in the nine member countries of the EEC is the series of directives on company law harmonization that is being formulated. Two are particularly relevant to international accounting standards: the Fourth and the Seventh.

The Fourth Directive deals with the annual financial statements of public and private companies, other than banks and insurance companies. Its purposes have been summarized as:

1. The co-ordination of national laws for the protection of members and third parties relating to the publication, presentation and content of annual accounts and reports of limited liability companies, and the accounting principles used in their preparation.

2. The establishment in the EEC of minimum equivalent legal requirements for disclosure of financial information to the public by companies which are in competition with one another.

3. The establishment of the principle that annual accounts should give a true and fair view of a company's assets and liabilities, and of its financial position and profit or loss.

4. The provision of the fullest possible information about limited companies to shareholders and third parties (with some relief for smaller companies).[17]

The directive sets out in considerable detail the information that is to be disclosed, and under what headings. It also has a section on "valuation rules" (i.e., principles of measurement), although alternatives are provided. For example, the purchase price or production cost of inventories may be computed by the use of weighted average prices, the FIFO method, the LIFO method, or "some similar method." However, a member state may eliminate one or more of these options.

Work on the directive started in 1968, and it was finalized in 1978. Member states are required to enact legislation to implement directives within two years of finalization, so the Fourth Directive will soon be having an impact in the nine EEC countries.

The Seventh Directive, which is still under consideration, will deal with consolidated financial statements.

Professional accounting bodies in the EEC countries have established a committee, the Group d'Etudes des Experts Comptables, to comment on all draft proposals that relate to accounting matters. It had a considerable effect on the content of the Fourth Directive.

Concluding Thoughts

In tracing the evolution of international accounting standards we have seen the significant progress made by the IASC. The IASC's willingness to respond to suggestions for change has been a key factor in this, and with the current interest and activities of the OECD and the UN, further changes may be needed in the future.

The lack of acceptance of IASs is presently a serious impediment to the development of truly international standards. Prime responsibility for acceptance rests with the IASC's member bodies, although the IASC may make surveys or suggest such actions as urging large companies to refer to IASs in their financial statements. However, there is no reason why either the OECD or the UN should not, if they see fit, prevail upon national governments to support the IASC. (The UN might be deterred from taking such a step through reluctance to recognize a private-sector committee which is dominated by member bodies from capitalist, industrialized nations, but the OECD should not be inhibited in this way.)

As we have seen, the IASC is planning to expand its board, so as to provide two seats for developing countries. In addition, those seats presently filled by Nigeria and South Africa will presumably be available for less-developed countries after 1982. The IASC should then: a) be more acceptable to the UN; and b) be less susceptible to criticisms that the projects it selects are unresponsive to the needs of developing countries—although, as was noted earlier, all IASC member bodies have been expected to suggest projects for study. (Developing countries are therefore only justified in voicing such criticisms if suggestions they have made have not been accepted.)

Apart from encouraging acceptance of IASs, national accounting bodies can contribute to international standardization by using their influence to see that national standards being developed will not cause the IASC problems. In other words, a new national standard on a subject covered by an IAS should preferably be compatible with a national standard recently developed by one or more countries whose support is vital to international acceptance of a future IAS. (This approach may not prove to be appropriate in every case—as Canada found in following the FASB's lead on foreign currency translation—but it should always be carefully considered.) Further, continuing efforts can be made to "tighten" national standards—or at least to refrain from criticizing an IAS for providing alternatives when national standards on the topic provide a similar range of alternatives.

This leads to three questions that merit the attention of researchers. Can further progress be made on setting international accounting standards without agreement being reached on the objectives of financial statements? And how practical would it be for the IASC to undertake such a project when so few national bodies have had the courage to do so? Or would the IASC's work be facilitated by the absence of entrenched national positions on financial statement objectives?

There are, of course, several other questions regarding international accounting standards that should be researched. They include the subjects on which international accounting standards are needed most urgently, and the aspects of existing IASs for which the present alternatives might be eliminated. Another key question is whether the efficient market hypothesis has any relevance to international accounting standards (considering that in many countries there is no financial market of any kind).

Several of the difficulties pertaining to international standardization stem more from national prejudice, than from the types of problems that can more readily be researched. However, researchers have a valuable role to play in ensuring that facts are available to the decision-makers, and that alternative approaches and methods are fully explored.

Notes

1. Jacob Kraayenhof, "International Challenges for Accounting," *The Journal of Accountancy* (January 1960): 34-38.

2. For example, in R. Douglas Thomas, "Accounting Research by Professional Accounting Bodies," in W. John Brennan, ed., *The Internationalization of the Accountancy Profession* (Toronto: CICA, 1979), p.109.

3. From review by Gerhard G. Mueller, *The Accounting Review* (July 1976): 692.

4. The concept of "vital countries" is discussed in Alister K. Mason, *The Development of International Financial Reporting Standards* (Lancaster: International Center for Research in Accounting, 1978), pp. 40-48 and 74-77.

5. The Royal Dutch/Shell Group of Companies attempts to follow accounting principles which are generally accepted in the Netherlands, the U.K. and the U.S. The auditors' report on the 1979 financial statements was qualified because under the new U.K. standard deferred taxes should only be provided on amounts considered to become payable in the foreseeable future.

6. Henry Benson, "The Story of International Accounting Standards," *Accountancy* (July 1976): 39.

7. R. Douglas Thomas, "International Accounting Standards," *CA Magazine* (October 1977): 49-50.

8. *Financial Reporting in Canada*, 13th ed. (Toronto: CICA, 1979), p.14.

9. *Survey of Published Accounts 1979* (London: Institute of Chartered Accountants in England and Wales, 1980), pp. 283-84.

10.   Michael Lafferty, David Cairns, and James Carty, *100 Major European Companies' Reports and Accounts* (London: Financial Times, 1979), p.19.

11.   Michael Lafferty and David Cairns, *Financial Times World Survey of Annual Reports 1980* (London: Financial Times, 1980).

12.   "The Time is Now," *CA Magazine* (November 1980): 68.

13.   *International Investment and Multinational Enterprises* (Paris: OECD, 1976), pp.14-16.

14.   Mason, op.cit., p.93.

15.   Published by the UN Department of Economic and Social Affairs, 1974.

16.   Group of Experts on International Standards of Accounting and Reporting, *International Standards of Accounting and Reporting for Transnational Corporations*, (New York: United Nations, 1977), p.17.

17.   *The Fourth Directive* (London: Deloitte, Haskins & Sells, 1978), p.1.

Part III

Overview

Introduction

The history of accounting is an international history. Thus, double-entry bookkeeping, as the basis of accounting as we know it today, reportedly migrated from southern to central Europe, then westward to the British Isles, the Americas, and on to the Far East. Despite its international origins, accounting has, paradoxically, become an intensely nationalistic affair. In the past, accounting nationalism has permeated not only professional standards and practices, but academic research as well.

This unfortunate state of affairs is, however, beginning to change. The movement to establish international professional accounting standards is a case in point. Accounting academics, cognizant of the needless redundancy that has often characterized international accounting research in the past, are also beginning to bridge the research gap through a variety of means, including: 1) attendance at international accounting conferences, 2) subscription to foreign accounting journals, and 3) participation in collaborative research projects with foreign colleagues.

Part III of this anthology presents a geographic overview of the state of the art of accounting research internationally. In addition to monitoring what is happening research-wise in other parts of the world, such an overview can provide useful insights into domestic accounting issues which often go unnoticed when viewed from a purely uni-national perspective.

European accounting issues are explored in the first essay to this section. In graciously accepting their charge, authors Busse von Colbe and Pohlmann undertake a difficult task, given the cultural and language heterogeneity of Europe. Despite such difficulties, the authors provide an interesting insight into the nature of accounting research in Europe. Especially helpful is their description of the institutional setting which shapes, to a large extent, accounting concerns in this region of the world.

In the next piece, Professor Hiramatsu of Kwansei Gakuin University provides a comprehensive narrative of accounting developments in Japan. What is particularly striking in this essay is the significant growth in attention accorded international accounting issues which appears to parallel, to some extent, Japan's international trade patterns and emergence as a world economic power (an untested hypothesis!). Reasons notwithstanding, international accounting issues are predicted to command even more attention in Japan in the future.

North America, encompassing both Canada and the United States, is the subject of the third essay. A prominent contributor to the accounting literature, Corbin posits that a major role of accounting research is to guide accounting policy decisions. This role is placed in historical perspective by examining the relation of accounting research to American accounting policy-formulation during the past twenty years. A direct outcome of this historical narrative is a list of research topics appropriate for the 1980s. Corbin does not fail in this regard; his list is both comprehensive and challenging.

Many of the research issues identified in this anthology have been espoused from the perspective of industrially-advanced and mature economies. Writing from an opposite perspective, Jacobsen reminds us that accounting has, and will continue to be, "culture-bound." Based on this premise and many years of "on-line" experience, Jacobsen enumerates a number of realistic research priorities tailored to the unique environment of Latin America.

Contemporary Issues in Financial Accounting:
A European Review

WALTHER BUSSE von COLBE and PETER POHLMANN
Ruhr University

I. Introduction

The task of surveying accounting systems in Europe is as attractive as it is difficult. At the present time, a "European Accounting System" does not exist. This is true even if one omits the socialist countries with their macro-economic oriented accounting systems for centralized governmental planning and concentrates on the European Community (EC). The reader should realize that in Europe (compared to the U.S.) a greater number of political, social, and legal units developed rather independently in a relatively small geographic area. People in ten EC-countries call seven different languages their mother tongue: those in the nineteen European OECD-countries talk in thirteen different languages.

Despite efforts to form a European Union especially enforced in the EC, differences between the environmental circumstances in those countries are still in existence and are diminishing very slowly. As the accounting system is part of the social system, it is influenced by differences in social, political, and legal environments.

In part II of this essay, characteristics of the social system and their importance for the structure of accounting systems are described without attempting to give a complete classification and correlation of types of accounting systems to the social framework as provided by Choi and Mueller in a much more general approach.[1]

Though one cannot talk about a "European Accounting System," one can find some common developments, which are reported in part III. Part IV gives a very personal and inevitably incomplete survey on the actual academic discussion topics concerning financial accounting in Europe.

II. The Influence of the Institutional Setting on Accounting Systems

1. Differences in Legal Systems

In the European countries, enterprise accounting is ruled differently with respect to the extent of regulations and the legal basis for regulations:[2]

- In some countries, as in Austria, Germany, Switzerland, France, Italy, and Sweden, accounting is ruled by law or authoritative decrees (e.g., German, Austrian, and Swedish Company Law or Corporation Acts). In others, only basic regulations are governed by law (e.g., the Italian and Swiss Civil Code). Nationally, there are also different GAAPs to be taken into account.
- In some other countries, such as the U.K. and Ireland, laws only give basic regulations, while professional accounting organizations elaborate detailed and generally accepted accounting standards.
- In a third group of countries, e.g., Denmark and the Netherlands, neither detailed legal regulations nor generally accepted accounting standards exist, thus allowing a wide range of different accounting practices.

Recently, the tendency in Europe is toward more legal regulation of accounting. For example, EC group accounts are now governed by legal statutes in Ireland, Germany, France, and Denmark. Accounting laws have been enacted in Scandinavia, with the "Plan Comptable Général" issued by the Conseil National de la Comptabilité in the case of France. This trend is enforced by the transformation of the 4th EC-Directive on financial statements of companies into national legislation. For the EC-countries, harmonization is attained to the extent that all member states are obliged to introduce legal minimum regulations.

The degree of compliance with legal requirements varies from country to country. Harmonization in legal requirements does not necessarily mean unification of practice.

Choi and Mueller mention a phenomenon that might be less obvious but materially more important. This relates to the fact that there are two different legal systems which exist in the European Community. While the Anglo-Saxon countries have a case law system, most continental countries are code law countries. This difference has important consequences. The acceptance of a basic standard, that goes much further than detailed regulations, will differ in both systems. An example of such a basic standard is the true-and-fair-view concept, as introduced by the British into the 4th EC-Directive.[3] Case law permits unique and special interpretation of basic standards not completely and generally defined in any detail. This interpretation is independent of earlier interpretations and is relevant only for the case in point. Thus, the true-and-fair-view concept is just a guideline in judging a special accounting procedure.

This approach is in direct contrast to that taken by a code law system, e.g., as in Germany. Code law requires that one first find a valid and universal interpretation of a basic standard. This interpretation is dependent on earlier attempts to find one universal interpretation of this basic standard. Not until then can the basic standard be used in finding the solution for a special problem. Thus, the basic standard operates less as a guideline in finding a solution to an accounting problem, more like a mathematical relation.

Consequently, in Germany it is extremely difficult to adopt an accounting-effect oriented regulation as the true-and-fair concept while using an accounting-technique oriented system of regulations. Most authors discussing this problem suggest, as a compromise, that the basic standard of "true-and-fair" not have a great deal of influence on balance sheet and profit and loss account presentation but apply more toward additional information given in notes to the financial statements.[4]

2. Capital Market Versus Creditor Protection Oriented Accounting

Though the annual report is a general purpose statement, the relative importance of a specific user group may influence the structure and information content of the accounting system. The predominance of information needs or requirements of equity investors, and, consequently, the capital market view of accounting information is typical for Anglo-American countries. In the German speaking countries (Austria, Germany, and Switzerland), it is typical to see much more importance placed on the information needs of creditors, i.e., the "principle of creditors' protection." This finds its reflection in the "principle of prudence" (*Vorsichtsprinzip*) that has a much stronger influence in asset valuation or calculation of contingencies in those countries and in France and Italy, than in the Anglo-American countries. The extent to which German, French, and, above all, Swiss balance sheet presentation of assets contains secret reserves is much higher than those of Anglo-American companies.[5]

Respect for the information needs of different interest groups in accounting reflects the different entity-concepts that are dominant internationally. In Anglo-American countries, stockholder-theory best reflects the attitudes of management. In contrast, on the European Continent the stakeholder-theory is dominant. In Germany, for example, equity shareholders of a largely-held public company are in a very weak position compared to creditors (especially banks) and employees. In Germany this situation is reflected in the inclusion of employees on the supervising

board (*Aufsichtsrat*) of larger companies and management's legal obligation to give a report on the actual situation of the company to representatives of the employees (*Wirtschaftsausschuß*).

In addition to entity-concepts, there is the different importance attached to equity and debt-capital, as represented in company debt-equity
ratios. A higher debt-equity ratio in German as opposed to British companies seems to call for much more conservatism in the preparation of
annual reports in Germany to protect the company against excessive dividend demands of share holders.[6] A more conservative valuation leads to
a lower equity capital shown in German balance sheets than in Anglo-
American accounting practice. An impressive example is given by the
German chemical group BASF. For purposes of world-wide consolidated
group accounts, for which there is no obligation in Germany, BASF evaluates the German part of the group in accordance with regulations of the
German Corporation Act and investments in foreign countries in accordance with SEC-regulations. Additional information given in the notes to
BASF's statements discloses that equity capital would be higher by 1,377
billions DM in 1979 and about 1,234 billions DM in 1978, if the German
investments were also evaluated according to SEC-regulations.[7] This would
increase its equity ratios in both years from 39 to 44 percent.

In the U.K., the equity capital of companies that are quoted on the
London stock exchange are higher than that of comparable companies in
other EC-countries. Thus, accounting requirements in the U.K. are influenced very much by the needs of fair information distribution in a
broadly based capital market. To a large extent, this means the accounting
system is big-company oriented.

On the other hand, in Germany the capital market for investment of
risk capital is not very important. Most companies (more than 250,000)
are organized as private companies (GmbHs) as opposed to the 2,100
public stock companies (AGs). Nonetheless, the largest companies are
AGs, so that their economic importance is much greater than the number
suggests.[8] Only about 450 AGs are quoted on the stock exchange and
only 150 have more than 1,000 shareholders. (In the U.S., there are about
11,000 companies with more than 1,000 shareholders.) Consequently,
German legal authorities take the mid-sized GmbH and not the large AG
or the multinational group as the standard type of company when drafting
new accounting regulations transforming the 4th EC-Directive into national law.[9] This explains why there are no legal requirements for a statement of funds' flow in the Draft Law. Practice, however, shows that
financial reporting of most large companies goes beyond minimum legal
requirements. This should be kept in mind when comparing accounting
systems of different countries. Consequences attending balance sheet pre-

sentation and especially profit presentation are an important criterion for judging accounting alternatives.[10] Those consequences are different from country to country; the influence on capital allocation is not as crucial in all countries as it is in the U.S.

3.   The Influence of Tax Law on Accounting

In Germany, France, and some other OECD countries, tax law has quite an influence on financial accounting.[11] The fact that tax advantages—e.g., accelerated depreciation—can only be realized if financial accounting follows tax accounting rules, is another important reason for conservative asset valuations in published financial reports in these countries.

4.   The Influence of Interest Conflicts on Accounting

At least in Germany, financial reporting can be looked upon as a means of solving conflicts of interest between those groups that are interested in the company, e.g., managers, owners, creditors, and employees.[12] Regulations requiring a minimum dividend for shareholders help to solve the conflict of interest between shareholders and management.

In Germany according to the Corporation Act (*Aktiengesetz*), the management of the AG has to pay out at least 50 percent of annual net income and is entitled to retain the rest. In contrast, the owners of equity capital of a GmbH can insist on a 100 percent dividend payout unless otherwise stated. Rules like these encouraging the use of secret reserves as financing from internal sources strengthens the position of management. Also, the conflict potential between management and employees encourages the showing of lower profits made possible through the use of secret reserves. High profits provoke employees' demands for higher social benefits and wages that can be negotiated for each company individually.

From different ways of accounting follow different ways of information distribution which, in turn, has a strong influence on the distribution of value-added between interested parties. Financial accounting thus becomes a tool in the distribution of income between social groups.

The emphasis on conflict regulation is a reason why in Germany, for example, reliability and uniformity are stressed in the development of financial accounting statements as opposed to relevance for financial statement users. This contrasts with the situation in the Anglo-American countries or the Netherlands.

5.   Harmonization of Accounting Systems in the Case of Different Environments

Given differences in the socio-economic setting of EC-countries, it seems impossible to find agreement on the objectives of financial accounting. A major conclusion from the above analysis for the development of a European accounting system is that deductive reasoning will not be helpful in trying to harmonize accounting systems. Defining objectives beforehand and deducing adequate accounting alternatives from those objectives, like the approach taken by the FASB's Conceptual Framework Project, will not be very successful in Europe. One has to start much more pragmatically by trying to find solutions for detailed questions.[13]

The latter approach is reflected in the 4th EC-Directive of 1978 governing financial accounting of a single company, the Exposure Draft of the 7th EC-Directive (consolidated financial accounting of a group of companies), as well as recommendations of the IASC concerning different details of accounting. Those concerned with European accounting should always be aware of the dangers inherent in harmonization efforts which portray uniformity in "form" rather than "substance."[14]

The same is true for comparisons between accounting regulations and accounting practices or their conformance with IASC recommendations. Differences in socio-economic environments must always be taken into account. Unfortunately, many empirical studies overlook this important point. Some Anglo-American studies neglect or do not notice these basic differences and take their accounting system as the only yardstick. If accounting is purpose-oriented, it is not surprising that accounting differs from country to country because of differences in purpose. Given this state of the world, ranking of national accounting regulations and practices does not make too much sense.

III. Contemporary Trends in Accounting in Europe

1. Extension of Disclosure Requirements

Until now disclosure requirements in the EC-member countries showed a wide range of variation. By means of the 4th EC-Directive, minimum disclosure requirements will be prescribed by law.[15] They will exceed present standards in most countries. In Germany, for example, all 250,000 GmbHs will have to fulfill the requirements of the 4th EC-Directive and publish their annual reports. Only some very large GmbHs had to disclose their annual financial statements prior to the 4th Directive. Extension of disclosure requirements is the most important sign of harmonization in the European Community. Together with the disclosure proposals of the OECD and UN, this trend seems likely to continue, at least for large companies in Europe.[16]

Despite such recent developments, success in harmonizing the material objectives of accounting regulations in Europe remains limited. This is because all member states may use the options given in the 4th EC-Directive in such a way that prior national accounting regulations will not be changed at all or only slightly. These options were written into the 4th EC-Directive partly to give member countries the chance to keep old regulations in effect. The comment on the draft of the German transformation law for the 4th EC-Directive states: "In using the options given to the member countries, attention was paid that there will be no changes compared to the actual practice." The interpretation of the new regulations will enforce this trend for practical accounting.

2. Inflation Accounting

The most debated question concerning financial reporting in Europe is how to handle price changes in financial accounting. In accordance with Article 33 of the 4th EC-Directive, the member states can allow or oblige all or special groups of companies to value depreciable fixed assets and inventories at replacement cost, to choose special inflation accounting procedures, or to undertake revaluations from time to time. These accounting procedures have to be reexamined after seven years. A common way to implement this specific regulation is not in sight right now. But this is not very astonishing given very different inflation rates in Europe. Inflation accounting options in the different EC member states vary. General price level adjustment is uncommon in Germany so far and will probably not be allowed in the near future. Denmark, France, and Italy have practiced, in special cases, a revaluation of depreciable assets sometimes required for tax purposes as well, and probably will continue to do so in the future. Companies in the U.K. are obliged to prepare complete current cost financial statements alongside historical cost statements. In the Netherlands, there is a probability that current cost information will be the only statement required if differences between historical and current cost statements become so pronounced that footnote disclosures will be insufficient.[17]

In the U.K. and the Netherlands, current cost accounting is favored over general price level accounting. In contrast, in the U.S. SFAS No. 33 has no specific preference for any of these alternatives. Still in discussion is the capital maintenance rule and profit definition. The most detailed pronouncement, British SSAP 16, is operating with two different profit measurements:[18]

• current operating profit (obviously also preferred in the Netherlands) including a purchasing power adjustment for net monetary working capital, and

- net profit attributable to shareholders including a gearing adjustment for the proportion of depreciation, cost of goods sold, and monetary working capital adjustments financed by borrowing.

Conceptually, this latter profit definition is similar to the German version of current cost accounting only for assets financed by equity capital (*Nettosubstanzerhaltung*), which had been recommended by the German Institute der Wirtschaftsprüfer as a voluntary supplement,[19] but is practiced only by a few large companies.

3. Consolidated Statement and Equity Method

In the countries of the European continent, consolidated statements have been published for two decades. In some countries, disclosure was mandatory for companies of specific legal form or size. Only the U.K. has a longer tradition of publishing group accounts on a world-wide basis.[20] Thus, the intended ratification of the 7th EC-Directive on group accounts will bring more extensive disclosure requirements in most member states especially for smaller and unquoted companies.

For majority-owned subsidiaries, the draft of the 7th EC-Directive requires a slight variation of the purchase method as prescribed in APB-Opinion No. 16 and IAS No. 3. This method is required in the U.K.,[21] normally used in the Netherlands, but not yet allowed in Germany. Nonetheless, this method is supported by German managers and academics because of its higher information content. According to the 7th EC-Directive, investments in associated companies should be accounted for according to the equity-method, commonly used in the Anglo-American area but not followed, for example, in Germany, Italy, or France.

Approval of the 7th EC-Directive has been delayed for several years because of differences in opinion as to what constitutes a *group* and the appropriateness of subgroup statements. While the French and Germans prefer a group definition based on actual control of subsidiaries by the parent company, the British prefer a definition based on the majority of stock and votes that connotes the possibility of control. Right now, the EC Commission is trying to find detailed regulations as to which companies are to be included in consolidated accounts without defining the concept of a group or its members. As discussed earlier, harmonizing accounting practices without first harmonizing the objectives and the socio-economic setting is dangerous. Take, as an example, the elimination of intercompany profit if the subsidiary's investment is accounted for on the equity basis[22] The proposed regulations of the 7th EC-Directive require equity accounting for investments of 20 to 50 percent.

Those who define the inclusion in consolidated statements by giving ratios of stock or vote held by the parent company may suggest the following treatment:

ratio of stock or vote held by the parent company	consolidation method	elimination of inter-company profit
more than 50%	purchase (full consolidation)	full/total
50% exactly	pro rata consolidation	proportional
20-50%	equity method (one-line consolidation)	proportional
20% and less	at cost	no

Those who define group companies as those actually controlled by the parent, take a dichotomizing approach; either a company is a member of the group or not. If a company is a member of the group, it has to be included in consolidation and intercompany profit has to be eliminated completely. If it is not a member of the group, it is an asset like other assets, and valuation has to follow the general rules. The equity-method in this case is no longer a consolidation procedure but a valuation rule.

If classification as a group member is rejected, no intercompany profits are eliminated. This is very much like the German approach. If the 7th-Directive avoids definition of the "group," there will be no systematic solution for problems like that shown above.

Another highly debated problem concerning group accounting is the translation of foreign currency statements of subsidiaries. The draft of 7th-EC-Directive presently does not include a regulation for this problem. Only in the U.K. is there the nearly uniform practice of translating foreign currency statements at the closing-rate. In contrast, the use of different exchange rates in Germany is predominant. Most of the twenty-three industrial parent companies voluntarily preparing group accounts on a worldwide basis for 1979 used a translation method on the basis of different rates.[23]

Translation according to the temporal method has been recommended by a working group of the Schmalenbach-Gesellschaft in cooperation with representatives of some of the biggest German industrial companies in 1979,[24] while the Institut der Wirtschaftsprüfer in 1977 rejected any standardization.[25] The reasoning for the choice of the temporal method was to guarantee a translation method that is in conformity with the accounting system, especially with historical cost accounting, the realization concept, and the lower of cost or market principle.

Taken from this point of view, the Exposure Draft of a new translation statement superceding SFAS No. 8 (dated August 28, 1980) as well as the British counterpart, Exposure Draft 27 (dated October 27, 1980), are regrettable, because the proposed closing rate method, recommended in both drafts, is not in conformity with a historical cost accounting system. There is also no evidence that the closing rate method reflects economic reality better than the temporal method. Both exposure drafts seem to be dictated by management wishes to avoid disclosure of exchange rate losses and yo-yo effects on quarterly earnings in times of a weakening dollar and pound sterling. If more and more detailed accounting problems are solved with respect to undesired economic consequences, instead of extent accounting systems, management may be free to orchestrate reported profits and losses as desired.

4. Fund Statements

Questions of segmental disclosure or quarterly reports, which evoked much interest in the U.S., did not find attention in Europe. Fund statements however became a point of growing interest. In the U.K., fund statements are an obligatory part of the annual report,[26] but are published voluntarily by nearly all big companies, as well as in Germany. Until now, fund statements are not presented in a single unified, common, and generally accepted structure (even in the U.K. a new way of presentation is being debated). Thus, it is very difficult to compare fund statements. They differ not only country by country but also company by company. The 4th EC-Directive does not prescribe the publication of fund statements. However, the record on the occasion of the ratification of the 4th EC-Directive included an authorization of the member states to make funds statements obligatory via national legislation.

5. Social Reports

The prevailing general objectives of management in Europe, especially the stakeholder-philosophy, is the basis of social reporting. Social reporting is of special importance in France where, since 1979, companies that have more than 750 employees are legally obliged to publish a social report disclosing special employee-oriented details.[27] On a voluntary basis, some German companies disclose similar information, but stress more governmental and environmental facts.[28]

In the U.K., the Corporate Report gave new incentives for the extension of financial reporting into the social reporting area.[29] Corporate response has been very strong thus far, except for discussions about value-added statements. Problems of measuring social revenues and social costs as well as their information content for decision-makers seem to be the crucial point of social reports. If social reports are voluntarily disclosed, they are very likely to be abused as public-relations instruments.

IV. Contemporary Research in Financial Accounting

Because there is no European communication forum and no European journal of accounting giving academics the possibility of reporting the results of their research projects, it is very difficult to obtain any survey on contemporary research issues in Europe. One reason may be language barriers. English has only slowly become the generally accepted communication instrument in Europe, with most acceptance in the Netherlands, Scandinavia, and the German speaking countries.

The European Accounting Association founded in 1977 has tried to become that missing European forum. The last two congresses at Amsterdam and Barcelona were attended by about 150-200 academics from ten to fifteen European countries and the number of attendees is increasing. Admittedly, the representation of various countries by the number of attendees is very different and not necessarily representative of the importance of accounting in those countries. The academic importance of accounting is very different from country to country in Europe. In the Netherlands, Scandinavia, the U.K., and the German speaking countries, academic accounting is much further developed than in the Romanic countries. Consequently, the following survey is fragmentary.

In Europe many more research activities are oriented towards interpretation and development of institutional accounting than in the U.S. Accounting regulations are a special point of interest. One may state that most of the German accounting professors look upon this point as their main task. The relatively strong link between financial and tax accounting in Germany and France, for example, requires deeper consideration even of the tax accounting regulations. Consequently, the transformation of the 4th and 7th EC-Directives and the other trends, as shown in part III of this article, are heavily discussed.

Another research field lies in analyzing the economic effects of different accounting systems on various user groups. Admittedly, the activities in this field are not as large as in the U.S. Incentives for developing an optimal macro-economic information system, like the research of Demski, has not found much attention until now. The U.K. might be an exception. The reason for this phenomenon might be the stress that is placed on the conflict-of-interest-regulating-function of the annual report in Germany and some other European countries in contrast to its information function.

One of the most important research topics in the field of economic consequences and information content of annual reports are predictive ability studies especially for business failure, and also the effect of inflation on financing the economic activities of a company. Because of the relatively small capital markets in continental Europe, research projects that ask for consequences of special accounting procedures on the capital market and its semi-strong efficiency are of minor importance.

A research field that should find a little more attention is international accounting. While German direct investment in foreign countries has been much higher than foreign investments in Germany for the past couple of years, only a few research projects have been dedicated to the accounting problems of internationally operating groups. Until now there are neither text books, monographs, nor special journals dealing with international accounting let alone chairs or special institutes at universities. There is a significant lack of synoptical expositions of accounting law and practice in Europe, though some articles have made a beginning in this area.

The harmonization of accounting in Europe through EC-Regulations may help to strengthen the understanding of the importance of international accounting. The work of Gerhard Mueller is a good basis for this new research field in Europe, too.

Notes

* The authors are very grateful to Bettina Hennig, research associate at the Ruhr-University, for drafting the translation of this manuscript.

1. Choi, F.D.S. and Mueller, G.G., *An Introduction to Multinational Accounting* (Englewood Cliffs, New Jersey: Prentice-Hall, Inc., 1978), pp. 21-46.

2. See W. Busse von Colbe, M. Lutter, (eds.), *Die Rechnungslegung in den Ländern der EG und in den USA* (1973); Institute of Chartered Accountants in England and Wales (ed.), *European Financial Reporting—1. West Germany* (1975);—2. *France* (1976);—3. *Italy* (1976);—4. *The Netherlands* (1978).

3. See for more details W. - D. Budde, "Überlegungen zur Umsetzung des True and Fair View in das deutsche Recht," in *Wirtschaftsprüfung und Wirtschafsrecht* (1980), pp. 109-35.

4. W. Busse von Colbe, "True and fair view—a German View" *Accountancy Age* (November 7, 1980).

5. See S.J. Gray, "The Impact of International Accounting Differences from a Security-Analysis Prespective: Some European Evidence" *Journal of Accounting Research* 18(1980): 69.

6. Ibid, pp. 73-74.

7. See BASF AG: *Annual Report* (1979), p.37.

8. See Otto Graf Lambsdorff, "Die Bedeutung der Aktie als Finanzierungsinstrument für die Wirtschaft," in *Zeitschrift für Unternehmens- und Gesellschaftsrecht* (1981), pp. 1-16.

9. See Comment to the Draft of the German Transformation Law 1980, p.20.

10. See e.g. S. Zeff, "The Rise of 'Economic Consequences', " *Journal of Accountancy* (Dec. 1978): 58-63.

11. According to a survey by the OECD in 15 out of 21 member states tax accounting follows more or less financial accounting rules. See OECD: International Investment and Multinational Enterprises—Accounting Practices in the OECD Member Countries, 1980.

12. See e.g. U.Leffson, *Die Grundsätze ordnungsmässiger Buchführung* (GoB), 5. ed., (1980), pp. 88-96; Moxter, A, *Bilanzlehre*, 2. ed., (1976), pp. 415-27. A similar approach can be found in the American Literature. See Ijiri, Y, *Theory of Accounting Measurement (1975), pp. X, 32-35.*

13. See W. Busse von Colbe, "The Search for Internationally Accepted Accounting Principles," *The Finnish Journal of Business* (1978): 217-19.

14. See W. S. Turley, "A Consideration of the Conceptual Issues underlying the E.E.C. Fourth Directive," University of Manchester Working Paper 8010, p. 15.

15. See the overview of the present state of the implementation process in Denmark, France, Germany, Italy, the Netherlands, and the U.K. recently given by Marlene Brown "Dramatic Changes: The EEC Fourth Directive" *The Accountant* (Feb. 5th, 1981): 136-38, and G. Gebhardt "Tendenzen in der Umsetzung der Vierten Richtlinie in das nationale Recht der EG-Mitgliedsländer" *Zeitschrift für Unternehmens- und Gesellschaftsrecht* 2(1981): (forthcoming), as well as the reports on the single member states: H.J. Block "The Effects on Accountancy Legislation in Belgium of the Fourth E C Council Directive relating to the Annual Accounts of Certain Types of Companies" *Journal UEC* 15(1980): 23-30; R. Johansen "The Effects of the 4th EEC-Directive on legislation in Denmark" *Journal UEC* 14(1979): 505-511; J. Clara, "The Repurcussions of the 4th Directive on Accounting Regulation in France" *Journal UEC* 14(1979): 502-5; R. Niehus, "The transformation of the Fourth Directive into German Law" *Journal UEC* 14(1979): 453-55; G. Bernard, "The effects of the 4th EC Directive on the presentation of accounts in Luxembourg" *Journal UEC* 14(1979): 396-402; S.A. Wessel, "The effects of the 4th EC-Directive on legislation in the Netherlands" *Journal UEC* 14(1979): 392-5; P. Rutteman, "Implementing the Fourth Directive in the U.K."

Journal UEC 15(1980): 18-22; B. Provstgaard, "Auswirkungen der 4. EG-Richtlinie auf Rechnungslegungsrecht und Rechnungslegungspraxis in Dänemark," *Die Wirtschaftsprüfung* (1981), forthcoming; C.W. Nobes, "Harmonization of Accounting within the European Communities: The Fourth Directive on Company Law," *International Journal of Accounting* 15.2(1980): 1-13.

16. See OECD: 1976 Declaration and Decisions on International Investment and Multinational Enterprises, III. Disclosure of Information; Commission on Transnational Corporations of the ECOSOC of the UN: International Standards of Accounting and Reporting for Transnational Corporations: Provisional Minimum Items for General Purpose Reporting Exposure Draft, 1976.

17. See J. Klaassen, "Die Durchführung der Vierten EG-Richtlinie in der Niederländischen Gesetzgebung," *Die Wirtschaftsprüfung* (1981), forthcoming.

18. Accounting Standards Committee (ASC), *Statement of Standard Accounting Practice No. 16: Current Cost Accounting* (1980).

19. Institut der Wirtschaftsprüfer in Deutschland e.V. (IdW): Stellungnahme HFA ²/hs "Zur Berücksichtigung der Substanzerhaltung bei der Ermittlung des Jahresergebnisses," *Die Wirtschaftsprüfung* (1975): 614-16.

20. See on the history of group accounts in Europe: R.H. Parker, "Explaining National Differences in Consolidated Accountings," *Accounting and Business Research* (Summer 1977): 203-7.

21. ASC: *Statement of Standard Accounting Practice No. 14: Group Accounts* (1978), par. 29.

22. See R. Bühner and K. Hille, "Anwendungsprobleme der Equity-Methode für die Konzernrechnungslegung in der Europäischen Gemeinschaft," *Die Wirtschaftsprüfung* (1980): 262-64.

23. See for further details and a survey of practice of consolidated statements in Germany W. Busse von Colbe and D. Ordelheide, *Konzernabschlüsse*, 3. ed., (1979), pp. 299-342.

24. "Arbeitskreis Weltabschlüsse der Schmalenbach-Gesellschaft: Aufstellung internationaler Konzernabschlüsse," *Zeitschrift für betriebswirtschaftliche Forschung*, Sonderheft 9 (1979).

25. IdW (ed.): *Die Einbeziehung ausländischer Unternehmen in den Konzernabschluß - Ergebnisse des Arbeitskreises "Weltbilanz" des IdW* (1977).

26. ASC: *Statement of Standard Accounting Practice No. 10: Statements of Source and Application of Funds* (1975).

27. See *Les Rapports Annuels des Sociétés Francaises* 1978, 1979, pp. 154-60.

28. See *"Sozial-Bilanz Heute," Empfehlungen des Arbeitskreises "Sozialbilanz-Praxis" zur aktuellen Gestaltung gesellschaftsbezogene Unternehmensrechnung* (1977).

29. See Accounting Standards Steering Committee, *The Corporate Report* (July 1975).

International Accounting Research in Japan: State-of-the-Art

KAZUO HIRAMATSU
Kwansei Gakuin University

Introduction

Accounting regulation and research in Japan have had an international heritage. Enacted in 1899, the Japanese Commercial Code, for example, was heavily influenced by German accounting regulations of that time. After World War II, revision of the Commercial Code and enactment of Japan's Securities and Exchange Law took place under the strong influence of U.S. accounting principles and practice. Accounting research in Japan has also drawn heavily on foreign accounting literature.

Despite such international underpinnings, it may be fair to say that research into the international dimensions of accounting is still at an early stage in Japan. In August 1969, the first Japanese book on international accounting was published. This, however, was simply the translation of Mueller's original monograph on the subject.[1] It was not until the latter part of the 1970s that serious studies on international accounting in Japan began to surface. In March 1978, Professor Someya published his *International Accounting*. This is the first book of its nature ever published in Japan by a Japanese scholar. In October of that same year, a collection of papers was published with the title, *Studies on the Internationalization of Accounting*. Edited by Professor Kazuo Mizoguchi, the anthology demonstrates the growing interest in international accounting among academic circles in Japan. Another publication entitled *International Accounting Standards*, edited by Professor Seigo Nakajima, is in preparation to be published soon. The appearance of this book in a sense signals the diffusion of interest in international accounting.

The purpose of this essay is to provide some insights as to the state-of-the-art of international accounting research in Japan. To this end data will be provided with respect to: 1) the increasing number of publications on international accounting, 2) major topics of interest, 3) leading scholars specializing in the international dimensions of accounting, and 4) key Japanese literature on international accounting. The characteristics of Japanese accounting research will then be summarized, followed by future research avenues.

The reader may have noticed that the term "international accounting" is used in this paper rather than "multinational accounting." This is because "international accounting" is used more often and the distinction between these two terms is not clear in Japan.

Increase in International Accounting Research in the 1970s

To give the reader a feel for the trend of international accounting research in Japan, I first made a survey as to the number of publications in accounting, in general, and in the area of international accounting in particular, for the most recent ten years. The "Monthly Report on Economic Literature," which is included in a journal entitled *Keizai Hyoron* (*Economic Review*), was used for this survey. Prepared by the Research Institute of Economics at Osaka City University, it covers articles from over 700 journals and books which are associated with the field of economics in a broad sense. The publications are classified into sixteen categories, with "accounting" as one of the sixteen. Table 1 summarizes the total number of accounting publications, the number of publications on international accounting, and its percentage of the total number for each year.

Although the *total* number of accounting publications for the last five years increased over the number for the first five years, it cannot be generalized on a year-to-year basis. On the other hand, the number of

Table 1.   Increase of Publications on International Accounting

	'70	'71	'72	'73	'74	'75	'76	'77	'78	'79	'80*	Total
Total Number of Accounting Publications	614	615	697	638	620	749	672	793	746	729	659	7532
Number of Publications on International Accounting	30	31	69	35	42	43	59	73	95	112	79	668
Percentage	4.9	5.0	9.9	5.5	6.8	5.7	8.8	9.2	12.7	15.7	12.0	8.9

*The numbers in 1980 are for the first eight months only.

publications on international accounting has increased steadily with only one exception (1972-73). In the early '70s, the number of international accounting publications per year was 30-40 (except 1972). Recently it has exceeded 100. In terms of percentage changes, international accounting publications was approximately 5% of the total compared to its present 10 percent. From this simple evidence, it can be seen that research on international accounting in Japan has increased considerably during the 1970s.

Needless to say, such observations are subject to limitations inherent in the methodological procedures of the survey. Major characteristics of the survey are presented below.

1. With regard to *total* number of accounting publications:
   a) It is the sum of the numbers of publications which were classified as accounting in "The Monthly Report."
   b) Different types of publications are included in "The Monthly Report"; books, articles, translations of foreign books and the records of discussions, etc. A book was counted as 'one,' even if it was a collection of several articles. Of all types of publications, articles were predominant in number.
   c) Determination of publication datelines was based upon the month and the year of each issue of *Keizai Hyoron* as opposed to the accounting publications original dateline. The difference between these two points of time was generally four to five months.
   d) Some non-accounting literature seemed to be classified as accounting in "The Monthly Report" and *vice versa*. No adjustment was made to avoid personal biases.
   e) *The Accounting Journal,* an important practical journal edited by the Japanese Institute of CPAs (like *The Journal of Accountancy*), had not been included in "The Monthly Report" until recently. Again, no adjustment was made since it could be judged that there was no significant change in the general result of the survey regardless of its inclusion.

2. With regard to number of publications on international accounting:
   a) The selection of the publications on international accounting was made by personal judgment, based solely on titles of the publications.
   b) The term "international accounting" is taken broadly to include comparative accounting as well as technical issues inherent in international accounting.

c) Even if a publication dealt with foreign accounting practice, it was eliminated in case it was too historic. Publications dealing with accounting theories espoused in foreign countries were also eliminated.

Major Topics of International Accounting Research in Japan

Six hundred sixty-eight publications on international accounting were classified based upon topical research. This classification procedure involved two subjective steps; namely, deciding 1) which criterion to use for distinguishing between broad research topics, and 2) how to fit given publications into these topical categories. I first broadly classified research areas into three categories: 1) technical issues inherent in international accounting, 2) international comparisons of accounting, and 3) introduction/explanation of foreign accounting regulations and practice. Each of these categories was then further subdivided as shown in table 2.

From table 2, the following points can be made.

1. Publications which introduce or explain foreign accounting are predominant in number. They acount for 71 percent or 477 out of the total of 668. Publications of this nature are still increasing.

2. In terms of introductory/explanatory publications, the United States is the country that is referred to most often, followed by France, West Germany, and the United Kingdom. In general, accounting in Europe and America is treated more frequently than accounting in Asia.

3. Studies on international comparisons or comparative accounting are relatively small in number. In the case of comparisons between Japan and a foreign country, U.S.-Japan comparisons predominate.

4. Publications which directly deal with technical issues account for approximately twenty-five percent of the total number. Most relate to financial accounting issues. Few are devoted to managerial accounting issues.

5. In terms of financial accounting issues, major topics include foreign currency translation and unification or harmonization of international accounting standards. Studies on international auditing are still limited. The number of publications on foreign currency translation is larger in 1972 and 1979. This is due to the issuance of accounting

Table 2. Major Topics of International Accounting Research in Japan

	'70	'71	'72	'73	'74	'75	'76	'77	'78	'79	'80	Total
Total Number of Each Year	30	31	69	35	42	43	59	73	95	112	79	668
I. Technical issues inherent in international accounting												
A. International accounting in general	4	1	1	1	1	2		1	3	1		15
B. Financial accounting issues												
1. Foreign currency translation	3	1	26	7	4	4	3	2	8	30	4	92
2. Unification of international accounting regulations (including IAS)		1		1	3	9	2	3	7	3		29
3. Disclosure by international companies		2		4				3	1	2	4	16
4. International auditing									1	1		2
C. Managerial accounting issues												
1. Performance evaluation										1		1
2. International transfer pricing												0
3. International taxation			1		1							2
D. Other issues												
1. Consolidation					4		2	2		1	1	10
2. Survey of accounting for foreign transactions					1							1
Subtotal (1)	7	5	28	18	9	17	7	9	20	39	9	168
II. International comparison of accounting												
1. Comparative accounting in general	1		1					2		1	1	6
2. International patterns of accounting		3		1	2							6
3. Comparison between Japan and a foreign country	1	1				2	1			3	3	11
Subtotal (II)	2	4	1	1	2	2	1	2	0	4	4	23

Table 2. (continued)

	'70	'71	'72	'73	'74	'75	'76	'77	'78	'79	'80	Total
III. Introduction/Explanation of foreign accounting regulations and practice												
1. Several nations	1	1	2		1	2	2	4	4	3	3	23
2. U.S.A.	8	3	13	6	11	8	18	16	32	20	22	157
3. Canada		1		1	1				1			4
4. E C				1	4	1	3	4	2	2	2	19
5. United Kingdom	2	1	4		2	3	2	8	9	8	13	52
6. Federal Republic of Germany (West Germany)	2	11	12	5	4	4	7	7	5	15	2	74
7. France	5	4	5	1	4	2	10	11	13	11	17	83
8. The Netherlands			1		1		1	1		1	1	6
9. Switzerland						2						2
10. Belgium							1		1			2
11. Sweden				1								1
12. Norway									1			1
13. Spain								1				1
14. Mexico		1						3	2	2		8
15. Argentina					2				1			3
16. Brazil			1			2	1	2		1	1	8
17. Australia	2		1						2	2	1	8
18. Republic of Korea									1	1	2	4
19. Republic of China (Taiwan)							2					2
20. Egypt					1							1
21. German Democratic Republic (East Germany)	1							2				3
22. U.S.S.R.			1		1	1	1	3	2		1	10
21. People's Republic of China				1			1			1	1	4
Subtotal (III)	21	22	40	16	31	24	51	62	75	69	66	477

standards on translation by the Business Accounting Deliberation Council of the Ministry of Finance during these years.[2]

Japanese Scholars of International Accounting

At the present time, there are not many scholars in Japan specializing in international accounting. Rather, those scholars who are already well established in other accounting areas are playing important roles as pioneers and leaders in studies dealing with the international dimension.

The 668 publications on international accounting were classified again by author(s) to identify the leading Japanese scholars in the field. The number of sole authors totaled 238. Table 3 lists sixteen scholars with eight or more publications in the area during the observation period.[3] Major areas of interest of each author are also shown in table 3. These areas of interest were tentatively determined by examining the titles of their publications. Determining the areas of interest of each scholar in such a manner might not be appropriate. It should be viewed as suggestive only.

Each scholar generally has his or her own research area which is characterized by a specific country or a geographic area. Some scholars further specialize in certain topics within a given national framework. There are several scholars who study major technical issues of international accounting. It might be proper to call them international accounting specialists. They are Professors Someya, Kuroda, Nakajima, and Shiratori. In fact, they are well-known for their research efforts in the area of international accounting. Further, Professors Kaneko and Arai often deal with technical issues. Professor Kurosawa has many publications in this area. This is by no means due to his specialization only in international accounting but mainly because of his status as the former chairman of the Business Accounting Deliberation Council and as the former president of the Japan Accounting Association.

Key Japanese Literature on International Accounting

Not many Japanese books are available in the area of international accounting. Four pioneering books are introduced first. Six books of practical import and three additional academic works on foreign accounting or tax systems will then be briefly examined. Although these books are by no means exhaustive, they represent most of the important ones now available in Japan.

Table 3. List of Scholars with Eight or More Publications on International Accounting

Name	University	Number of Publications	Research Area
Arai, Kiyomitsu	Waseda U.	8	translation, U.S.A.
Iioka, Toru	Komazawa U.	12	U.S.A., U.K.
Kaneko, Shunzo	Hosei U.	8	internationalization, translation, consolidation
Kato, Yasuhiko	Konan U.	9	auditing in West Germany
Kuroda, Masatoshi	Kobe U.	15	international accounting in general
Kurosawa, Kiyoshi	Dokkyo U. (Emer., Yokohama National U.)	14	translation, IASC
Morikawa, Yasuo	Meiji U.	25	Europe
Murakami, Jin-ichiro	Ryukoku U.	11	social accounting in France
Nakagawa, Misako	Kanto Gakuin U.	30	Latin America, comparative accounting
Nakajima, Seigo	International Christian U.	10	IASC, comparative accounting
Nomura, Kentaro	Kobe U. of Commerce	27	France
Nishikawa, Yoshio	Tokyo U. of Economics	8	public utility accounting in U.S.A.
Otaka, Yoshizumi	Nanzan U.	10	translation, Asia
Shiratori, Shonosuke	Seijo U.	10	translation, inflation accounting
Someya, Kyojiro	Waseda U.	12	international accounting in general
Tachibana, Tokuo	Aichi Gakuin U.	9	West Germany

Four Most Important Books

Kyojiro Someya (Waseda University), ed., *Internationalization of Economy and Contemporary Accounting—The Way to International Accounting,* Tokyo: Chuo Keizai Sha, 1970, 230 pp.

This is the first book published in Japan that directly deals with the problems of international accounting, and is thus a pioneering work in the development of international accounting research in Japan. It explains major problems of international aspects of accounting which became important with the internationalization of the Japanese economy. Under the editorship of Professor Someya, the book was written by ten scholars who were deemed to be the most qualified for each topic at the time. Following is the title and author of each chapter.

Introduction: Advent of International Accounting (Prof. Kyojiro Someya, Waseda University)

    Part I.   Accounting for International Business Operations
1.   Consolidation of Financial Statements of Foreign Companies (Prof. Shonosuke Shiratori, Seijo University)
2.   Financial Reporting of Oversea Operations to Management (Prof. Osamu Nishizawa, Waseda University)
3.   Financial Reporting of Joint Venture Under Inflationary Conditions (Prof. Kichinosuke Takahashi, Keio University)

    Part II.   Differences of Accounting and Auditing Among Countries
1.   Differences of Accounting Theory and Practice (Prof. Fujio Inagaki, Chuo University)
2.   Differences of Financial Statement Audit (Prof. Yoichi Kusakabe, Waseda University)

    Part III.   International Accounting and Auditing Standards
1.   Expectations of International Accounting and Auditing Standards (Prof. Akira Wakasugi, Yokohama National University)
2.   Problems of International Tax Accounting (Prof. Ryuji Takeda, Kobe University)

Supplement I. The Problem of Selecting a Basic Currency in International Enterprises (Prof. Kazuo Morito, Meiji Gakuin University)
Supplement II. Development of International Accounting Research in the United States (Prof. Yukio Fujita, Waseda University)

Kyojiro Someya (Waseda University), *International Accounting—A New Area of Business Accounting,* Tokyo: Chuo Keizai Sha, 1978, 254 pp.

This is the first and the only book ever published in Japan by a single Japanese scholar with the title "International Accounting." It includes research results published by Professor Someya for the last ten years. Major topics covered are the background of the advent of international accounting and its problems, accounting for fluctuating foreign exchange rates, comparative study of financial statements, international accounting standards, and the survey results of accounting for foreign transactions of Japanese corporations. The title of each chapter is:

1. Development of International Accounting in the 1960's
2. Economic Internationalization and Accounting
3. Currency as the Accounting Unit of Measure
4. Exchange Rate Fluctuations and Accounting
5. Accounting Problems of Foreign Currency Translation
6. A Comparative Study of Financial Statements in Six Nations—U.S.A., U.K. and West Germany
7. A Comparative Study of Financial Statements in Six Nations (Continued)—France, Canada and Australia
8. International Patterns of Financial Statements
9. Annual Reports to Foreign Stockholders
10. International Accounting Standards
11. A Survey of Accounting Aspects of Foreign Operations of Japanese Large Corporations

Kazuo Mizoguchi (Kobe University), ed., *Studies on Internationalization of Accounting,* Tokyo: Chuo Keizai Sha, 1978, 364 pp.

The Committee on Internationalization of Accounting was formed by thirty-six representative Japanese accounting scholars, Professor Mizoguchi being the chairman. The activities of the committee were subsidized by the Ministry of Education. Twenty-three papers which directly or indirectly deal with international aspects of accounting were submitted by the members of the Committee to be published in this anthology. Its publication has added a significant dimension to the development of international accounting research in Japan in that it was the result of a collaborative effort by Japanese accounting academicians. The title and the author of each chapter is:

Part I. International Unification of Accounting Standards

1. Revolution of Paradigms in the History of Accounting Thought (Prof. Kiyoshi Kurosawa, Emer., Yokohama National University)
2. International Accounting Standards and the Japanese Business Accounting System (Prof. Seigo Nakajima, International Christian University)
3. An Examination of International Accounting Standards No. 2 (Prof. Naomi Tsumagari, Tokyo University)
4. Structural Analysis of Price Level Change "Financial Information" in International Accounting Standards No. 6 (Prof. Ichiro Katano, Emer., Hitotsubashi University)
5. Harmonization of Regulations on Corporate Financial Reporting in the EEC (Prof. Masatoshi Kuroda, Kobe University)

Part II. Accounting Problems Caused by the Internationalization of Business Operations

6. Reports of the Committee on International Accounting of AAA (Prof. Shigeo Aoki, Waseda University)
7. Financial Reporting by Multinational Enterprises (Prof. Masatoshi Kuroda, Kobe University)
8. Social Disclosure by Multinational Enterprises (Prof. Hiroshi Yoshida, Kobe University of Commerce)
9. Accounting Rules for Consolidation of the U.S. Securities and Exchange Commission (Prof. Ryuji Takeda, Kobe University)
10. Problems of Accounting for Exchange Rate Fluctuations—An Interpretation (Prof. Shonosuke Shiratori)

Part III. International Trend of Financial Accounting Systems
11. Two Systems of Inflation Accounting (Prof. Kaichiro Bamba, Emer., Hitotsubashi University)
12. Forms of Price Level Accounting and Its Trend in Several Nations (Prof. Kiyomitsu Arai, Waseda University)
13. Trend of Annual Reports in the United States (Prof. Hirohisa Masutani, Kwansei Gakuin University)
14. The Accounting Disclosure System in France (Prof. Kaichi Kiuchi, Matsuyama University of Commerce)
15. Formation of Corporate Social Accounting and Its Trend in the United States (Prof. Yasuichi Sakamoto, Emer., Kobe University of Commerce)
16. Trend of Corporate Social Accounting—A Critical Perspective (Prof. Kenji Aizaki, Yokohama National University)
17. An Epitome of Accountants and Its Trend in West Germany (Prof. Masaatsu Takada, Kobe University)

Part IV. International Trend of Management Accounting Systems
18. The Trend of Controllership in the United States (Prof. Kazuo Mizoguchi, Kobe University)
19. The Trend of Management Accounting Theory in the United States (Prof. Kiyoshi Okamoto, Hitotsubashi University)
20. The Trend of Productivity Analysis in the United States (Prof. Tatsundo Yamagami, Osaka City University)
21. The Trend of Optimal Fund Management Theory—With an Emphasis on the Literature in the U.S. and West Germany (Prof. Yukio Goto, Kobe University of Commerce)
22. The Trend of Long Range Business Planning in West Germany (Prof. Masaaki Miyamoto, Osaka University)
23. The Trend of Cost Accounting Theory in West Germany (Prof. Tetsuo Kobayashi, Kobe University)

Seigo Nakajima (International Christian University), ed. *International Accounting Standards,* Tokyo: Chuo Keizai Sha, 1980, 320 pp.

To celebrate its thirtieth anniversary, Chuo Keizai Sha, one of the major publishers of accounting literature in Japan, is now publishing a series of fourteen books on accounting which cover most of the important areas of contemporary accounting and are edited and written by leading accounting scholars. This volume, *International Accounting Standards,* edited by Professor Nakajima, is to be published soon as one of these fourteen books. Chuo Keizai Sha had published the same types of books for its tenth and twentieth anniversaries, respectively. However, this is the first time that a volume devoted to international aspects of accounting is included in the series. It shows that the importance of international accounting has now come to be widely recognized. The title and the author of each chapter are:

Introduction: Necessity of International Accounting Standards and Its Difficulty (Prof. Seigo Nakajima, International Christian University)

Comparative Accounting System
1. An Introduction to Comparative Accounting Systems (Prof. Seigo Nakajima)
2. Accounting Systems in the United Kingdom (Prof. Kiyomitsu Arai, Waseda University)
3. Accounting Systems in West Germany and the Netherlands (Prof. Akira Wakasugi, Yokohama National University)
4. Accounting Systems in France (Prof. Osamu Aoki, Nagoya Industrial University)
5. Accounting Systems in North America (Prof. Morihiro Kato, Doshisha University)
6. Accounting Systems in Latin America (Prof. Misako Nakagawa, Kanto Gakuin University)
7. Accounting Systems in Asia and the Pacific (Prof. Seigo Nakajima)
8. Possibility of the Establishment of International Accounting Standards and Its Direction (Prof. Seigo Nakajima)

Foundation of IASC and Its Activities
9. Foundation of IASC and Its Circumstances (Prof. Shozo Tatsumi, Soka University)
10. Activities of IASC (Prof. Jun-ichi Kawaguchi, Senshu University)

Practical Guides

The Japan Development Bank, Research Institute of Capital Formation, ed., *Case Study: Business Accounting of Foreign Countries,* Tokyo: Nippon Keizai Shimbun Sha, 1971, 464 pp.

The Japan Development Bank performed a series of basic research with the purpose of developing a data bank of international financial information. This book is a pioneering work which compiled part of the research results on foreign accounting. It explains regulations on financial statements, shows real examples of financial statements, and refers to issues of business accounting for each of the six nations: U.S.A., U.K., Canada, France, West Germany, and the Netherlands.

Fumio Takagi, ed., *Accounting and Taxation for Overseas Transactions* (Revised Ed.), Osaka: Seibun Sha, 1979, 627 pp., & *Accounting and Taxation for Overseas Operations* (Revised Ed.), Osaka: Seibun Sha, 1979, 849 pp.

These two big volumes are the most comprehensive practical guides on accounting and taxation for overseas business. Major topics are: accounting and taxation for imports and exports, foreign investment, introduction of foreign capital, transfer pricing, tax havens, foreign subsidiaries, foreign branches, etc. Emphasis is placed on tax issues. Most of the authors are practitioners.

Yoshiaki Komatsu, *Tax Systems of Various Countries* (Fifth Ed.), Tokyo: Zaikei Shoho Sha, 1980, 1100 pp.

Recent movements in the elimination of double taxation, regulations on transfer pricing, and policies against tax havens were the reasons for the fifth edition of this book. It covers tax systems of 30 countries. Since its first edition (1967), it has been an important information source for researchers as well as for practitioners.

JICPA, Tokyo Chapter, ed., *International Financial Statements*, Tokyo: Toyo Keizai Shimpo Sha, 1976, 363 pp.

Daiichi Audit Corporation, *How to Prepare International Financial Statements*, Tokyo: Chuo Keizai Sha, 1979, 258 pp.

Deloitte, Haskins & Sells, *Introduction to International Financial Statements*, Tokyo, Zaimu Kenkyukai Shuppan Kyoku, 1979, 256 pp.

Each of the above three books explains U.S. accounting regulations and disclosure systems from a practical point of view and thus offers guidelines for the preparation of international (U.S.) financial statements. Differences between U.S. and Japanese accounting systems are also explained.

Other Academic Books

Osamu Aoki, *The French Accounting System*, Tokyo: Moriyama Shoten, 1977, 254 pp.

With the understanding that French accounting will mature by the establishment of the new Plan Comptable and the value added accounting system, the author studies the French accounting system mainly focusing on the process of the development of value added accounting.

Mitsuru Mashita, *Soviet Accounting,* Tokyo: Mirai Sha, 1975, 396 pp.

Soviet accounting is in principle restricted by the economic laws of socialism and by the self-supporting system of planned management. With such recognition, the book deals with the object, problems, methods, systems, and characteristics of Soviet accounting.

Misako Nakagawa, *Studies on New Business Accounting Systems in Brazil,* Tokyo: Kokusai Shojiho Kenkyu Sho, 1980, 180 pp.

Corporation Law in Brazil was revised in 1976 to include certain regulations for inflation. In 1977 the Income Tax Law was also revised. This book explains the new accounting system in Brazil. Its main contents are: Financial Statements Under the New Corporation Law, Accounting Regulations by the Income Tax Law, Financial Statements of Listed Companies and Auditing Systems.

Problems and Prospects of International Accounting Research in Japan

As mentioned previously, research on international accounting in Japan has increased throughout the 1970s. Leading scholars in this area are generally financial accounting specialists. Professors Someya, Kuroda, Nakajima, and Shiratori all possess strong backgrounds in financial accounting. This is also the case with practitioners. The JICPA has been playing a central role in this area, especially with respect to international accounting standards. Thus, as pointed out by Professor Shigeo Aoki of Waseda University, president of the Japan Accounting Association, studies on management aspects of international accounting are lagging behind both among academicians and practitioners.[4] It is, therefore, expected that management accounting scholars as well as business firms will contribute to the development of international accounting research in Japan.

As to future research avenues, it was indicated that the introductory/explanatory publications of foreign accounting were predominant in number, especially those of Europe and the United States. Taking into account Japan's status and role in Asia, it will soon become urgent to further study Asian accounting systems and practice. Within the technical issues inherent in international accounting, again, financial accounting issues were treated more often, while less attention has been given to issues of management accounting, tax, or auditing. These areas should be developed further. The problem of the teaching of international accounting should also be discussed more.

What then are the characteristics and problems of research methodology? Even when the technical issues inherent in international accounting are dealt with, many publications develop inferences based upon descriptions of foreign literature. Often cited are *International Accounting* by Professor G. G. Mueller and Reports of the Committee on International Accounting of the American Accounting Association. And in case international accounting standards are treated, they are for the most part explanatory descriptions of the content or background of the Standards. There have been very few research type publications in the sense of empirical research with hypothesis testing or survey research in relation to Japanese business firms. It is well recognized that the descriptive and/or comparative data are of prime importance for research purposes. But in the near future, more empirical studies should also take place.

Research on international accounting in Japan in the 1980s presents many challenges. However, one thing is clear. The 1980s certainly will be a decade witnessing the advancement of international accounting in Japan.

Notes

1. Gerhard G. Mueller, *International Accounting* (New York: The Macmillan Company, 1967). (Japanese translation) Shunzo Kaneko and International Accounting Study Group, *Kokusai Kaikei Ron* (Tokyo: Perikan Sha, 1969).

2. At these times, the Business Accounting Deliberation Council of the Ministry of Finance issued the following opinion and standards, respectively: "Opinion on Accounting Treatment of Foreign Assets, and so forth, Under the Existing Foreign Exchange System" (July 7, 1972); and "Accounting Standards on Foreign Currency Translation, and so forth" (June 26, 1979). The latter is effective today.

3. In addition to these individuals, the Management Accounting Study Group of Kobe University (Prof. Kazuo Mizoguchi and others) published a series of thirteen papers on the Cost Accounting Standards Board of the United States.

4. Shigeo Aoki, "Problems of International Accounting," *Kaikei*, III. 3 (March 1977): 1-16.

Research in Accounting: A North American Overview

DONALD A. CORBIN
University of Hawaii

Introduction

The outlook for new research projects to aid policy setters in North America is bright. This applies to both a priori and empirical research. Policy setters, such as the Financial Accounting Standards Board (FASB) in the U.S. and the Accounting Research Committee (ARC) of the Canadian Institute of Chartered Accountants (CICA) in Canada, have a great need for research, especially in controversial problem areas: first, for background facts and concepts; then, for choosing among alternatives, in terms of objectives, consistency, and consequences; and finally, for ammunition to persuade dissenters to go along with given choices.

Regarding research and policy in the two countries, several clarifications are in order. In Canada the title of the ARC, the equivalent standard-setting body of the FASB, is a misnomer. The ARC is not a research body. It uses research studies commissioned by the CICA's Research Department to aid in policy decisions. Up to June 18, 1980, the CICA has issued twenty-five research studies in its published series. The ARC is responsible for issuance of Accounting Recommendations for inclusion in the *CICA Handbook*. The *Handbook* is equivalent to the FASB's statements of Accounting Standards.

Further differences exist. The ARC is a committee of the profession, whereas the FASB is an independent body. As to enforcement power, Accounting Recommendations of the ARC have the force of law, under the provisions of the Canada Business Corporation Act; whereas the FASB has primarily only the power of "general acceptance" by the profession and the business community. In the U.S., the Securities and Exchange Commission (SEC) has the legal power to set accounting standards, but has extended this power at present to the FASB in the private sector. To December 1980, the FASB has issued forty-four standards. Its research department commissions ad hoc studies, but no series is published.

In the discussion which follows regarding research and policy setting, most of the illustrations will come from U.S. experience. This is not due to bias, but because of this writer's limited geographical knowledge. Fortunately, it appears that both countries have had similar experiences: research on the same topics and dissatisfaction in similar areas, such as the lack of a conceptual framework, poor inflation disclosures, leases, pensions, deferred taxes, and foreign currency translation, to name only a few. Both also have come to recognize the problems of politicization of the standard setting process.

Although challenging research projects abound today, if the U.S. past may be used as a guide, the outlook for research having great impact on standard setters is not exceptionally bright—but the climate is improving. Both the Accounting Principles Board (APB) during its tenure, (1959-1973) and the FASB (1973-present) seemingly ignored much of their own sponsored research. They did, however, give growing lip service to empirical research of academia, especially in finance related areas such as portfolio theory, the efficient market hypothesis and discounted cash flow theory. More recently, concern with the "economic consequences" of a new accounting standard, and the new "Statement of Accounting Concepts" series of the FASB have elicited a rash of new sponsored research.

Earlier sections of this book have already treated many aspects of research. In this section on North America we shall review briefly policy making and related research in the area of financial accounting. First, recent history will be highlighted to examine some "hot issues" faced by the APB, the FASB, and the SEC in the U.S. This will be followed by some suggestions for future research, both in Canada and the U.S.

Accounting Principles Board Era (1959-1973)

The APB served as a board of the American Institute of CPAs. Among its most important charges at its inception were the "narrowing of alternative methods in practice" and "the development of a broad set of accounting principles." The members of the APB were part-time, with a director of Research who commissioned fifteen Accounting Research Studies between 1961 and 1973. The first was Maurice Moonitz's "The Basic Postulates of Accounting." Also in 1961 Perry Mason authored APBO No. 2, "Cash Flow Analysis and the Funds Statement." These two were followed by No. 3 in 1962 by Robert Sprouse and Maurice Moonitz, "A Tentative Set of Broad Accounting Principles for Business Enterprises."

The APB's use of these first three research studies may be characterized as neglect and rejection. The "Postulates" were ignored, the "Funds Statement" recommendations were not adopted, and the "Principles" were explicitly *not* accepted in 1962 in APB Statement No. 1. It characterized them as ". . . too radically different from present generally accepted accounting principles for acceptance at this time. . . ." (The principles had stated that accounting data included, past, present, and future prices.)

Several observations on this important bit of history are appropriate before proceeding. First, as most readers know, the APB was considered unsatisfactory and was replaced by the FASB in 1973. Many explanations of its failure have been offered, such as subservience to clients' and SEC pressures, part-timers, lack of regard for the views of all concerned members of society, and ignoring economic consequences. Another important factor, often slighted, was undoubtedly the failure to build on this early normative research to develop an improved theory of accounting—a set of logically integrated principles. When expressed, this type of objection rather has been in terms of the board's preoccupation with putting out "brush fires" (ad hoc compromise solutions); but the important point may have been the board's failure to meet its original missions. Recent counter arguments proclaim the impossibility of developing a grand theory of accounting. Economic reality is believed to be too elusive to prescribe, especially since user's decision models are not known.

In the U.S., these types of arguments have led to two clearly discernable approaches. One school argues against developing improved principles and champions empirical, positive research to discover the behavioral, financial, economic, communications, political, etc. aspects of policy-setting. The research results would then somehow reveal the appropriate accounting policies, feasible for practice. The other school argues for both more a priori and empirical research, in order to develop an improved set of tested accounting principles. These would then serve as guides, both for judging and improving current practice and for solving future (unknown) accounting problems as they arise.

In effect, it appears that the latter approach is the one now being followed by the FASB in its many faceted "Conceptual Framework" project. (This project includes objectives of accounting; qualitative characteristics of accounting information; elements of financial statements; recognition criteria; measurement; reporting earnings; funds flows, liquidity and financial flexibility; and financial statements). In many respects the project is an enlarged repeat of Sprouse and Moonitz's work on principles. It differs, however, in that much has been learned about the politics of policy-setting in the intervening decades. The FASB has cleverly disassociated the conceptual project from its accounting standards. It has set up a new "Concepts" series, which the board gradually will use as fundamentals upon which to base standards. Inconsistencies between current standards and the concepts will be handled "in due course." Thus, the process of improvement and change is to be evolutionary—similar to the one recommended for the Canadian ARC (and believed to be the present approach in Canada) by Edward Stamp in his 1980 CICA research study "Corporate Reporting: Its Future Evolution." The FASB approach hopes to forestall immediate rejection of new concepts as being "too revolutionary"—the fate of Sprouse and Moonitz.

Returning to opponents of the principles (now called concepts and standards) approach, one group relies on the results of "efficient market" research. There has been strong evidence (recently weakened somewhat by contrary research) that the aggregate stock market impounds all public information rapidly and unbiasedly in stock prices. As a consequence, one of the researches, William Beaver concluded that *full disclosure* is the main criterion for reporting. Others have gone further and concluded that it does not make any difference what principles are followed in the basic statements, as long as alternative information is also disclosed. Many studies have confirmed that the market is not fooled by accounting changes; so it is concluded, for example, that it makes no difference whether FIFO or LIFO (or straight-line or accelerated depreciation) is the standard, as long as the counterpart is disclosed. Contrarians argue, however, that it *does* make a difference. In the Platonic ideal sense, one method *is* preferable to another. Further, a completely different method may be even more preferable; and giving up, as it were, may preclude the discovery of the best solution. In his Canadian research report Stamp went further: others besides investors use financial reports, the market may be efficiently impounding *mis*information, and full disclosure may lead to overload and unsuitable reports for users.

This writer concludes that research and arguments regarding efficient markets is far from over and that its importance in accounting has been grossly overstated.

In the above observations, the reader may have noticed a somewhat loose, interchangeable use of the words principles and standards. In the U.S. this comes about primarily from a subtle change, hardly noticed and seldom mentioned. The accountant's report (clean certificate) states ". . . fairly presented in accordance with generally accepted accounting *principles*. . . ." The APB was charged with developing these principles.

When it failed, it was replaced by the FASB, which now issues FASB Statements of Accounting *Standards*. The certificate still says "principles." (To make matters worse, the auditing standards of reporting of the AICPA state that "principles" include *"methods"* of application). Thus, in the U.S., we now have certification to principles of accounting which are codified as standards (standards may be high or low, incidentally); without any specification of this change in wording. A present move by the AICPA to modify the wording of the accountant's report may clarify this anamoly.

A final observation on the early research for the APB will be made. Failure to follow the implications of its own early research studies seems to have set the pattern for much of the ensuing work of the APB. The full fifteen research studies and thirty-one opinions are too numerous to detail, so only a few will be reviewed to illustrate this point.

The research studies typically grew out of critical problem areas which had arisen in practice. Examples are accounting for business combinations and reporting the effects of price-level changes in 1963, accounting for the cost of pension plans in 1964, interperiod income tax allocation in 1965, financial reporting in the extractive industries in 1969, reporting foreign operations in 1972, and accounting for research and development cost in 1973. Each of these had been preceded by difficulties or criticisms of accounting reports. In the merger era, conglomerates which used the pooling method were showing "instant earnings" and were able to by-pass amortization of purchased goodwill. As price-levels rose, businesses were believed to be reporting phantom operating profits and omitting real holding and debtor gains during inflation. Companies with huge pension liabilities using the cash basis of accounting for pensions were able to avoid showing either the expense or the liability for pensions. Shortages of energy and the OPEC oil price increases brought alternative oil and gas accounting methods into question. The rise of multinational firms and fluctuating currency values brought about concern with foreign exchange translation. Business failures of companies which had large capitalized research costs causes reconsiderations of accounting methods for R&D.

Before tackling these problems, the APB prudently commissioned research. Much of the research involved literature review and a priori reasoning; only a small part was empirical. However, the empirical research of academia on these topics during this period seems to have had little noticeable effect on the opinions issued by the board; although research methodology greatly improved.

Additionally, in most of the problem areas cited above, the board countered the recommendations of its researchers in their final opinions.

(As will be discussed in the next section, one of the consequences of this was the *re*consideration later and modification of most of these opinions by the FASB). Examples follow.

In his research on business combinations, Arthur Wyatt made recommendations which would have precluded most poolings, but APB No. 16 ended with a loose compromise, permitting both pooling and purchase accounting. The APB research staff recommended required disclosure of price-level changes in annual reports but no APB opinion was forthcoming. The research on pensions greatly aided the APB for opinion No. 8, but the pension *liability* problem was not fully solved for past service costs.

Income tax allocation proved an exception—APBO No. 11 coincided fairly well with the research. No opinions were issued following the research on oil and gas, on reporting foreign operations (foreign currency translation) or on R&D. These were areas undertaken later by the FASB.

Since most of the important areas covered by APB opinions were (or are) being re-examined by the FASB, they will not be reviewed at this point. Instead we shall end the APB era on one topic for which the APB had no research. This was the investment credit controversy. It came about early in 1962. A new tax law had allowed an income tax credit for investments in qualifying property. Was the credit a reduction in tax expense, a reduction in the asset's cost, or a deferred credit (liability)? Without the benefit of research or a set of principles defining expense, asset or liability, the APB, in a split decision, decided to defer the investment credit; rather than reducing expense immediately. Some believed this violated the intent of the law; the SEC permitted either; and several Big Eight CPA firms bolted, using the "credit to expense" method. Not receiving general acceptance, and having no authority to impose its principle, the board backed down and permitted either method in APBO No. 4. In a scathing dissent M. Moonitz, then a board member, chastised the majority for having contradictory principles. Later the board tried once again to assert its "deferred credit" method (also questioned by Moonitz for being an item appearing in the liability section of the balance sheet which is not an obligation); but this time the U.S. Congress passed a law permitting either method of accounting. Politics had entered in full force and the opposing lobbies had succeeded.

In spite of its "unprincipled" solution to the investment credit controversy, the APB was able to survive for another full decade.

Financial Accounting Standards Board Era (1973-present)

The era of the FASB, although short, has been one of increasing activity. Both in public exposure and written pronouncements (FASB Statements of Financial Accounting Standards) (FAS), the volume has increased. Through December 1980, forty-four standards and almost as many interpretations have been issued. The increased number of reporting requirements has resulted in what some critics call "information overload." Others have complained that accounting in the U.S. has become overly legalistic. The profession's expertise partially rests on the ability to search for the proper rules. Professional judgment is being seriously weakened. Alternatively, some fear that the results could be, as Edward Stamp observed regarding a possible approach to the Canadian *Handbook*: "if it is not in the *Handbook*, anything goes."

Because of their large number, no attempt will be made here to review all of the controversies and related research during the FASB era. Instead a few "hot topics" will be selected. As background information, it should be noted that when the FASB took office in 1973, it decided to retain all prior principles of the APB until the board had time to reconsider unsettled problems.

First, let us examine an area not satisfactorily handled by the APB, lease accounting. It involves the questions of "off-balance-sheet financing" and "what is a liability." The topic was purposely omitted in the previous section on the APB (although it is the clearest example of the APB ignoring its own research study), because the FASB felt compelled to redo the APB opinion, still ignored the previous research, and after issuing several standards on various aspects of leases, as well as several related interpretations, it finally issued a booklet over 140 pages long to describe the latest rules.

In an interview in a national magazine only last year, Arthur Wyatt, partner of a Big-Eight CPA firm, described the latest rules on capitalizing leases as "easy to beat" by lessees so as to still accomplish off-balance-sheet financing.

It may be that if attention had been paid to the original APB Research Study No. 4 on reporting of leases by John Myers in 1962 (which recommended showing the present value of both the asset and the liability whenever property rights were exchanged) many man hours and many volumes of paper work could have been avoided. The whole story for lessee accounting would probably have fit on a few pages and the requirements would not be "easy to beat."

So unsatisfactory were the APB principles for lease accounting in the view of the SEC, it felt compelled to issue rules in 1973 requiring disclosure of the appropriate total present value of all lease commitments in its filings. Further, use of M. Moonitz's research in that period, regarding the concept of liabilities, would have precluded off-balance-sheet financing. He defined liabilities, in essence, as the expected amount of future outlays arising out of past occurrences, which fits the usual lease case perfectly.

Next, let us examine the mode of operation during the first year or so of the FASB, in order to gain insight into their procedures. The first "full-process" statement was No. 2 on research and development. No. 1 on foreign currency translation merely called for disclosure of foreign currency translation policies, because the FASB's initial research had indicated non-comparable methods in practice. The board planned to investigate the problems of translation more thoroughly, and simply called for disclosure until they could do further research.

The upshot of FASB Statement No. 2, "Accounting for Research and Development costs," was that "all R&D costs . . . shall be charged to expense when incurred." Procedures for reaching this conclusion involved a task force of sixteen persons with varying backgrounds, a review of APB Research Study No. 14, a review of published research studies and articles, interviews with knowledgeable parties, issuance of a Discussion Memorandum, a public hearing, a review of responses to an Exposure Draft of the proposed statement, and adoption of the statement, unanimously, by the seven members in October, 1974. (This is called the independent FASB's "due process" cycle.) The "basis for conclusions" is given in an appendix. Briefly, since the cost of R&D is not a good measure of its value, and the timing of the benefits cannot be accurately measured, the costs must be expensed immediately.

Although the final statement received many adverse comments, including one by this writer; and although many national and international bodies still call for capitalization of certain R&D, the FASB has continued the standard. It has a policy of reviewing standards after a five-year period; but in this case has not rescinded the statement.

The next statement of the FASB, No. 5, turned out to be even more controversial. It was titled "Accounting for Contingencies" and called for recording estimated expenses only if they met two tests: 1) asset impairment or liability incurrence, and 2) reasonably accurate estimation. These reasonable tests ruled out the customary recording of insurance expense by self-insurers, giving rise to a hue and cry. In response to an FASB request for letters regarding reconsiderations of statements after five years, No. 5 was the second most unpopular (foreign currency translation was first). However, to date the FASB still has the request under consideration.

Issued in 1975, FAS No. 8 on foreign currency translation turned out to be the most controversial statement of all. Building on research for the APB, the Canadian Institute of CAs, and itself, the board adopted requirements similar to the temporal method described in the APB's 1972 Accounting Research Study No. 12. Most unpopular was a new requirement that unrealized translation gains or losses be included in current income. In the past, most concerns deferred these items. However, the many immediate requests for re-consideration were turned down by the Board. Disapproval continued and was reported in a survey by F. Choi and H. Lowe in 1978. Almost all respondents objected to the inclusion of the "non-deferral" requirement. An amendment to FAS No. 8 and several interpretations were published, but the complaints did not subside. They centered specifically on 1) the necessity for uneconomic exchange risk activities, required to offset the income reporting requirements, and 2) the negative effect on stock market share prices due to fluctuating earnings, caused by translation gains and losses.

In 1978 the FASB sponsored research projects on these two problems. The first study, done by a Foundation at the University of South Carolina, surveyed 156 Fortune 500 companies and found that management practices of risk management were definitely affected. The study, however, was unable to find significant net gain or loss effects. The second study by R. Dukes of Cornell University found no significant effect of FAS No. 8 on stock prices. It carried the impressive title "An Empirical Investigation of the Effects of Statement of FAS No. 8 on Security Return Behavior." Requests for consideration continued nevertheless, and finally early in 1979 the subject was put on the Board's technical agenda. "Due process" was again followed—and is still in progress. The latest report on the December, 1980 public hearing showed 47 oral presentations and 317 written comments. A new exposure draft had indicated changes involving translation at *current* exchange rates and *deferral* of translation gains to later dates. To the surprise of some observers, many divergent views were still expressed. The chairman of the FASB indicated that since the Board had not completed its conceptual framework, it was struggling to communicate the realities of foreign currency items. Its current research indicated to board members that FAS No. 8 often did not reveal "economic reality," but they were still bound by the historical cost model. In inflationary foreign economies this model precludes reality, so any method of translation the board chooses is likely to receive criticism. Research on this problem by F. Choi in 1978, which had recommended restatement to "economic reality" before translation, has probably again been considered "too revolutionary." The outcome of the board's deliberations on foreign currency translation is too difficult to predict.

Two exceptionally hot potatoes in the FASB era involved conflicts with the SEC. One was accounting for price changes; the other involved accounting for oil and gas producers. Since the SEC has full authority to set standards, the FASB lost the battle in both cases. Not only its power but also its survival were at issue; but in the final analysis the SEC formally treated the problems as unusual incidents. It continues to delegate accounting standard-setting to the FASB, keeping it in the private sector.

Briefly, in the price-change area, double-digit inflation put such strains on the credibility of accounting reports that the FASB in late 1974 called for mandatory disclosure of inflation effects in an exposure draft titled "Financial Reporting in Units of General Purchasing Power." This was labeled "Pupu" accounting by the SEC's chief accountant. The FASB delayed a final statement in order to do further research in 1975, and finally in June 1976 announced deferral of action. The explanation of why the FASB backed down really had come earlier, in March of 1976, when the SEC issued ASR No. 190. It called for disclosure of replacement cost information in both income statements and balance sheets by large companies.

Neither approach was to survive. Comprehension of the empirical and a priori work of H. W. Sweeney back in the 1930s would have revealed that both general price-level adjustments (for a uniform measuring unit and debtor gains) and current value adjustments (for real operating measures and holding gains) are required for full disclosure of the effects of significant price changes. Thus, in September 1979 the FASB finally issued statement No. 33 "Financial Reporting and Changing Prices." It called for a five-year experiment, with disclosure of both types of adjustments as supplementary information. The SEC withdrew its replacement cost requirements.

A similar undercutting of the FASB's standards took place in 1978 in oil and gas reporting. Failure to require reporting of "economic reality," through reliance on the historical cost model, again seems to have been the cause of the disagreement with the SEC.

Building on the 1969 Research Study No. 11 and other research of the APB, the FASB reached the conclusion in FAS No. 19 (1977) that only "successful efforts" reporting (immediate expensing of the costs of dry holes) be used by oil and gas producers. This was under a mandate of the U. S. Congress, and delegation by the SEC regarding uniform U. S. reporting in the energy field. However, conflicting research ignored by the FASB had indicated that the "full cost" method (capitalization of all costs of developing wells) was preferable in cases where the value of underground reserves greatly exceeded total costs.

To the dismay of the FASB, in August 1978, the SEC adopted not only the successful efforts method, but also permitted the full cost method; and it stated further that *neither* was satisfactory, because both methods relied on historical costs. Current valuation of proved reserves should also be developed. This was called "reserve recognition accounting" (RRA) and is being developed by the SEC. The FASB after much political maneuvering, decided to suspend the effective date for requiring successful efforts reporting. Again, the final outcome is unknown, as companies struggle with the new requirements of RRA in filings with the SEC, but continue using either of the cost methods in annual reports.

In retrospect, the a priori and empirical work of scholars like J. B. Canning, in his 1929 *Economics of Accounting,* and H. W. Sweeney, in his 1936 *Stabilized Accounting,* indicated that not reporting the billions of dollars of underground oil and gas discovered each year, as well as changes in values of these reserves as prices increased wildly each year— the essence of RRA—omitted some of the most important changes in oil and gas companies' fortunes. It is a question of "soft" relevant vs. "hard" unrealistic data.

The Future

The above brief review of some of the controversial problem areas and related research during the APB and FASB eras indicates the vast scope of future research possibilities. Most of the problems have not been fully resolved and research of all types is still needed. While some proceed with normative and a priori work, such as the facets of the FASB conceptual framework, others will choose empirical testing or the development of positive theories. The various approaches will be competing to a certain extent, but also will be complementary, in the sense of validating or disproving various aspects of normative models. This leads to improvement.

A great deal of research will be needed on the FASB's conceptual framework project to complete the recognition criteria, the measurement, and the reporting aspects. The implications of the empirical research on capital and efficient markets need further study, and in spite of the proliferation of work supporting efficient market theories, recent research casts serious doubt on its validity, not to mention its relevancy. Investor decision models are not fully known, so a wide-open field for research exists here. Even the "fundamentalist" approach in the investment area, implicit in many normative theories of accounting, needs further work. This leads to the area of *forecasting,* to which the SEC has given its blessing for the first time in its history. How one-year forecasts fit the model is a most important question.

The information overload problem has not been settled. Further empirical research is called for here also.

The research to date on "economic consequences" of accounting standards has not been very extensive. It also suffers from clearcut relevance. Should a change to an improved standard be stalled because it may have adverse consequences for certain sectors of the economy? Which sectors take precedence if conflicting consequences arise? Or, is Kenneth MacNeal's "truth," regardless of consequence, sufficient? This writer believes that the FASB must be congnizant of consequences for political and implementation achievements—hence the need for the research, but agrees with the board's "even handed" and "building a concensus" approaches. Permitting low standards (even falsehoods) or preventing improvements in order to achieve economic goals does not appear to be a supportable approach. But this writer's biases should not preclude the research on this important topic.

Positive research, described above, offers many possibilities, and should advance our knowledge of the political process of policy setting. Its use for choosing policies, on the other hand, is another question, because the problem really may be one of what should the standard be, not what is it or how was it chosen.

Without repeating all of the problem areas faced in early history, which still call for further research, what areas are likely to become significant topics in the 1980s? Basic to all, of course, will be the research needed to complete the conceptual framework. Just published by the FASB, for example, is "Recognition of Contractual Rights and Obligations" by Yuji Ijirii. In process are research projects on "Users Decision-Making Processes" and the use of "Summary Indicators" in analyzing financial reports. When completed, the "Concepts" series will serve as guidelines for improvements in past and future standards.

A list, with short comments or questions on each research topic, follows:

1. Accounting for price changes. When the five-year experimental period ends in 1984, the FASB will face the hard choice among general price level vs. specific price vs. both general and specific price adjustments. Should the information be supplementary or incorporated in GAAP? The conceptual framework may be crucial, and additional research beneficial to decision making. At bottom is the question of whether more soft data should be admitted to generally accepted accounting principles (GAAP).

2. Oil and gas accounting. Of greatest significance will be discovery of whether RRA can be implemented without too great a loss of objectivity, and without material errors necessitating constant changes.

3. Foreign exchange translation. To make foreign exchange gains and losses meaningful, should the historical cost model be abandoned in order to take price changes into account, before translating foreign subsidiaries?

4. Lease accounting. Before reconsidering and possibly "tightening" lease accounting, the FASB is investigating the effects of FAS No. 13 on stocks prices, bond risk premiums, and the perceptions and actions of preparers and users, in a research project headed by Professor A. Rashad Abdel-khalik. Should the present value of all property rights and lease obligations be required to be capitalized?

5. Pension accounting. Should expected future pension cash flows for past service costs (often significantly omitted at present) be shown as liabilities? Is the offset really an asset; or is it a loss, associated with prior periods?

6. Corrections of prior periods (and restatement of prior income statements). Are changes in accounting principles, changes in estimates, and accounting errors false classifications—are they all errors? When material, should all changes affecting prior periods require restatement?

7. Stock option accounting. Is it possible to reasonably estimate in advance the salary expense associated with stock options, so that current, arbitrary rules resulting in minimal salary expense can be avoided?

8. Marketable securities accounting. Although no great opposition to FAS No. 12, "Accounting For Marketable Securities," has been expressed, it inconsistently permits recognition of appreciation in some cases, but not in others; and it is based on the historical cost model. William Beaver's survey of research in 1974 indicated that all decision-models in the area relied on current market values of securities, but the research has been ignored.

9. Materiality. The FASB removed materiality from its technical agenda and included it in its conceptual series. In Concept No. 12 (1980) the board took the position that "no general standards of materiality can be formulated," especially quantitative ones. Is their position too timid?

10. Human resource accounting. Research is continuing in this important area. Progress is being made on quantification in the managerial area. Although not on the FASB's agenda, possible huge values for employee talent are being omitted from financial reporting. If reported, should a cost or a value approach be used?

11. Social accounting. Another important area of continuing research has to do with social costs and social benefits—"externalties," as

they are often called. Interest in social reporting waxes and wanes, as interest in corporate social responsibility varies, but many researchers have made a serious start in this relatively new measurement area. Again, is it the costs of activities in solutions to pollution control, safety, discrimination, etc., problem, or is it the value of the performance results that are important? How should they be reported?

12. Governmental (not-for-profit) accounting. Probably the weakest and lowest-level accounting standards are found in the governmental accounting area. A jurisdictional battle is occurring in the political arena, with the FASB taking some steps forward. The outcome is uncertain, but important, because the standards being developed for private businesses appear to hold great promise for improving governmental accounting. Research opportunities here are unbounded, both behavioral and conceptual.

13. Goodwill accounting. Although not a hot topic at present, the problem of improper valuation of total net assets always lurks in the background of accounting. J. B. Canning's "Master Valuation" account "Goodwill" is currently ignored in financial reporting. Should attempts be made to value it, as recommended in a research study by R. Gynther (U. of Queensland)? Or, should its omission be specifically disclosed? Research on Goodwill has not yet been completed.

14. Computer processing. Although not specifically in the standard-setting area, computers have had such a pervasive influence on accounting and auditing in recent decades that data processing should not be omitted when thinking of accounting research. Special areas are internal controls, audit trials, and fraud.

15. Funds flows and liquidity. The last topic to be discussed, but one of the most important is the area of "cash flow." The retiring Chairman of the SEC in recent speeches, hot on the tail of the FASB for its slowness in dealing with changing prices and off-balance-sheet financing, has gone so far as to say that cash earnings have become more important than accrual-basis earnings. The FASB's vehicle for addressing these issues is a phase of the conceptual framework project called "Funds Flows, Liquidity and Financial Flexibility." In its Concept No. 1 on objectives, the FASB calls for information about a firm's cash flows, because investors and creditors need to assess cash receipts from dividends or interest *and* the proceeds from sale or maturity of securities or loans.

Perceptive readers will see a flaw in the above reasoning, which should open wide the door for research. If investors, for example, look forward to cash from dividends *and* the sale of their stock (*not to the firm*) then it is *not* primarily the firm's cash flows that they look to. What determines the market selling price is the main question, after dividends feasibility has been determined. Is it really a firm's historical cash flows that determine stock prices? Could the more relevant total lifetime cash flows ever be ascertained by accountants? Or, are cash flows only important in assessing dividend and liquidity problems (not stock market prices directly)? Put another way, if earnings calculations were made more relevant, under improved standards, would they then be reinstated to a place of importance? Again, research opportunities abound.

In conclusion, apologies are repeated to our colleagues in the north for emphasizing U. S. topics. Past experience indicates, however, that Canadian researchers will be necessary and cooperative partners in the many research opportunities of the future.

Multinational Accounting: Research Priorities for the Eighties—Latin America

LYLE JACOBSEN
University of Hawaii

Accounting research activities relative to Latin America are discussed in the literature in various contexts because several different developments which have taken place are all accounting-related. One can only be convinced about accounting research priorities for the future in Latin America by first examining the recent history of accounting developments in Latin America and noting the present status of some of the forces which influence accounting there.

Some Relevant Recent Historical Highlights

Accounting in Latin America has received increased attention in the last fifteen years mainly as an adjunct to such actions as the major allocation of international agency resources for industrial development and economic growth in developing countries.[1] (Literature cited in this chapter is by no means all-inclusive and there is no attempt to mention the most significant works—a judgment readers must make themselves. Rather, the goal is to provide examples of the directions research has taken or is taking.)

Institution-building and up-grading in Latin American education for business (and therefore accounting) were stimulated by the 1963-64 founding in Lima, Peru, of Latin America's first graduate school of business exclusively for university graduates. The school was given the acronym ESAN (Escuela de Administracion de Negocios para Graduados—School of Administration of Business for Graduates). Instruction and teaching materials were in Spanish.[2]

Accounting research efforts specific to Latin America naturally accompanied this push for industrialization and the formation of the ESAN institution.[3]

The goal of standardization, universalization, or harmonization[4] of accounting methods, which began in a serious way in 1905 with the convening of the first World Congress of Accountants,[5] became increasingly important because of the growth of international business. The emergence of multinational corporations opened a new area for international accounting research which has relevance to Latin America, host to many multinational corporations.[6] The first comprehensive textbook in multinational accounting was published in 1978.[7]

To sum up, the recent history of accounting research output relevant to Latin America includes research emanating from several streams of activity: 1) the industrialization movement in underdeveloped countries; 2) the founding in Latin America of a quality graduate school of business with instruction and teaching materials in the indigenous language to serve as a model for other Latin American countries as well as to provide an institution for research; 3) renewed institutional efforts to harmonize diverse accounting practices in the world; and 4) increasing predominance of multinational corporations.

Implications for accounting research will be discussed with respect to the second and third of the above mentioned forces which have had an impact on the accounting scene—improvement in Latin American educational institutions, and attempts to harmonize accounting worldwide. Although accounting research related to industrialization and multinational corporations is encouraged to continue, it is from the other two areas primarily that the research priorities suggested in this chapter arise.

Improvement in Educational Institutions

The push for industrialization of underdeveloped countries subsided with changes in the world economic political situation—especially the assassination of U. S. President John F. Kennedy who championed the Alliance for Progress idea. Accounting research in this area waned naturally, perhaps mainly from lack of funds to finance it adequately. The upgrading of educational institutions offering business and accounting education which was to accompany Latin American industrialization continued, however.

The Peruvian graduate school of business, ESAN, has been a "shining light in the midst of darkness" for full-time business and accounting education in Latin America. The school survived the entire spectrum of political revolution under both democratic and military junta systems.

In 1965 Latin American universities typically lacked *graduate* courses in accounting and administration, served mainly *part-time* students, utilized mainly *part-time* professors, and lacked adequate specialized libraries and technical journals. The importance of a lack of full-time dedication by students and professors can be seen in the fact that in a 1965 survey of 136 Latin American universities 94.4 percent of the faculty were *part-time* in universities with departments of accounting.[8] Because of tradition and economic necessity, students also were predominantly part-time. This was to change, however.

In the last fifteen years there has been a remarkable growth in the institutionalizing and development of accounting and managerial education in Latin America. CLADEA (Consejo Latinoamericano de Escuelas de Administracion—Council of Latin American Schools of Administration) was an adjunct part of the ESAN project, but was headquartered in another country.

CLADEA was designed, among other things, to set standards for stimulating the improvement of Latin American university education in industrial and public administration, including accounting, in both private and public universities. Improvement in four specific areas is required by CLADEA for membership status. Member schools are to have 1) postgraduate courses in administration, 2) full-time professors, 3) courses in which students have the option to study full time, and 4) specialized libraries and technical journals.

At the 1974 (9th) regular annual meeting of CLADEA, in Saõ Paulo and Rio de Janeiro, Brazil, it was noted that six new Latin American institutions were accepted to the group of eleven members for an increase of over 50 percent *in one year,* bringing the number of *professors* of the CLADEA schools to about 150.[9] In correspondence with the author, Paul Garner suggests that CLADEA is now "more solid, useful, and wider-based with about thirty-eight members."

This group of professors and schools serves as a leadership group for inspiring other universities to upgrade their educational quality. Member institutions of CLADEA, consequently, provide a more professional, rigorous, and relevant alternative for superior Latin American students.

Research Priorities

B. L. Jaggi (1973) has categorized accounting research relating to developing countries as 1) descriptive studies, 2) conceptual studies, and 3) hypothesis-testing studies, giving examples of each type in the literature. He noted that "little has been done in this field (of accounting research in developing countries) so far" and that "an immediate need exists for descriptive studies of various countries in order to develop conceptual and hypothesis-testing studies."[10]

More recently, Gerhard G. Mueller discusses different ways that have been proposed to categorize research and suggests a composite list of 1) descriptive, 2) comparative, 3) empirical, 4) traditional-normative, 5) bibliographical-historical, and 6) behavioral. He mentions examples of each with annotations for each.[11]

One of the hopes of the builders of ESAN and CLADEA was that, eventually, research would be stimulated in the Latin American countries and done by Latin American professors rather than by foreigners. This goal has only partially been realized. Several factors are responsible for this lack of success. There is no incentive for research and adequate, sustained financial support is lacking. (As usual in universities almost everywhere, teaching takes priority over research when financial support wanes.) Another reason for lack of great accomplishment of this goal is a lack of "temperament" for doing scholarly, relevant and pragmatic research. A third factor is a lack of training in research design and methodology.

It may not be easy to develop a "research temperament" in Latin American countries, but much could be done to develop research design and methodology skills. This is an area which has been neglected by foreigners in developing educational institutions in accounting and related areas in Latin America.

First Priority: Develop and Transfer a Technology for Accounting Research Design, Method, and Technique in Latin America

An expertise in accounting *research* design, analytic technique, and method could be developed which would be applicable to all Latin American countries and exported to them as a *transfer of technology* in which Latin American accounting professor-researchers could be trained. The technology might rely on tools or modifications of them from other disciplines. These researchers could then apply this technology to regional and local situations.

The idea of a transfer of research technology from one country to another has been confined largely to the production function or to product research. The thesis proposed here is that accounting research design and analytic techniques and methods can be developed and transferred from countries with the required financial and intellectual resources to those that do not have these resources.[12]

The development of this professional and managerial accounting research talent will not be an easy task for several reasons;

1. In the U. S., for example, there are not many professor-researchers with exceptional interest and/or talents of the type envisioned here in this area. Research models tend to quickly become unintelligible even in English and communication through Spanish or Portuguese translation would be a disaster. Translators who are proficient in languages usually are lost when confronted with technical areas of accounting research and, conversely, experts in technical areas such as accounting usually do not have sufficient language proficiency.

2. Experience shows that in Latin America, because of cultural pride and independence-autonomy constraints, the indigenous language (Spanish or Portuguese) is the language to use, rather than English or some Asiatic or European language.

3. Developing a U. S. skill in both accounting research design technology to be transferred *and* a proficiency in Spanish and or Portuguese would require more than modest financial underwriting to attract someone to invest the considerable time and effort required to develop the area.

    A 1967 preliminary research study under the auspices of the International Committee for Accounting Cooperation (ICAC) conducted in Columbia was part of a "Proposal for International Accounting Aid" to Latin American countries. The sponsors of the project had hopes of stimulating large-scale financing from various *stakeholders* in Latin American development (the American, Mexican, and Canadian accounting professions; national and international financing agencies; foundations; etc.). The aggregating of sufficient funds for further research and implementation never materialized. A colleague suggests that foundations who were approached believed this to be a province of the private sector. The U. S. government at this time was scaling down foreign aid.

4. Follow-through in the countries receiving the "accounting research technology transfer" must somehow be assured or the effort will be wasted. Development and change take time and follow-through, a fact too often forgotten. There is a general disinclination to "follow-through." Government emphasis on developing one type of project or another comes and goes with political change. Similarly, the organized, practicing accounting profession also changes its priorities for project interest and support as circumstances change. Universities could, perhaps, provide the needed continuity.

To sum up the first priority for accounting research in Latin America: a major thrust is needed to enrich the accounting research capabilities in the graduate schools of business developed in Latin America with international assistance in the last fifteen years. Those institutions which are members of CLADEA are dedicated to maintaining high standards and to improving education in accounting and administration. They have for the most part maintained an independent professionalism enabling them to survive political change.

The thrust should be in the form of a "transfer of technology" focusing on accounting research design, method, and technique utilizing scholars encouraged and motivated financially to "gear up" in both the accounting research technology relevant to these countries and the Spanish and/or Portuguese language capability. It will require time and a long term financial investment to do this.

Second Priority: Research the Extent to Which Accounting is, and Should be, "Culture-Bound"

Accounting has been culture-bound and will be for decades to come—as much in the managerial accounting area as in the public accounting area. The accounting fraternity has not recognized the extent to which it is and, therefore, the extent to which our concepts are relevant to the Latin American cultures. A related, but separate, problem is that of language—finding equivalencies in English, Spanish, and Portuguese for accounting terms and concepts.

In teaching accounting in Spanish one is constantly faced with accounting terminology quandaries. Spanish accounting terms even differ from one Latin country to another. The prevalence of slang (not easily translatable) in accounting terms in English (e.g., sunk costs, goodwill, plugged figure) poses a dilemma.

César A. Salas, a well-known accounting scholar, notes that "to translate the term 'goodwill' (universally accepted among North American accountants) seven different words are used in Spanish Latin America. The term 'board of directors' has, to my knowledge, four different usages. Pure Castilian language cannot offer a solution, because accounting in Spain has not made sufficient progress. We must look, therefore, to a continental Spanish terminology of the Western Hemisphere as the practical solution."[13]

The biggest quandary of all, however, is trying to determine whether to impose a transferred technology as something new to the students or to adapt to their accounting tradition. For example, in the U. S. we use the concept of working capital (current assets minus current liabilities). In Peru, a traditional balance sheet employed more gradations of liquidity in the asset section of the balance sheet than current, fixed, other, etc.

Should Latin American classifications be changed so that our concept of "capital de trabajo" (working capital) can be accommodated?

This brings us to a second accounting research priority for the eighties: research the extent to which accounting is culture-bound and then develop the areas of universality and new concepts appropriate to Latin American cultures.

The accounting fraternity in developed countries has been the impetus for accounting harmonization in the world. Too few colleagues in these developed countries, however, realize the "culture-bound" nature of accounting and its importance as a force in retarding improvement in accounting until cultural "lags" are overcome. These deterrents should be faced realistically in order that research toward constructive approaches to the problem can be organized.

Irving Fantl, an accounting scholar noted for his long time interest in international accounting, commented in reviewing the manuscript for this chapter that "despite the long history of involvement of U. S. accountants and accounting academicians in Latin America, awareness of the real condition of accounting education and practice there is lacking. Conditions you describe as existing in 1965 have changed very little in fifteen years."

Robert Seiler, a former professor of accounting at ESAN, suggested in his review of the manuscript for this chapter that the efficient market theories of the United States may not work in Latin American and other developing countries. He suggests that their information processes may be such that these theories do not hold.

This need to recognize the importance of culture and environment has been pointed out in the literature of economic development and other non-accounting areas such as in the 1965 paper by William F. Whyte titled "Culture, Industrial Relations, and Economic Development: The Case of Peru."[14]

Whyte chose the relevant aspects of culture in his paper to be "the way people think and feel about the world around them—particularly the values that they hold in areas that seem to us relevant for economic development." He then sought to measure some of these thoughts and feelings concluding, for example, that manual work has a low status. The "obrero," "empleado" distinction in Peru is much sharper than our "blue collar," "whyte collar" classification. Whyte noted that "for generations the typical Peruvian economic activity has been concentrated on the land—ownership of haciendas (ranches), buying and selling of real estate—and commerce, the buying and selling of goods. Manufacturing has not been a part of that pattern." He concludes that culture does have an impact on industrial development. The author of this chapter maintains that culture has an impact on accounting research and teaching which has not been sufficiently explored. Whyte searched for cultural forces that have held back industrial development in Peru. Other cultures should be researched to isolate the cultural forces that impact on accounting (both managerial and public-professional) and determine how culture-bound accounting is. This has not been done.

Gerhard G. Mueller has mentioned cultural factors in South America in the context of comparing accounting principles in the U. S. with those in other countries at different *and* similar stages of development: "Many instances are present of significant economic underdevelopment along with social and educational underdevelopment. The business base is narrow. Agricultural and military interests are strong and often dominate governments. There is considerable reliance on export/import trade. Currencies are ususally soft. Populations are increasing heavily."[15]

A more specific beginning effort in this area is Lee H. Radebaugh's article, "Environmental Factors Influencing the Development of Accounting Objectives, Standards, and Practices in Peru."[16] Radebaugh undertook an extensive research assignment in Peru and reported in 1975 on "the major environmental factors that influence the development of accounting objectives, standards, and practices" using Peru as his model. B. L. Jaggi had reminded us a couple of years earlier that the usual classifications of scientific inquiry apply also to accounting—descriptive research, conceptual research, and hypothesis-testing research. He has categorized completed international accounting research studies into these three groups.[17] Hypothesis-testing research builds upon conceptual research which builds upon descriptive research.

Radebaugh points out that descriptive research "is by far the most common and involves a discussion of the current state of the art." Continuous research of a descriptive nature is the basis for research of the "higher" two orders, just as "environmental scanning and intelligence gathering" are a necessary prerequisite for developing normative planning and control systems in a given situation.[18]

Radebaugh then applies to Peru an interesting conceptual framework depicting the evolution of accounting and reporting practices. This research piece not only attempts to give structure but, perhaps more importantly, gives real importance to the environmental factors of 1) nature of the enterprise; 2) enterprise users; 3) government; 4) accounting profession; 5) other external users such as creditors, financial institutions, and entities; 6) academic influence; 7) international influence; and 8) local environmental characteristics.[19]

The last three of these areas have been given little recognition in accounting research, yet they represent the fertile area for our future international accounting researches because they *are the relevant cultural factors* quoted from Radebaugh earlier in this chapter. The details of these areas are:

Academic influence:
   1.   educational infrastructure
   2.   basic and applied research
   3.   academic associations
International influences:
   1.   colonial history
   2.   foreign investors
   3.   international committees
   4.   regional cooperation
   5.   regional capital markets
Local environmental characteristics
   1.   rate of economic growth
   2.   inflation
   3.   public versus private ownership and control of the economy
   4.   cultural attitudes

Third Priority: Engage in More Conceptual Research, Building on Continuing Descriptive Research Results

Research into any new intellectual area begins with descriptive research, the foundation for conceptual and theoretical research. Such research should be continued and expanded.

It is the *linkage* between environmental factors and the normative accounting system of objectives, standards, and practices which needs most to be researched. Studies in this area may help determine how culture-bound accounting really is, and, in Radebaugh's words, "will help identify common situations where compromise may be necessary or where uniform standards and practices are simply impracticable," This is, indeed, the challenge ahead as is demonstrated in the next section of this chapter.

International Harmonization of Accounting

In 1973, Dhia D. AlHashim suggested the concept of "purposive uniformity" in the context of international standardization.[20] His concept puts a premium on user utility so that a necessary condition for "purposive uniformity" is that accounting control must rest with users rather than with providers of accounting information. A second necessary condition is the ability to make user needs "operative" in order to call into action the appropriate accounting control responses.

Efforts by the accounting profession to standardize, and thus universalize, accounting have been made within countries, within regions, and within the world of capitalism and free enterprise—particularly in the financial accounting and auditing area. Most recently the universalization movement has extended to the *entire* world as countries such as the People's Republic of China and Russia adopt accounting techniques from "outside" their countries, especially in the management accounting area.

Research activities, albeit not necessarily formally structured, underlie the actions of the agencies dedicated to this movement at internationalization. No significant amount of research has been done to see how various regional organizations have solved similar problems. Such research might provide insight into solving a particular region's problems.

Preceding most of the international accounting organizations is the founding in 1949 of the Inter-American Accounting Conference (Conferencia Interamericana de Contabilidad) with Señor Juan Gil of Puerto Rico as president of the first organizing committee. This first conference which met in Puerto Rico consisted of thirteen Latin American republics, plus the United States and Canada. The conference was repeated every two or three years or so and celebrated its eleventh conference in 1974 as the silver anniversary of the organization's founding with twenty Latin American republics, plus Canada and the United States participating. The conference became sufficiently institutionalized that after twenty-five years it "renovated" itself and became officially the Inter-American Accounting *Association* (rather than Conference), i.e., Asociacion Interamericana de Contabilidad—the permanent body which would continue to sponsor the conferences periodically.

The week-long conferences provide not only an important opportunity for professionals and academics within the hemisphere to meet and develop contacts, but technical sessions are held in which research papers are presented in Spanish and English. The "areas of study" under which the research papers fit were broadened and restructured for the Fourteenth Conference in Santiago, Chile (1981). They are under several commissions: Accounting Research, Auditing Standards and Practice, Governmental Accounting Standards, Education, Administration and Finance, and Professional Practice. Ten specific areas delineated are: income determination, leasing, new approaches to the auditing function, auditing minicomputer systems, government financial statements, formation of the accountant—non-technical aspects, specific methods for the control of professional updating, financing under inflation, reconsideration of the code of ethics, quality control in the professional office.[21]

Although research papers on such traditional academic and practical topics as development of the accountant, the future of the accounting profession, generally accepted accounting principles, social accounting, and impact of computers on auditing are predominant, papers on multinational accounting, continuing education programs, and management accounting now are receiving attention.

In November 1968, Stephen A. Zeff founded and edited for the Inter-American Accounting Association its pioneering *Boletín Inter-Americano de Contabilidad (Inter-American Accounting Bulletin)*. From 1971 to 1975 the Mexican Institute of Public Accountants undertook this responsibility, and later it was issued under Argentine sponsorship. Out of the *Boletín* has come both the *Revista Interamericana de Contabilidad* (Inter-American Accounting Review), which began publication in early 1980, and the *Carta Interamericana* (Interamerican Letter) which is still published as the internal newsletter of the Inter-American Accounting Association. This set of periodicals has been very useful as an instrument for the exchange of ideas and developments among the republics of the hemisphere.

There has developed recently a linkage between the Inter-American Accounting Association and the European and newer international agencies. Committees of the International Federation of Accountants (IFAC) and the Board of the International Accounting Standards Committee have greater responsibility and involvement in the technical program of the Twelfth International Congress of Accountants (Mexico City, 1982). The Fifth International Conference on accounting education follows in Monterrey, Mexico.

In "standardizing" accounting and auditing practices between and among Canada, the United States, and the Latin American republics, the intense nationalistic spirit of some Latin American countries thwarts standardization even among themselves, let alone with those of the "Anglo giants" to the north. This provides a good reason to use the concept of "harmonization" rather than "standardization." Mexico has played a remarkable buffer role in this process of adaptation between the English-speaking, Spanish-speaking, and Portuguese-speaking countries. More recently, however, Mexico has exhibited a more nationalistic spirit in this area. This situation points more strongly to the urgency of the earlier suggested priority of researching the culture-bound nature of accounting and then developing accounting rules for specific cultures.

Roy Nash, who from November 1977 to October 1979 served as Secretary of the International Accounting Standards Committee (IASC), concludes that, "In reality, however, universally-agreed-upon accounting and reporting standards are far from fruition . . . Harmonization efforts by other bodies, such as the UN and OECD, have also failed to command general international acceptance."[22]

Nash also hints that a major restraining force is the jurisdiction dispute over whether governments or non-government, professionally-represented organizations should have the responsibility for accounting universalization worldwide.

In Nash's words:

> Government involvement is another pivotal element in the efforts to harmonize international accounting and reporting. In the U. K., the U. S., and most of the other English-speaking countries, accounting standards are issued by private bodies. In the other countries of the world, however, accounting standards usually are determined by government. The International Accounting Standards Committee (IASC) work is made more difficult because governments—always reluctant to concede any of their powers to outside groups—would have to change their local legislation so as to conform to IASC standards.[23]

He notes further that in Europe governments are involved through the EEC (European Economic Community), and that "internationally the United Nations and the Organization for Economic Cooperation and Development have gone on record saying that, while they support the work of the IASC, they believe that *cooperative government efforts* are needed in order to achieve uniform worldwide accounting and reporting standards."

Radebaugh describes the Peruvian committee to develop a national Plan Contable General (General Accounting Plan): "Several representatives of the accounting profession served with government personnel on the commission; conspicuously absent were any representatives of the private industrial sector of the economy."[24] We may find, indeed, that there is often an antagonism between government and business and that the accounting profession is caught in the middle.

This author believes that universalization progress in the Latin American area has even less hope than Nash expresses on the international scene *unless the cultural factors are researched and accommodated* in a spirit of "harmonization." In this sense, this author agrees with the pessimistic outlook of B. L. Jaggi.

Jaggi has started us along this line by drawing on cultural studies outside the discipline of accounting. He suggests, for example, that the sociologist's concepts of *universalism* versus *particularism* are relevant to the development of accounting in different cultures.[25]

Jaggi notes that "the *universalistic* value orientation will be predominant in societies which exhibit complex technology, emphasize individual independence and mobility, and value competition and achieved status.

In these societies, friendship is valued mainly in terms of material or status gain. The economically developed countries, especially the United States, are considered to be universalistically oriented societies. . . . Societies which are less technical, less scientific, and less urban are considered to be predominantly *particularistic*. The main cultural characteristics of these societies are exhibited in the extended family system, in the distrust and disregard for the authority of government and laws, and in the lack of responsibility to societal obligations. The societies of developing countries, such as Mexico and India (author's note: and Polynesia), exemplify particularism.''[26]

In development economics, econometric studies have been attempted along this line.[27] Such studies are useful to suggest to international accounting researchers what a sister discipline perceives the relevant cultural and other non-economic variables to be.

This author believes the Jaggi approach is a fruitful one for international accounting research, both financial and managerial, and that it should be given a high priority.

Focusing research efforts on developing accounting research design and on the cultural linkage of accounting is not without problems. This would be a departure from what many professional accounting practitioners and scholars believe to be the urgent areas for research. George M. Scott's DELPHI study aimed to focus upon problems that are of greatest concern in international accounting. These tended to be the pragmatic problems long held to be crucial, such as: exchange rate and currency translations, international education, international accounting standards, disclosure problems, and international auditing problems.[28]

It will take some hard work to convince accounting colleagues, for example, that, as stated in correspondence from an accounting professor, "behavioral matters (such as) the Latin temperament, moral structure, value structure, and life values are different and that the behavioral research which relates to accounting here (the U. S.) and in other developed non-Latin countries may not apply at all in Latin America."

The final pessimistic note shared by colleagues in correspondence is the lack of financial resources for accounting research.

Summary and Conclusions

During the last fifteen years a good beginning has been made as a foundation for accounting research appropriate to Latin American countries. Institutions emphasizing upgraded teaching and providing an infrastructure for research have been founded and continue in operation. Exchange of information through the Inter-American Accounting Association's

"Conferences" and the Association's publication, *Boletín Interamericano de Contabilidad,* which later became the *Revista Interamericana de Contabilidad,* have made the Latin and Anglo members of the profession in this hemisphere aware of accounting problems and proposed solutions of the neighbor countries.

The international link of the Latin American organization is strengthening as the professional groups of individual Latin American countries join IFAC—International Federation of Accountants. Further prospects of progress in internationalizing accounting via international agencies appear dim because more bureaucratic government agencies consider themselves important *stakeholders* in the process and the independent, profession-oriented agencies view this as a restraining force.

Research activity needs to be implanted in the young educational institutions recently established or revitalized under CLADEA philosophy. An accounting research design expertise needs to be developed by countries which have the financial and human resources. This expertise then needs to be exported as a transfer of technology to Latin American countries and tailored to their cultures. This could be done in much the same way as the transfer of production technology or product research technology takes place.

Developing an expertise in accounting research design, analytic technique, and method will not be an easy task for several reasons. First, there are not many academicians interested and/or talented in this area. Second, there are not many academicians skilled in both accounting research design technology to be transferred and in Spanish or Portuguese language proficiency. Third, journals which would publish research findings are lacking. Finally, follow-through is quite necessary and yet oftentimes forgotten. Despite these obstacles, a transfer of technology is needed to enhance accounting research in Latin America.

In research, accounting must not be excised from its environment as is so often the case. Colleagues still raise questions about what economics or business administration, let alone the cultural, historical, anthropological, and behavioral areas have to do with accounting research! These areas have everything to do with accounting; they provide the context in which accounting has developed and exists today.

Several colleagues have urged the author to make suggestions for how needed accounting research might be given higher priority and how it may be financed. This is a particularly relevant point to make when resources are not sufficient to satisfy the basic priorities of life—food, housing, the 3 R's of education. The only suggestion which comes to mind is that the case must be made stronger and, more importantly, that the directions for accounting research as suggested in this chapter be given consideration—concentrate on relevant research methodology and the cultural and environmental factors which impact on accounting.

Tailoring managerial and financial accounting models to a specific country requires research into the impact of culture on accounting. This is the new area for accounting research. The extent to which accounting is "culture-bound" in Latin America might be determined by exploring further the impact of the following environmental factors on accounting: academic influence, international influence, and local environmental characteristics. It is a legitimate role of universities to be the locus of a solid base for accounting research and international technology transfer and follow-through.

Notes

The author is grateful to the following colleagues for taking the time to respond to the invitation to review this chapter during its preparation: Dhia D. AlHashim, Michael Chetkovich, Irving Fantl, Paul Garner, Howard Keefe, Roy Nash, Lee H. Radebaugh, George M. Scott, Robert Seiler, R. D. Thomas, C. J. Trunkfield, James P. Wesberry, Jr., and Stephen A. Zeff.

1. See George M. Scott, *Accounting and Developing Nations* (Seattle: University of Washington Graduate School of Business, 1970). See also Adolph Enthoven, *Accountancy and Economic Development Policy* (Amsterdam: North Holland Publishing Company, 1973) for a comprehensive treatise supporting accounting as a requisite for successful economic development.

2. The financial responsibility for this institution-building project resulted from negotiations between the government of Peru and the U. S. government—inspired by then U. S. President John F. Kennedy's Alianza para el Progreso (Alliance for Progress). Stanford University's Graduate School of Business managed the project.

3. The research of Edward L. Elliott, among others, comes to mind. Edward L. Elliott, *The Nature and Stages of Accounting Development in Latin America* (Urbana, Illinois: Center for International Education and Research in Accounting, 1968). See also, Robert E. Seiler and Harold R. Dilbeck, "Latin America—A Challenge in Development Assistance, "*Journal of Accountancy* (October 1967): p. 46-50.

4. The word "harmonization" is preferable because it is a newer concept indicating accommodation and compatibility. The older terms in the literature, "universalization" and "standardization" connote a conformity to one ideal worldwide, which is an unacceptable notion to many who prefer more recognition of individual differences.

5. For a summary of highlights in this area, consult Paul Garner, *The Development of International Accounting Standards and Conventions* (University, Alabama: University of Alabama Graduate School of Business Center of Business and Economic Research, March, 1971).

6. See Gerhard G. Mueller, *International Accounting* (New York: The Macmillan Company, 1967).

7. See Frederick D. S. Choi and Gerhard G. Mueller, *An Introduction to Multinational Accounting* (Englewood Cliffs, New Jersey: Prentice Hall, 1978).

8. *International Handbook of Universities,* 1965 edition. For a modern study of influences on the development of scholarly institutions in Latin America, see Joseph Maier and Richard W. Weatherhead (eds.), *The Latin American University* (Albuquerque: University of New Mexico Press, 1979). Chapters 5, 7, 8, and 9 have particular relevance here.

9. *Boletín Interamericano de Cantabilidad,* No. 24, August-October, 1974, p. 19.

10. B. L. Jaggi, "Accounting Studies of Developing Countries: An Assessment," *International Journal of Accounting,* pp. 168-69.

11. Gerhard G. Mueller, "The State of the Art of Academic Research in Multinational Accounting," reprinted in *Essentials of Multinational Accounting,* Frederick D. S. Choi and Gerhard G. Mueller, eds. (Ann Arbor, Mich.: University Microfilm Intl., 1980), pp. 249-68.

12. See for example, B. N. Bhattasali, *Transfer of Technology Among the Developing Countries*(Tokyo: Asian Productivity Organization, 1972).

13. César A. Salas, "Accounting Education and Practice in Spanish Latin America," *The International Journal of Accounting* (Fall 1967): p. 67-85.

14. Published in *Industrial and Labor Relations Review* 16: 583-93.

15. Gerhard G. Mueller, "Accounting Principles Generally Accepted in the United States Versus Those Generally Accepted Elsewhere," *The International Journal of Accounting* (Spring 1968): 95.

16. Lee H. Radebaugh, "Environmental Factors Influencing the Development of Accounting Objectives, Standards, and Practices in Peru," *The International Journal of Accounting* (Fall 1975): p. 39-56.

17. B. L. Jaggi, "Accounting Studies of Developing Countries: An Assessment," *The International Journal of Accounting* (Fall 1973): p. 159-70.

18. Jerry Dermer, *Management Planning and Control Systems* (Richard D. Irwin, Inc., Homewood, Illinois, 1977) presents a planning and control system design process which might serve well in training for the structure of research design in international accounting areas.

19. From a FASB discussion memorandum "Conceptual Framework for Accounting and Reporting," based on a Study Group report published by the American Institute of Certified Public Accountants (AICPA) in October, 1973 entitled *Objectives of Financial Statements,* which later was issued as FASB *Statement of Financial Accounting Concepts No. 1,* "Objectives of Financial Reporting by Business Enterprises," November, 1978.

20. Dhia D. AlHashim, "Accounting Control Through Purposive Uniformity: An International Perspective," *The International Journal of Accounting* (Spring 1973): 24.

21. *Carta Interamericana* (November, 1980).

22. Arthur Young *Client Memorandum,* Arthur Young and Co., March 31, 1980. The sub-

stance of this memorandum was prepared as an article for *The Financial Times of London* by Roy C. Nash, Arthur Young and Co. partner.

23. *Ibid.*

24. Radebaugh, *op. cit.,* p. 51.

25. B. L. Jaggi, "The Impact of the Cultural Environment on Financial Disclosures," *The International Journal of Accounting* (Spring 1975): p. 75-84. See also Talcott Parsons and Edward A. Shils, eds., *Toward a General Theory of Action,* (Cambridge: Harvard University Press, 1950); Clyde Kluckhohn, "The Study of Culture," *The Policy Sciences,* ed. Danial Lerner and Harold D. Lasswell (Stanford: Stanford University Press, 1951), p. 86; Louis A. Zurcher, Jr., Arnold Meadow, and Susan Lee Zurcher, "Value Orientation, Role Conflict, and Alienation from Work: A Cross-Cultural Study," *American Sociological Review* (August, 1965); p. 539-48; and also, Talcott Parsons, *Essays in Sociological Theory* (Glencoe, Ill: Free Press, 1954), p. 79.

26. Jaggi, *op. cit.,* p. 79.

27. Irma Adelman and Cynthea Taft Morris, "An Econometric Model of Socio-Economic and Political Change in Underdeveloped Countries," *American Economic Review* (December 1968); p. 1184-218.

28. George M. Scott, *Eighty-eight International Accounting Problems-In Rank Order of Importance* (Sarasota, Florida: American Accounting Association, 1980).

Appendix: About the Contributors

VINOD B. BAVISHI is assistant professor of accounting at the University of Connecticut (Storrs) and received his Ph.D. from The Ohio State University. Formerly associated with Price Waterhouse and Co., his research interests span both international accounting and finance. He is currently director of the Center for Transnational Accounting and Financial Research, University of Connecticut, and is a holder of the CPA, CMA, and CFA certificates. Professor Bavishi is a member of the American Accounting Association, National Association of Accountants, Academy of International Business, and European Accounting Association.

W. JOHN BRENNAN is professor of accounting and dean of the College of Commerce, University of Saskatchewan. He received his Ph.D. from The University of Michigan. Formerly secretary of the International Accounting Standards Committee, he is the editor of *The Internationalization of the Accountancy Profession: A Collection of Views by Leading International Accountants* (Canadian Institute of Chartered Accountants). Dean Brennan is a member of the Institute of Chartered Accountants of Saskatchewan, the Institute of Chartered Accountants of Quebec, the American Accounting Association, and is president-elect of the Canadian Accounting Association.

RICHARD C. BURKE is associate professor of accounting at the University of Saskatchewan and received his Ph.D. from the University of Washington. Previously with IBM, he has worked, studied, and taught in a number of countries. His present interests include working with native peoples in Canada and the development of operational social accounting information systems. He is a member of the Canadian Academic Accounting Association and the American Accounting Association.

WALTHER BUSSE VON COLBE is professor of accounting at Ruhr University (Bochum, Germany) and received his doctorate from the University of

Cologne. He is co-author of *Konzernabschlusse* (on group accounts) and author of numerous articles on inflation accounting, cash flow accounting, financial statement analysis, consolidated statements, international accounting, and EEC harmonization efforts. He has previously taught at Keil University and Pennsylvania State University. A board member of the management development institute (Universitatsseminar der Wirtschaft) at Cologne, Professor Busse von Colbe is past president of the European Accounting Association.

FREDERICK D. S. CHOI is professor of accounting and international business at New York University and received his Ph.D. from the University of Washington. He is the co-author of *An Introduction to Multinational Accounting* (Prentice-Hall), *Essentials of Multinational Accounting: An Anthology* (University Microfilms International), *Assessing the Performance of Foreign Operations* (Business International), and author of numerous monographs and articles in the field of international accounting and finance. He has previously taught at the University of Hawaii, Cranfield School of Management (England), the University of Washington, the Japan-America Institute of Management Science, and served as founding professor of the National Center for Industrial Science and Technology Management Development in the People's Republic of China. On several editorial boards, he is an active member of the American Accounting Association, the National Association of Accountants, and the Academy of International Business.

DONALD A. CORBIN is professor of accounting and business economics at the University of Hawaii and received his Ph.D. from the University of California at Berkeley. He is the author of *Accounting and Economic Decisions* (Dodd, Mead) and numerous articles on topics such as accounting for price changes, funds statements, forecasting, and social accounting and reporting. He has previously taught at MIT, the University of Washington, University of California (Riverside), and Tachikawa AFB, Japan, and is a member of the American Accounting Association, National Association of Accountants, and American Institute of CPAs.

ROLAND E. DUKES is professor of accounting at the University of Washington and received his Ph.D. from Stanford University. Formerly with Cornell University, his articles have appeared in such prestigious journals as the *Accounting Review, Journal of Accounting Research,* and *Journal of Accountancy.* He currently serves on the editorial boards of *The Accounting Review, Journal of Accounting Research,* and *Survey of Accounting and Auditing Literature.* Dukes holds memberships in the American

Accounting Association, the American Finance Association, and Western Finance Association.

HELEN MORSICATO GERNON is assistant professor of accounting at the University of Oregon and received her Ph.D. from Pennsylvania State University. Her research interests center on financial control and she is the author of *Currency Translation and Performance Evaluation in Multinationals* (UMI Research Press). Professor Gernon sits on the board of directors of the Oregon State Society of CPA's, is an NAA director of professional development, and is a member of the American Accounting Association and the American Institute of CPA's.

KAZUO HIRAMATSU is associate professor of accounting at Kwansei Gakuin University and received his advanced degrees from that university. He is the author of *Gaibu Joho Kaikei (Accounting Information for External Users)*, co-author of *Gendai Boki Souron (An Introduction to Contemporary Accounting)* and co-editor of *Gendai Kaikei no Kihon Mondai (Fundamental Problems of Contemporary Accounting)*. He is a member of the Japan Accounting Association, the American Accounting Association, the National Association of Accountants, and the Institute of International Accounting Studies in Japan.

LYLE JACOBSEN is professor of accounting at the University of Hawaii and received his Ph.D. from the University of Illinois (Urbana). Formerly with Stanford University, he is founding professor of Escuela de Administracion de Negocios (ESAN) in Lima, Peru. Professor Jacobsen is co-author of *Cost-Accounting: A Managerial Approach* (McGraw-Hill) translated into Spanish, Portuguese, Turkish, and Japanese, and has traveled extensively in most of the free world as well as the People's Republic of China, Mongolia, and Russia. He is a member of the American Accounting Association, National Association of Accountants, and Academy of Accounting Historians.

ALISTER K. MASON is a partner in the executive office of Deloitte, Haskins and Sells (Toronto) and holds a Ph.D. from the University of Lancaster. His dissertation, *The Development of International Financial Reporting Standards*, was published by the International Center for Research in Accounting, Lancaster, England. He is the author of several articles and two studies: *Social Responsibility and Canada's Largest Corporations* and *Related Party Transactions*. He previously served as associate director of research, and research studies director of the Canadian

Institute of Chartered Accountants and is president-elect of the Canadian Academic Accounting Association.

PETER POHLMANN is research assistant at the School of Business Administration, Ruhr University, and holds the Ph.D. from the School of Business Administration, Ruhr University. His major research fields are inflation accounting and valuation of the firm.

LEE H. RADEBAUGH is associate professor of accounting and international business at Brigham Young University (Provo) and received his D.B.A. at Indiana University. Formerly at the Pennsylvania State University, Radebaugh is the co-author of *International Accounting and Multinational Enterprises* (Warren, Gorham, and Lamont) and *International Business: Environments and Operations* (Addison-Wesley). He is a member of the American Accounting Association, Academy of International Business, European Accounting Association, advisory board of the International Accounting Section of the AAA, and past chairman of the section.

GEORGE M. SCOTT is professor of accounting at the University of Connecticut and received his Ph.D. from the University of Washington. Formerly at the Wharton School and the University of Texas (Austin), he is the author of *Accounting and Developing Nations* (University of Washington), and co-author of *An Introduction to Financial Control and Reporting in Multinational Enterprises* (University of Texas), and *Eighty-eight International Accounting Problems in Rank Order of Importance* (American Accounting Association). His journal contributions have covered subjects such as management information systems and control, current value accounting, development accounting, and computer auditing. He is an active member of the American Accounting Association.

LEE J. SEIDLER is Price Waterhouse Professor of Auditing at New York University and general partner at Bear, Stearns & Co. He received his Ph.D. from Columbia University. In addition to Columbia, he previously taught at Robert College of Istanbul. He is co-editor of *The Accountant's Handbook,* 6th ed. (Ronald/Wiley) and author or co-author of *Social Accounting: Theory, Issues, and Cases* (John Wiley), *The Equity Funding Papers: Anatomy of a Fraud* (John Wiley), and *Accounting and Economic Development* (Praeger). He is editor of the Financial Reporting Section of the *Accounting Review* and is a member of the Five Times All Star Team of Financial Analysts chosen by *Institutional Investor.*

HOSSEIN SHALCHI is assistant professor of accounting at Simon Fraser University and received his Ph.D. from the University of Illinois (Urbana). Having previously taught at the University of Illinois and the University of Tehran, he is the author of a management accounting text (University of Tehran Press).

CHARLES H. SMITH is Peat Marwick Mitchell Professor of Accountancy and director of the Ph.D. program at the University of Illinois (Urbana) and received his Ph.D. from Pennsylvania State University. He is the co-editor of *Accounting: A Book of Readings* (Dryden Press) and is the author of numerous articles which have appeared in both U. S. and foreign journals. He has previously taught at the University of Cape Town (South Africa), the University of Washington, the University of Texas (Austin), and Arizona State University and is consulting editor of the Random House accounting textbook series.

Index